Sociolinguistic Perspectives on Migration Control

LANGUAGE, MOBILITY AND INSTITUTIONS
Series Editors: Celia Roberts, *King's College London, UK* and
Melissa Moyer, *Universitat Autònoma de Barcelona, Spain*

This series focuses on language and new ways of looking at the challenges facing institutions as a result of the mobility and connectedness characteristic of present day society. The relevant settings and practices encompass multilingualism, bilingualism and varieties of the majority language and discourse used in institutional settings. The series takes a wide-ranging view of mobility and also adopts a broad understanding of institutions that incorporates less studied sites as well as the social processes connected to issues of power, control and authority in established institutions.

All books in this series are externally peer-reviewed.

Full details of all the books in this series and of all our other publications can be found on http://www.multilingual-matters.com, or by writing to Multilingual Matters, St Nicholas House, 31-34 High Street, Bristol BS1 2AW, UK.

LANGUAGE, MOBILITY AND INSTITUTIONS: 5

Sociolinguistic Perspectives on Migration Control

Language Policy, Identity and Belonging

Edited by
Markus Rheindorf and Ruth Wodak

MULTILINGUAL MATTERS
Bristol • Blue Ridge Summit

DOI https://doi.org/10.21832/RHEIND4672
Library of Congress Cataloging in Publication Data
A catalog record for this book is available from the Library of Congress.
Names: Rheindorf, Markus – editor. | Wodak, Ruth – editor.
Title: Sociolinguistic Perspectives on Migration Control: Language Policy, Identity and Belonging/Edited by Markus Rheindorf and Ruth Wodak.
Description: Blue Ridge Summit, PA: Multilingual Matters, [2020] | Series: Language, Mobility and Institutions: 5 | Includes bibliographical references and index.
Identifiers: LCCN 2019018871 (print) | LCCN 2019020082 (ebook) | ISBN 9781788924689 (pdf) | ISBN 9781788924696 (epub) | ISBN 9781788924702 (Kindle) | ISBN 9781788924672 (hbk: alk. paper) | ISBN 9781788924665 (pbk: alk. paper)
Subjects: LCSH: Emigration and immigration – Government policy. | Immigrants – Government policy. | Immigrants – Language. | Language policy. | Language and languages – Political aspects. | Discrimination. | Sociolinguistics.
Classification: LCC JV6271 (ebook) | LCC JV6271 .S63 2019 (print) | DDC 325 – dc23
LC record available at https://lccn.loc.gov/2019018871

British Library Cataloguing in Publication Data
A catalogue entry for this book is available from the British Library.

ISBN-13: 978-1-78892-467-2 (hbk)
ISBN-13: 978-1-78892-466-5 (pbk)

Multilingual Matters
UK: St Nicholas House, 31-34 High Street, Bristol BS1 2AW, UK.
USA: NBN, Blue Ridge Summit, PA, USA.

Website: www.multilingual-matters.com
Twitter: Multi_Ling_Mat
Facebook: https://www.facebook.com/multilingualmatters
Blog: www.channelviewpublications.wordpress.com

Copyright © 2020 Markus Rheindorf, Ruth Wodak and the authors of individual chapters.

All rights reserved. No part of this work may be reproduced in any form or by any means without permission in writing from the publisher.

The policy of Multilingual Matters/Channel View Publications is to use papers that are natural, renewable and recyclable products, made from wood grown in sustainable forests. In the manufacturing process of our books, and to further support our policy, preference is given to printers that have FSC and PEFC Chain of Custody certification. The FSC and/or PEFC logos will appear on those books where full certification has been granted to the printer concerned.

Typeset by Riverside Publishing Solutions
Printed and bound in the UK by the Short Run Press Ltd.
Printed and bound in the US by NBN.

Contents

Contributors		viii
1	Sociolinguistic Perspectives on Migration Control: An Introduction *Markus Rheindorf and Ruth Wodak*	1
	Crises of Migration, Crises of Control	1
	Theorizing Discourses of Migration Control: Securitization, Culturalization and Symbolic Politics	3
	European Language Policies	7
	Sociolinguistic Perspectives	9
2	Migrants from Other States of the Former Yugoslavia in Slovene Language Policy: Past, Present and Future *Kristof Savski*	17
	Introduction	17
	Migration in Socialist Yugoslavia	18
	Ex-Yu Communities in 1990s Independent Slovenia	23
	Ex-Yu Communities in 21st-Century Slovenia: Drafting and Debating Language Policy	31
	Conclusions: When Does a Migrant Become Indigenous?	35
3	Resisting Discriminatory Immigration Procedures and Practices in the UK and Pakistan: A Discourse-Ethnographic Approach to Exploring Migration Literacies *Tony Capstick*	41
	Introduction	41
	Mirpuris in Britain	43
	Theoretical Orientations	45
	Resistance in Language and Literacy Resources	46
	Methodology	48

Analysis	49
Resistance as Action Through Vernacular Literacy	57
Conclusion	60

4 Biography as Political Tool: The Case of the Dreamers   64
Anna De Fina

Discourse and Storytelling	65
The Dreamers Movement	68
Storytelling Practices among the Dreamers	70
Data and Methods	72
Analysis	74
Discussion and Conclusions	81

5 Moving for a Better Life: Negotiating Fitting in and Belonging in Modern Diasporas   86
Jo Angouri, Marina Paraskevaidi and Federico Zannoni

Introduction	86
Identity Construction in Modern Diasporas	87
Belonging and the Process of Fitting in	92
Data and Methodology	95
Findings and Discussion	96
Concluding Remarks	109

6 Building 'Fortress Europe': Legitimizing Exclusion from Basic Human Rights   116
Markus Rheindorf and Ruth Wodak

Introduction	116
Historical Context	117
Immediate Context	119
Discourse, Legitimation and Argumentation	120
Research Design: Data and Methods	125
Results	127
Qualitative Results: Legitimizing Immigration Control	136
Discussion	141

7 'Youth should be sent here to absorb Zionism': Jewish Farmers and Thai Migrant Workers in Southern Israel   148
Iair G. Or and Elana Shohamy

Introduction	148
Scope and Methodology	151

Thai Migrant Workers in the Israeli News and Media 152
The Findings: Main Entities and Attributes 154
Discussion and Conclusions 165

Index 170

Contributors

Jo Angouri
Tony Capstick
Anna De Fina
Iair G. Or
Marina Paraskevaidi
Markus Rheindorf
Kristof Savski
Elana Shohamy
Ruth Wodak
Federico Zannoni

1 Sociolinguistic Perspectives on Migration Control: An Introduction

Markus Rheindorf and Ruth Wodak

Crises of Migration, Crises of Control

In times of an international crisis in migration policy – widely referred to as a 'refugee crisis' – that is linked to conflicts and wars in Africa, the Middle East and Asia, this book brings together timely analyses of the manifold and yet context-specific ways in which migration affects globalized societies. Indeed, due to the very different sociopolitical histories of each country (colonial versus non-colonial country; country of immigration versus country of emigration; Eastern versus Western country and so forth) and each migrant/refugee community as well as migration movements examined (EU migrants versus migrants from outside the EU; Christian versus Muslim migrants/refugees and so forth), attitudes towards migrants and refugees differ, as do the implemented migration and asylum policies. Moreover, media coverage foregrounds and backgrounds different dimensions of the arrival and integration of migrants and refugees, depending on their respective editorial policy, their readership and their outreach.

Simultaneously, we are able to observe growing tendencies of *re-nationalization* in many countries (Heller, 2010; Wodak, 2015a, 2018a) and a concomitant proliferation of new policies to keep 'strangers' out (Bauman, 2016; Penninx *et al.*, 2008; Triandafyllidou, 2018). This trend can be seen as a counter-movement to globalization and transnational cooperation that has moved from merely populist rhetoric or oppositional party programmes to actual policy and implementation. It is arguably built on exclusionary discourses and cultural Othering that has become *normalized*, even in its extreme forms.[1] We thus observe a range of locally specific linguistic, cultural and economic nationalisms that potentially relate to migration in terms of legitimizing and re-building walls and borders, restricting or stopping migration (including refugees), and defending or enforcing languages, cultures, religions or values against real and imaginary threats (Krastev, 2017; Krzyżanowski et al., 2018; Rheindorf & Wodak, 2018). Instead of focusing on how to cope best with (language) education, employment and housing for migrants and refugees, a *culturalization* of discourses is being instrumentalized by a politics of fear, dominating both media and politics, thus constructing seemingly insurmountable obstacles for a successful acceptance of diversity and difference. This development poses substantial challenges for sociolinguistics and sociolinguists, in the EU and beyond, both theoretically and analytically (Delanty et al., 2011; Duchêne et al., 2013). In this volume, we restrict ourselves – in our case studies – to the Western world, i.e. to EU member states, Israel and the US. Nevertheless, we believe that our theories and methodologies could be applied elsewhere, in context-dependent ways.

Many apparent similarities in reactions to migration and flight differ among European nation states and political parties. In this, the voices of migrants and refugees are rarely heard – usually, they are debated about, summarized and reported but not included in the debates, and as a result their authentic stories are seldom heard. This fact was evidenced, for example, in a large quantitative and qualitative study about the representation of refugees, migrants and asylum-seekers in the British press (over a period of 10 years; Baker et al., 2008; KhosraviNik, 2009). Usually, refugees and migrants were placed into a single threatening category of strangers; their plight and suffering were seldom reported – and, if they were, only focusing on women and children. Krzyżanowski and Wodak (2009) and De Fina (2003) were able to interview migrants and refugees, and thus make their stories visible. In a longitudinal project, the journalist and author Ernst Schmiederer (2013) is attempting to capture autobiographical narratives told by migrant adolescents and refugees. These young people are asked to write essays about themselves, their feelings and experiences, which are then published in an anonymized form, distributed in schools and workshops. In the public sphere, however, fear and anxieties abound, fuelled by misinformation and instrumentalized by various politicians to gain votes, smear a political opponent, legitimize a particular policy or distract from other issues. In the fields of politics and media, rational and factual discussions are increasingly pushed into the background.

In this toxic climate – perhaps best illustrated by Donald Trump's populist demand for (and simultaneous promise of) a wall against Mexico, to be paid for by Mexico itself, and the 2018 alliance between

Austria, Italy and Visegrád states against refugee movements in Europe, self-labelled as an 'axis of the willing' – migration is easily reduced to a matter of security of the nation and the individual, i.e. protection of the economy, the labour market, the social welfare system, the education or medical system, the national culture and language, but also protection against crime and terrorism (Van Leeuwen & Wodak, 1999; Bauböck & Tripkovic, 2017; Wodak, 2018b). In short, discourses of migration have been subject to securitization on many different levels and across the globe. Borders of all kinds – territorial, material, cultural or linguistic – and the social, discursive practices that construct, transform or maintain them abound and signal new regimes of belonging, identity and language policy (Lehner, forthcoming). In this way, in many countries, in particular in so-called liberal democracies, the existent legal and political consensus is being challenged and/or changed to accommodate new regimes of migration control, both in terms of physical entry at territorial borders and restrictions imposed on migrants, or refugees once arrived, pertaining to language policy, identity and belonging. In some cases, new migration control regimes conflict with the respective host country's constitution, legal tradition, international obligations or history of migration, leading to public and sometimes extensive campaigns to legitimize them (Rheindorf, 2019; Lehner & Rheindorf, 2018) as well as to resistance from NGOs and parts of civil society (Wodak, 2018c).

Theorizing Discourses of Migration Control: Securitization, Culturalization and Symbolic Politics

To provide a counter-perspective to the symbolic and highly charged debates which populism thrives on, it is important to discuss the concept of 'culture' in more differentiated terms. As Miller (2016: 9) maintains, migration control and the control of immigrants residing in the country are linked and relatively recent phenomena: 'In earlier times [...] immigrants were left to their own devices so long as they did not become involved in illegal or antisocial behaviour'. Today, he continues,

> the contemporary democratic state cannot take such a hands-off view: it wants and needs immigrants to become good, upstanding citizens. And achieving this may involve encouraging or even requiring them to shed some of the cultural baggage they bring with them.

It is obvious that such requirements cannot be easily translated into policies – which cultural or religious beliefs are perceived as integral to a given society, and which actually clash with common and widely accepted routines and knowledge? While this volume cannot address the important political and philosophical debates on this matter in a comprehensive fashion, it provides sociolinguistic perspectives on many of the issues that pervade related discourses and practices in specific European countries and beyond. In doing so, the contributions in this book emphasize that views on the rights and obligations (increasingly even fundamental human rights) on the side of both migrants and host societies are strongly influenced by contextual factors such as the numbers of migrants, their countries of origin, the history of migration in the host country, levels of xenophobia in the host country, hegemonic media reporting, programmes and policies of governmental parties, relationships between country of origin and migrants' levels of education, cultural similarities and so forth.

When following the dominant debates about migration in politics and the media, throughout Europe and beyond, one is also struck by a remarkably pervasive appeal to *'values'*. Although these values are rarely specified, they are often described as 'ours' (e.g. European) and vaguely linked to 'culture', 'religion' and 'language'. Apart from the central role of the national language(s) which migrants and refugees are expected to acquire (Wodak, 2015a: 90ff; see below), the respective in-group is characteristically constructed as a homogeneous national 'us' defined by 'birth', 'heritage', 'culture', 'language' or even 'genetics' rather than citizenship. In European countries, the category of 'cultural heritage' is often extended to 'common European values' and thus a potentially much more expansive 'us' (for a case study on the appeal to 'European values' in Austrian political debates, see Rheindorf, 2019).

Invariably, such constructions underpin a Manichean contrast between a positively valued 'us' and a backward, threatening 'them' – two solidified and homogenous blocs with nothing in-between – which can subsequently serve as the naturalized setting for a range of threat scenarios in which 'they' threaten 'us' as a matter of course, as 'cultural difference' is translated into 'threat' within a logics of homogeneity. The above-mentioned development has been described as a *culturalization of discourse* (Yilmaz, 2016: 17), a process through which legal principles such as citizenship or freedom of speech are transformed into a cultural value, although such rights certainly did not develop via cultural evolution but rather as a result of political struggles, revolutions and/or abrupt breaks with the past (e.g. Chanock, 2000). Indeed, as Soysal (2009: 5) argues, culture has become the *dominant frame* for political issues and policies linked to migration, including citizenship, security, education, the economy and so forth; i.e. culture has been appropriated as the floating/empty signifier onto which politicians, media and laypersons are able to project whatever problems or categories they choose (Yilmaz, 2016: 18–20; Wodak, 2017: 119–121).

In this notable *culturalization* of migration-related debates, strict *language requirements* in many contexts are among the most salient and important components (e.g. in the Austrian government's long-standing regime of 'integration through language'; Wodak, 2012; Rheindorf, 2019). Many countries are promoting a nationalist agenda with respect to language and culture, including European countries that are part of the multilingual and multicultural EU (see below). The concept of 'language competence in the host country's language' as a salient prerequisite for *belonging* has become part and parcel of new citizenship laws, regulations and requirements, and is advocated or even championed not only by far-right populist parties but also by mainstream politicians.

More recently, however, the public salience of national languages (if not yet their legal significance) has been eclipsed by *religion*, e.g. in discussions regarding a potential ban on religious symbols in many different national contexts (Mourão Permoser & Rosenberger, 2012). Culturalization is evident in both cases insofar as language and religion are articulated as inherently cultural expressions of a particular people/ethnos and/or nation: to be Austrian means to speak German, to become Austrian (attain residency, citizenship), one has to pass language competence tests etc. Perchinig (2010: 27) convincingly debunks the underlying understanding of language as prerequisite for citizenship as a veiled 'ethno-cultural demand for assimilation', while Mourão Permoser and Rosenberger (2012) similarly recognize, on the discursive level, the culturalist emphasis on cultural assimilation.

Language thus plays multiple roles in *migration control*: it is regulated by legal provisions; it must be acquired by migrants; it is tested in language exams; it is used to argue and legitimize such measures. Culturalization is recognizable in all these perspectives, but it is perhaps most evident in the fact that the language is simultaneously the medium, mechanism and purported aim of migration control (e.g. de Cillia & Dorostkar, 2013).

Beyond the instrumentalization of language, restrictive, contemporary regimes of migration control also rely heavily on *symbolic politics* as part and parcel of their restrictive, exclusionary identity politics. In order to be able to do so, they also exploit, foment or create symbolic conflicts between 'us' and 'them', e.g. bans on the 'headscarf' of

Muslim women or on kosher/halal slaughtering practices.[2] Such policies and the public debates about them are symbolic in the sense that they do not address an actual conflict between the majority and a migrant minority but demand a symbolic gesture of deference or submission in lieu of cultural assimilation. Joppke (2007: 14–16) argues that such regimes of migration control betray a 'repressive liberalism' based on 'power and disciplining'. A particularly illustrative example for this trend can be recognized in the debate over instituting new criminal laws against migrants' 'unwillingness to integrate' that occupied the attention of Austrian politics and Austrian media in early 2015 (Rheindorf, 2019). In the context of regional elections, Austrian mainstream politicians had sought to attract far-right voters by linking integration to security or, rather, linking an alleged unwillingness to integrate to terrorism. Migrants who were unwilling to integrate should be heavily penalized, they proposed, with punishments ranging from fines to prison sentences or even deportation. Asked by journalists to provide 'examples' of behaviours that indicated such an unwillingness, said politicians recounted anecdotes about Muslim schoolboys refusing to shake hands with their female teachers and Muslim schoolgirls failing to appear for swimming lessons. Both behaviours were described as in conflict with 'European values' and – predictably – as the seeds of 'future terrorist threats'.

Obviously, such populist demands conflate *public and private culture*: on the one hand, the culture of the wider society (i.e. its language, symbols and institutions) and, on the other hand, individuals' religions, forms of art and literature, cuisines, languages and so on (Miller, 2016: 141–143). This distinction does not, of course, eliminate all conflicts: it is, after all, a particularly thin and easily blurred line. Immigrants may wish to retain practices and symbols of their own culture, including language, and integrate them with the host culture. Host societies, however, increasingly expect a demonstrable and exclusive identification with their national identity and symbols, largely overlapping with those of 'banal nationalism' (Billig, 1995). A problem arises most vehemently – as can be observed across Europe and beyond – in the case of religion, i.e. when migrants' religious beliefs and religious practices are perceived as colliding with elements of the host society's culture. In view of the highly controversial debates about the burqa or headscarf as metonymic tropes for Islam and, more recently, political Islam and the related oppression of women, Miller's proposals might be dismissed as purely academic and rather philosophical (Wodak, 2015b: 151–153).

Cultural Otherness, especially if displayed publicly and proudly, is often seen as disloyal, even treasonous behaviour. A case in point is the initial outrage and subsequent debate over a prominent and previously popular German football player: Mezut Özil, of Turkish descent but born in Germany and a German citizen, was photographed with Turkish president Recep Tayyip Erdoğan. Rather than a debate over the latter's politics, the picture triggered a deluge of hate speech and threats against Özil that denigrated him as an ungrateful traitor and argued that one could not be Turkish and German at the same time. Özil then resigned from the national football team, explaining his disappointment at being blamed for the team's bad performance at the 2018 World Cup games in Moscow. This incident demonstrates that migrants' belonging, even the status as a 'national hero', can be challenged and contested by members of the majority on grounds of a lack of exclusive cultural and symbolic identification. Indeed, Özil summed up the hypocrisy he had experienced in one sentence: If we win, I am considered a German citizen; if we lose, I become a migrant (Spiegel, 2018).

Even economic arguments that used to dominate migration control regimes appear to have been eclipsed by culturalization. Trained and economically needed workers have become the subject of political campaigns, e.g. to reduce welfare benefits solely based on their country of origin. At the same time, however, economic arguments can still be used to argue that asylum laws must be changed so that refugees can be turned back at the border, without due process, because they represent an 'unbearable economic burden'. Thus, economic arguments can be used to legitimize changes to existing laws, but they are no defence against deportation according to existent law (Rheindorf & Wodak, 2018).

Next to religion, language use and (the testing of) language skills have played a major role as markers of cultural difference in contexts of migration control – thus, languages are simultaneously potential resources for migrants and potential tools of exclusion or inclusion by the host society (Extramiana *et al.*, 2014). In contrast with religion, however, language competence is used less to construct resistant, unalterable Otherness and more to test for migrants' capacity and readiness to assimilate.

European Language Policies

Arguably, the tensions between recent re-nationalization and long-standing liberal principles are nowhere more evident than in the increasingly glaring discrepancies between the language policies of European Union member states and the Council of Europe or EU Commission. The *European Cultural Convention*, opened for signature by the Council of Europe in 1954, defines European multilingualism as a vital component for European identity/ies and the preservation of multilingualism on the national, regional, local, societal and individual level. Along similar lines, the importance of language learning has been repeatedly stressed in European authorities' policy declarations on language, education and pedagogy (e.g. 'Recommendation No. (98) 6 to member states concerning modern languages' and its predecessors from the Committee of Ministers and Parliamentary Assembly (PACE) since the 1950s).

In the pivotal Maastricht and Amsterdam treaties of 2000, the EU again committed to European multilingualism. The aforementioned recommendation No. 98 warns explicitly 'of the dangers that might result from marginalisation of those who lack the skills necessary to communicate in an interactive Europe'. Specifically, it recommends that steps be taken to 'ensure that there is parity of esteem between all the languages and cultures' so that children growing up in multilingual environments, e.g. the children of migrants, are able to 'learn to understand and appreciate the language and culture' of multiple languages (Council of Europe, 1998: 34). Indeed, migrants and immigrants are specifically mentioned in the recommendations for governments 'to promote bilingualism' (Council of Europe, 1998: 34).

Although the Council of Europe holds a more nuanced position on plurilingualism, the European Commission's 'White Paper on Education and Training' regards languages as 'the key to knowing other people' and states that '[p]roficiency in languages helps to build up the feeling of being European with all its cultural wealth and diversity and of understanding between the citizens of Europe' (European Commission, 1995: 67; see also Krzyżanowski & Wodak, 2011). When the 'new framework strategy for multilingualism' was published in 2005 as part of the multilingualism portfolio of the Union's Commissioner on Education and Culture, it reaffirmed the Commission's commitment to 'promoting multilingualism in European society' on the grounds that multilingualism is good not only for the European economy but also for a 'social Europe' and the democratization of the EU. It also offered a policy-relevant definition of multilingualism as 'both a person's ability to use several languages and the co-existence of different language communities in one geographical area' (European Commission, 2005: 3). The document recognizes that the European Union is founded on 'unity in diversity', including languages, as 'a source of wealth and a bridge to greater solidarity and mutual understanding' (European Commission, 2005: 2). Arguably as a result of the European crises that have plagued the EU since 2008 as well as the transfer of the Multilingualism Portfolio to Education, Culture and Youth in 2010, most of the policies elaborated in the European Multilingualism Strategy have not been implemented. Nonetheless, multilingualism and support for both individuals' and collectives' language identities are integral to language policies at the European level.

These policies are contradicted more and more by the national language policies of many EU member states. Since national policies exert a substantial influence on the language requirements imposed on migrants from non-EU countries, these have largely counteracted both the recommendations of the Council of Europe and the guidelines of the EU Commission. Indeed, many political parties on the national level, and increasingly also those in government, propagate the so-called 'Leitsprachenmodell', which posits that the language of the majority should serve for all communicative purposes in public life and thus contradicts the European language policies mentioned above (de Cillia, 2003).

Naturalization conditions pertaining to language competence vary enormously among the current 28 members of the European Union. These regulations determine who is permitted to move 'inside' the European Union and thus also who must remain 'outside' (e.g. Bauböck & Goodman-Wallace, 2012). In 1998, only 6 of the then 15 member states had citizenship and/or language tests; by 2010, this number had grown to 18 out of 27; and by 2014 to 23 out of 28. Moreover, the requirements and the content of tests also vary greatly, indicating the strong national interest in language for migration control by naturalization (Extramiana *et al.*, 2014).

Sociolinguistic Perspectives

The above-outlined theoretical perspectives on migration control in and by means of language, including securitization, culturalization and language policies, have also been taken up and developed in sociolinguistic studies, in particular with respect to migrants' investment in language(s) (e.g. Martín Rojo, 2014; Blackledge *et al.*, 2014) and language policy (e.g. Barakos & Unger, 2016; de Cillia & Dorostkar, 2013), while discursive approaches to the representation of migrants and refugees have increasingly paid attention to the intersection of media and politics (e.g. Baker *et al.*, 2012; Gabrielatos & Baker, 2008; Baker *et al.*,

2008), the legitimization of migration control regimes, and the resurgence of xenophobic sentiment and discriminatory practices (Lehner & Rheindorf, 2018; Wodak, 2018b; Colombo, 2018; Uitz, 2015).

The contributions in this volume pursue – inter alia – the following questions in the respective national or international contexts:

- How are refugees and migrants portrayed in politics and the media?
  - What distinctions – and relationships – do such portrayals construct between these two groups?
  - Which cultural, economic or moral categories are used in constructions of 'us' versus 'them' in the specific national contexts?
  - Do such constructions allow for integrative practices or do they reinforce exclusionary and discriminatory regimes of migration control?
- Which sociolinguistic problems are salient in today's complex sociocultural-political migrant societies (for example, second language acquisition, intercultural communication, religious practices and so forth)?
  - How do specific national politicians and political parties position themselves in relation to these groups?
  - Which argumentative and legitimation strategies are used with respect to policies and practices related to migration control, in particular to asylum, residency, integration and citizenship?
  - How do migrants position themselves in such discourses and make use of the linguistic resources available to them?
- And, finally, what contribution might sociolinguistic theories and methodologies offer to practitioners for developing adequate new policies to confront discrimination and support integration?

While this volume's contributions are mainly empirical, they are informed by a view on the sociolinguistic realities of migration – e.g. social practices associated with it, its representation in the host society (politics, media etc.) and the legitimization of efforts to control it – that focuses on multiple intersections between linguistic practices and migration. Indeed, the individual chapters focus on discourse in terms of representation, narrative and argumentation, with many chapters pursuing a critical or historical perspective in their analyses. All of the contributions analyse language use in context, but Chapters 3, 4, 5 and 7 also draw on ethnography and sociolinguistic fieldwork.

The linguistic data analysed varies between chapters, demonstrating the rich and nuanced perspectives sociolinguistic approaches to migration enable. In terms of data and methodology, then, the volume encompasses different sociolinguistic and in particular discourse-analytic approaches to how *language* relates to migration:

- through the *negative representation and low prestige of migrant languages* in the context of language policy and the media (Chapter 2);
- as *migration literacies* allowing migrants to counter discriminatory immigration procedures in an institutional context (Chapter 3);
- as *strategic and contextually embedded identity claims* in biographical narratives that allow migrants to *enact resistance* to discriminatory policies (Chapter 4);
- as the *construction of 'home' or 'belonging' in narratives* of people who migrated for 'a better life' at an early age (Chapter 5);
- as the *mediatized political negotiation* over closing borders and limiting the number of refugees accepted (Chapter 6);
- and as *exclusionary discourse* that celebrates a national/Zionist ideal of (agricultural) labour (Chapter 7).

In his contribution to this volume, Kristof Savski covers the past, present and future of Slovene language policy towards Serbo-Croat-speaking migrants from other states of the former Yugoslavia. Although this is the largest minority language in Slovenia, speakers of Serbo-Croatian enjoy no special rights in education or dealing with state institutions, because Slovenia grants such minority rights only to indigenous language communities. Savski demonstrates how language policy and the representation of migrants from the other post-Yugoslav states has changed in Slovene public discourse, both historically and recently, due to factors such as the violent break-up of Yugoslavia, their upward social mobility since the early 2000s, and the economic slowdown in the wake of the Eurozone crisis.

In his chapter on resisting discriminatory immigration procedures in the UK and Pakistan, Tony Capstick reports the in-depth results of a four-year study of transnational migration between Pakistan and the UK using a discourse-ethnographic approach to migration literacies. The chapter focuses on the role of migration literacies in countering discriminatory immigration procedures by tracing, on the one hand, the ways in which institutions shape particular literacies and, on the other hand, how migrants appropriate the dominant literacies to negotiate the barriers that separate 'insiders' from 'outsiders' and how they counter-impose identities in their vernacular literacies of migration. To do so, Capstick studies literacy practices in relation to their context by focusing on particular uses of texts and text production, e.g. health bureaucracies and visa applications.

In Chapter 4, Anna De Fina explores biography as political tool in studying the case of the so-called Dreamers, the children of undocumented immigrants to the United States of America, whose legal status remains for the most part in limbo. From their precarious position, they have launched the powerful United We Dream movement that pushes for the recognition of their right to stay in the country and for migration reform in the United States. De Fina approaches the Dreamers' biographical narratives in terms of the interplay between narrative and identity from a sociolinguistic and interactional perspective, emphasizing the strategic and context embeddedness of identity claims. Specifically, the chapter traces the way their self-presentation and enactment of resistance against discriminatory policies have evolved from the Obama presidency to the 2016 presidential election campaign and shortly after the election of Donald Trump.

The joint contribution of Jo Angouri, Marina Paraskevaidi and Federico Zannoni explores the nexus of narrative, identity and belonging through the narratives of people from Greece and Italy between 15 and 25 years of age who moved either with their families or individually as young professionals. These stories of 'moving for a better life' from two countries severely affected by the ongoing financial crisis were collected through ethnographic interviews and analysed following the principles of critical discourse analysis and interactional sociolinguistics. The authors explore perceptions of the economic crisis and the new era of globalized mobility, but specifically focus on the ways in which the individual positions 'self' and 'other' in relation to the traditional home/host dichotomy with respect to family and society.

In Chapter 6, Markus Rheindorf and Ruth Wodak analyse legitimization strategies in the context of changing border practices in Austria during the so-called refugee crisis of 2015–2016. During the time period studied, the Austrian government's stance shifted from a policy of 'open borders' to building a border fence and setting an annual limit on asylum applications. Although both policies effectively contributed to exclude asylum seekers from basic human rights, they were recontextualized in mediatized politics as positive contributions to building the 'Fortress Europe'. Combining corpus linguistic results from a large media corpus and qualitative analyses conducted on a smaller sample downsampled to identify the changing representation of refugees and migrants, the authors link specific discursive shifts in representational as well as argumentative strategies to the events in the local and international context.

Finally, Iair G. Or and Elana Shohamy's contribution focuses on the discourse surrounding the media coverage of agricultural workers from Thailand in the sparsely populated Central Arava region (Israel), where they outnumber Jews. Agriculture in the region displays a unique configuration of power relations, since tensions exist between the state, the farmers, consumers, human rights groups and the workers. While the discourse about Jewish farmers traditionally celebrates the pioneering, entrepreneurial spirit of Zionism, they have recently been criticized for exploiting migrant workers and charging exaggerated prices for their produce. The migrant workers themselves are not traditionally seen as part of Israeli society and its immigration policy, as they are expected to leave after a few years and have no viable way of becoming permanent residents, let alone citizens. Using the discourse-historical approach, the paper examines a wide range of materials, focusing on comments related to news items in the national press, but also integrates insights from the linguistic landscape of the region.

Taken together, all the sociolinguistic studies included in this volume share a common interest in the position of migrants and social practices related to migration in relation to language(s) in several domains of society. Similarly, they all engage with questions of power (or empowerment) and discrimination or exclusion in relation to language(s) and semiotic practices. While each chapter thus makes a very specific contribution, the overall aim of the book is to shed light on the multi-faceted and multi-layered interdependence between language(s) and migration.

Notes

(1) See Link (2013) for a definition of the concept of normalization (*Normalismus*).
(2) Only recently, Gottfried Waldhäusl, a local politician of the Social-Democratic Party of Austria, demanded that all butchers who produce kosher meat according to Jewish doctrine as well as anyone buying such products should be registered by the state. He claimed only to be acting in the interest of 'humane' treatment of animals (DerStandard, 2018).

References

Baker, P., Gabrielatos, C., KhosraviNik, M., Krzyżanowski, M., McEnery, T. and Wodak, R. (2008) A useful methodological synergy? Combining critical discourse analysis and corpus linguistics to examine discourses of refugees and asylum seekers in the UK press. *Discourse & Society* 19 (3), 273–306.

Baker, P., Gabrielatos, C. and McEnery, T. (2012) Sketching Muslims: A corpus driven analysis of representations around the word 'Muslim' in the British press 1998–2009. *Applied Linguistics* 34 (3), 255–278.

Barakos, E. and Unger, J.W. (2016) *Discursive Approaches to Language Policy*. London: Palgrave Macmillan.

Bauböck, R. and Goodman-Wallace, S. (2012) *EUDO Citizenship Policy Brief 2*. Florence: European University Institute.

Bauböck, R. and Tripkovic, M. (eds) (2017) The integration of migrants and refugees. An EUI Forum on Migration, Citizenship, and Demography. Florence: EUI.

Bauman, Z. (2016) *Strangers at Our Door*. Cambridge: Polity.

Billig, M. (1995) *Banal Nationalism*. London: Sage.

Blackledge, A., Creese, A. and Tahki, J.K. (2014) Discourses of aspiration and distinction in the local school economy. In J.W. Unger, M. Krzyżanowski and R. Wodak (eds) *Multilingual Encounters in Europe's Institutional Spaces. Advances in Sociolinguistics* (pp. 173–193). London: Bloomsbury.

Chanock, M. (2000) 'Culture' and human rights: Orientalising, occidentalising and authenticity. In M. Mamdani (ed.) *Beyond Rights Talk and Culture Talk* (pp. 15–37). Cape Town: David Philip.

Colombo, M. (2018) The representation of the 'European refugee crisis' in Italy: Domopolitics, securitization, and humanitarian communication in political and media discourses. *Journal of Immigration and Refugee Studies* 16 (1–2), Special Issue: Mediatization and Politicization of Refugee Crisis in Europe, 161–178.

Council of Europe (1998) *Recommendation No. (98) 6 to Member States Concerning Modern Languages*. Council of Europe. See https://rm.coe.int/16804fc569 (accessed 7 October 2019).

de Cillia, R. (2003) Grundlagen und Tendenzen der europäischen Sprachenpolitik. In M. Mokre, G. Weiss and R. Bauböck (eds) *Europas Identitäten. Mythen, Konflikte, Konstruktionen* (pp. 231–256). Frankfurt am Main: Campus.

de Cillia, R. and Dorostkar, N. (2013) Integration und/durch Sprache. In J. Dahlvik, Ch. Reinprecht and W. Sievers (eds) *Migration und Integration: Wissenschaftliche Perspektiven aus Österreich. Jahrbuch 2/2013* (pp. 143–161). Göttingen: V&R unipress, Vienna University Press.

De Fina, A. (2003) *Identity in Narrative: A Study of Immigrant Discourse*. Amsterdam & Philadelphia: John Benjamins.

Delanty, G., Wodak, R. and Jones, P. (eds) (2011) *Identity, Belonging and Migration*. Liverpool: Liverpool University Press.

DerStandard (2018) Regeln für koscheres Fleisch, newspaper article, 18 July 2018. See https://derstandard.at/2000083723212/ (accessed 28 August 2018).

Duchêne, A., Moyer, M. and Roberts, C. (2013) (eds) *Language, Migration and Social Inequalities*. Bristol: Multilingual Matters.

European Commission (1995) *White Paper on Education and Training* COM 590, Brussels, 3 November 1995.

European Commission (2005) *A New Framework Strategy for Multilingualism* COM 596, Brussels, 22 November 2005.

Extramiana, C., Pulinx, R. and Van Avermaet, P. (2014) *Linguistic Integration of Adult Migrants (LIAM): Policy and Practice*. Final Report on the 3rd Council of Europe Survey 2014.

Gabrielatos, C. and Baker, P. (2008) Fleeing, sneaking, flooding: A corpus analysis of discursive constructions of refugees and asylum seekers in the UK press, 1996–2005. *Journal of English Linguistics* 36 (1), 5–38.

Heller, M. (2010) *Paths to Post-Nationalism: A Critical Ethnography of Language and Identity*. Oxford: Oxford University Press.

Joppke, C. (2007) Beyond national models: Civic integration policies for immigrants in western Europe. *West European Politics* 30 (1), 1–22.

KhosraviNik, M. (2009) The representation of refugees, asylum seekers and immigrants in British newspapers during the Balkan conflict (1999) and the British general election (2005). *Discourse & Society* 20 (4), 477–498.

Krastev, Ivan (2017) *Europadämmerung*. Frankfurt/Main: Suhrkamp.

Krzyżanowski, M. and Wodak, R. (2009) *Politics of Exclusion: Debating Migration in Austria*. New Brunswick: Transaction Press.

Krzyżanowski, M. and Wodak, R. (2011) Political strategies and language policies: The 'rise and fall' of the EU Lisbon strategy and its implications for the Union's multilingualism policy. *Language Policy* 10 (2), 115–136.

Krzyżanowski, M., Triandafyllidou, A. and Wodak, R. (2018) The mediatization and the politicization of the 'refugee crisis' in Europe. *Journal of Immigration and Refugee Studie* 16 (1–2), Special Issue: Mediatization and Politicization of Refugee Crisis in Europe, 1–14.

Lehner, S. (forthcoming) Diskurs und Grenze/n. In D. Gerst, M. Klessmann and H. Krämer (eds) *Handbuch Grenzforschung*. Baden-Baden: Nomos.

Lehner, S. and Rheindorf, M. (2018) 'Fortress Europe': Representation and argumentation in Austrian media and EU press releases on border policies. In G. Dell'Orto and I. Wetzstein (eds) *Refugee News, Refugee Politics: Journalism, Public Opinion and Policymaking in Europe* (pp. 40–55). London: Routledge.

Link, J. (2013) *Versuch über den Normalismus: wie Normalität produziert wird*. Göttingen: Vandenhoeck & Ruprecht.

Martín Rojo, L. (2014) The genealogy of educational change: Educating to capitalize migrant students. In J.W. Unger, M. Krzyżanowski and R. Wodak (eds) *Multilingual Encounters in Europe's Institutional Spaces. Advances in Sociolinguistics* (pp. 195–220). London: Bloomsbury.

Miller, D. (2016) *Strangers in Our Midst: The Political Philosophy of Immigration*. Harvard: Harvard University Press.

Mourão Permoser, J. and Rosenberger, S. (2012) Integration policy in Austria. In J. Frideres and J. Biles (eds) *International Perspectives: Integration and Inclusion* (pp. 39–58). Montreal & Kingston: McGill-Queen's University Press.

Penninx, R., Spencer, D. and Van Hear, N. (2008) *Migration and Integration in Europe: The State of Research*. ESRC Centre on Migration, Policy and Society (COMPAS). Oxford University.

Perchinig, B. (2010) All you need to know to become an Austrian: Naturalisation policy and citizenship testing in Austria. In R. van Oers, E. Ersbøll and D. Kostakopoulou (eds) *A Re-Definition of Belonging? Language and Integration Tests in Europe* (pp. 25–50). Leiden & Boston: Martinus Nijhoff.

Rheindorf, M. (2019) Disciplining the unwilling: Normalization of (demands for) punitive measures against immigrants in Austrian populist discourse. In M. Kranert and G. Horan (eds) *Doing Politics: Discursivity, Performativity and Mediation in Political Discourse* (pp. 179–208). Amsterdam: Benjamins.

Rheindorf, M. and Wodak, R. (2018) Borders, fences and limits – protecting Austria from refugees: Metadiscursive negotiation of meaning in the current refugee crisis. In *Journal of Immigration and Refugee Studies* 16 (1–2), Special Issue: Mediatization and Politicization of Refugee Crisis in Europe, 15–38.

Schmiederer, E. (2013) *Wir in Wien – Berichte aus Margareten und der Donaustadt*. Wien: Import/Export.
Soysal, L. (2009) Introduction: Triumph of culture, troubles of anthropology. *European Journal of Anthropology* 55, 3–11.
Spiegel (2018) Özil-Statements im Wortlaut, newspaper article, 22 July 2018. See http://www.spiegel.de/sport/fussball/nach-erdogan-affaere-das-oezil-statement-im-wortlaut-a-1219615.html (accessed 28 August 2018).
Triandafyllidou, A. (2018) A 'refugee crisis' unfolding: 'Real' events and their interpretation in media and political debates. *Journal of Immigration and Refugee Studies* 16 (1–2), Special Issue: Mediatization and Politicization of Refugee Crisis in Europe, 198–126.
Uitz, R. (2015) Can you tell when an illiberal democracy is in the making? An appeal to comparative constitutional scholarship from Hungary. *I.Con* 13 (1), 279–300.
Van Leeuwen, T. and Wodak, R. (1999) Legitimizing immigration control: A discourse-historical analysis. *Discourse Studies* 1 (1), 83–119.
Wodak, R. (2012) Language, power and identity. *Language Teaching* 44 (3), 215–233.
Wodak, R. (2015a) *Politics of Fear: What Right-Wing Populist Discourses Mean*. London: Sage.
Wodak, R. (2015b) 'Normalisierung nach rechts': Politischer Diskurs im Spannungsfeld von Neoliberalismus, Populismus und kritischer Öffentlichkeit. *Linguistik Online* 73 (4), 27–44.
Wodak, R. (2017) Integration and culture: From 'communicative competence' to 'competence in plurality'. In R. Bauböck and M. Tripkovic (eds) *The Integration of Migrants and Refugees: An EUI Forum on Migration, Citizenship, and Demography* (pp. 116–137). Florence: EUI.
Wodak, R. (2018a) Discourses about nationalism. In J. Flowerdew and J.E. Richardson (eds) *The Routledge Handbook of Critical Discourse Studies* (pp. 403–420). Abingdon: Routledge.
Wodak, R. (2018b) 'Strangers in Europe': A discourse-historical approach to the legitimation of immigration control 2015/16. In S. Zhao, E. Djonov, A. Björkvall, M. Boeriis (eds) *Advancing Multimodal and Critical Discourse Studies* (pp. 31–50). London: Routledge.
Wodak, R. (2018c) The revival of numbers and lists in radical right politics. CARR: Center for the Analysis of the Radical Right. See www.radicalrightanalysis.com/2018/06/30/the-revival-of-numbers-and-lists-in-radical-right-politics/.
Yilmaz, I. (2016) *Muslim Laws, Politics and Society in Modern Nation States*. London: Routledge.

2 Migrants from Other States of the Former Yugoslavia in Slovene Language Policy: Past, Present and Future

Kristof Savski

Introduction[1]

Between 1945 and 1991, while Slovenia was part of the Socialist Federal Republic of Yugoslavia, it experienced a considerable amount of immigration, with large numbers of skilled labourers arriving from the less developed parts of the federation. As a result of this internal migration, recent census data shows that there are presently around 135,000 individuals living in Slovenia who migrated there as adults (Medvešek, 2007). In addition, there are also nearly 130,000 individuals living in Slovenia who can be considered second-generation migrants, having been born in Slovenia or having arrived as children and grown up there (Medvešek, 2007). Among these are representatives of all the other five constitutive nations of Yugoslavia – Croats, Bosnians, Serbs, Montenegrins and Macedonians – as well as of other ethnic groups in the Yugoslav space, in particular Kosovar Albanians.

The purpose of this chapter is to analyse in detail the historical and present-day status of this diverse set of communities (henceforth: Ex-Yu communities) in Slovenia. Given the differences that exist between the various groups as well as the complexities brought about by inter-ethnic marriages, this necessarily involves a level of generalization. In this chapter, while clearly different from each other based on ethnicity, the time of arrival in Slovenia as well as the purpose and place to which they migrated, the individuals that constitute the Ex-Yu communities are seen as joined by both their history – having migrated during the existence of socialist Yugoslavia – and by their present-day position in

Slovene language policy – characterized by a lack of collective linguistic rights.

This chapter therefore combines diachronic and synchronic analysis of language ecology in Slovenia with regard to Ex-Yu migrant communities. It examines the roots of the migration that brought their development, in the postwar processes of inter-ethnic reconciliation and economic modernization. Then, it examines the position of the communities in independent Slovenia, examining in particular the debates surrounding their position in language policy. These analyses of language ecology are complemented by an examination of the social and linguistic forces that shaped the language repertoires of Ex-Yu community members in Slovenia, in particular the typological closeness of Slovene and Serbo-Croat.

Migration in Socialist Yugoslavia

Economic and sociopolitical factors in internal migration

Upon its establishment and international recognition in the aftermath of World War II, socialist Yugoslavia was a state whose population had been engaged in active warfare for several years, as was the case across Europe at that time. However, the Yugoslav state faced an additional challenge in legitimizing its power, as in many cases armed conflicts had erupted between the different ethnic groups that now co-existed in the new country, with Axis aggression igniting centuries-old hatreds between groups of different religions, yet often similar traditions. In the interwar period, the Kingdom of Yugoslavia, dominated by the Serb Karađorđević royal family, had attempted to quell such tensions by pursuing a 'melting pot' cultural policy, intending to create a nation of 'Yugoslavs' with a single language and culture. To this end, the state was centralized, and while regional administrative units existed, their borders were deliberately drawn along the lines of major rivers rather than along ethnic boundaries. In practice, this policy failed and as a result the kingdom suffered from continuous political instability, fuelled in part by building inter-ethnic tensions. Socialist Yugoslavia differed from the kingdom in the formal sense, as it was from its inception a federalist state built around six constitutive republics, each of them with some extent of autonomous control over its own territory and, most crucially, legitimated through its association with a particular ethnic nation. At the same time, the legitimacy of the state as a whole stemmed from the socialist revolution which had overthrown the previous order, nominally transferring power from the bourgeoisie to the workers, and from the collective resistance of the Communist Party, led by Josip Broz Tito, against Axis occupation.

From its inception, therefore, socialist Yugoslavia attempted to reconcile two powerful ideologies, nationalism and communism, by drawing on both to legitimate its power and sovereignty. This quest for dual legitimacy was supported by its official language policy, which to a large extent codified equality between the different languages of the various ethnic groups, though with some limitations. The official language of command in the Yugoslav People's Army, for instance, was exclusively Serbo-Croat, a fact which was tacitly linked to the numerical dominance of ethnic Serb officers. The status of Serbo-Croat, which includes several dialect groups whose boundaries only loosely coincide with ethnic and religious borders and whose speakers – Serbs, Croats, Bosniaks and Montenegrins – had engaged in some of the bloodiest inter-ethnic fighting during the preceding war, was resolved by treating it as a single language with two possible scripts, Latin and Cyrillic (Bugarski, 2012). Officially, therefore, Yugoslavia was trilingual, with Slovene and Macedonian seen as the only distinct 'languages' other than Serbo-Croat[2] (Tollefson, 1981). In practice, however, Serbo-Croat was dominant in most domains at the federal level (particularly in politics, business and culture), while the two smaller languages were each the main official language in their own republic, with Serbo-Croat playing the role of a second language (Stabej, 2007).

Initially, the new Yugoslav leadership under Tito pursued Stalinist economic policies and embarked on widespread collectivization. However, after the Tito–Stalin split in 1948, the new country changed directions and, while continuing to pursue socialist economic policy, distanced itself from the rest of the Eastern Bloc and eventually began trading with both the East and West, all the while following the policy of 'non-alignment' in international affairs. After a period of crisis during the 1950s, the Yugoslav economy gradually began to grow with the support of loans from Western states and international organizations, though unemployment remained high. During this period, Yugoslavia experienced a large amount of initially illegal and later legal emigration, with many skilled workers seeking better salaries in western Europe, particularly in Germany. In parallel, with enrolment in high schools and universities becoming more accessible, the education level of the workforce increased rapidly, leading to a shortage of skilled labour, particularly in Slovenia, the federation's most developed republic (Zorn, 2010).

As a result of this shortage, numerous skilled labourers began to migrate from less developed parts of all other republics of Yugoslavia to

Table 2.1 Migrants from other Yugoslav republics according to year of arrival and gender (Statistical Office of the Republic of Slovenia, 2002)

	1948–1952	1953–1960	1961–1970	1971–1975	1976–1980	1981–1985	1986–1990
Total	3959	12496	24992	22278	27047	17391	13529
Average per year	791.8	1562	2499.2	4455.6	5409.4	3478.2	2705.8
Men	2096	7338	14451	12884	13929	8269	6545
	53%	59%	58%	58%	51%	48%	48%
Women	1863	5158	10541	9394	13118	9122	6984
	47%	41%	42%	42%	49%	52%	52%

Slovenia in order to support the growing manufacturing and construction sectors in major Slovene cities (Zorn, 2010). This process started in the mid-1960s and continued until the downfall of the Yugoslav state (see Table 2.1), with net migration numbers remaining positive throughout this period (Zorn, 2010). The majority of the arriving workers were initially male, mirroring the sectors in which the demand for labour existed, with the gender gap later reducing and eventually disappearing during the 1980s. In terms of language, this migration was supported both by the large degree of mutual intelligibility between Slovene and Serbo-Croat as well as the widespread knowledge of the former among ethnic Slovenes. Therefore, migrants arriving during this period were in most cases able to rely on their first language for basic communication (see below). In official situations, this was also supported by the right of citizens of all Yugoslav republics to use their first language with officials, even if located in another republic (e.g. Constitution of SFRY, 1974, Art. 171).

Intra-state migration to Slovenia began to slow down during the economic recession that followed the death of President Tito in 1980. During this time, ethnic tensions began to once again brew between the different Yugoslav nations, with Croat and Serb leaderships in particular engaged in a long-term struggle for dominance over federal politics. Relations between the Slovene and Serb leaderships also deteriorated as a result of various events, which included the ascendance of Slobodan Milošević and his nationalist followers to the top of Serbian politics, Slovene support for striking ethnic Albanian miners in the historically Serb province of Kosovo, perceived Serb-led moves towards political centralization of power in Belgrade and perceived reluctance of the Slovene leadership to crack down on media outlets critical of the federal government and the Yugoslav People's Army. These conflicts eventually led to the secession of the Slovene League of Communists from the parent

Yugoslav organization and its partial withdrawal from power following the 1990 parliamentary and presidential elections, in which a centre-right coalition gained the parliamentary majority while the communist candidate Milan Kučan was elected president. The election was followed by Slovene secession from the Yugoslav federation – to be joined by Croatia – and in the summer of 1991 by a brief 10-day armed conflict between the Yugoslav army and the Slovene defence forces, which ended after an agreement was brokered by the European Community. Despite its short-lived nature, the conflict in Slovenia is significant in the sense that the withdrawing Yugoslav army was subsequently taken over by the Serbian political leadership and soon deployed to other crisis areas involving ethnic Serbs in both Croatia and Bosnia, where the war was to last until 1995.

The linguistic repertoires of first-generation Ex-Yu migrant workers in Slovenia

While different groups of migrants arriving from other Yugoslav republics had at least three distinct mother tongues, i.e. Serbo-Croat, Macedonian and Albanian (for arrivals from Kosovo), the largest and most prominent of these was without doubt Serbo-Croat, which also merits special consideration for its typological proximity to and mutual intelligibility with Slovene. Typologically, while the Slovene- and Serbo-Croat-speaking space can be seen as a single dialect continuum, the dialectal diversity of both languages also means that different varieties display different levels of phonological, grammatical and lexical proximity when compared to each other. The closest relationships exist between the two main varieties of Slovene, i.e. Eastern and Western Slovene, and their counterparts in the Kajkavian language/dialect spoken in the north-west of Croatia and to some extent the Chakavian variety spoken in Istria and northern Dalmatia (Greenberg, 2000). However, the Shtokavian dialect spoken in eastern Croatia, Bosnia, Serbia and Montenegro, which is also the basis for all present-day Serbo-Croat standard varieties, is sufficiently distinct from all three of these varieties to prevent complete mutual intelligibility. Therefore, although Slovene and Shtokavian Serbo-Croat – the main first language of Ex-Yu immigrants residing in Slovenia – belong to the same subgroup, i.e. Western South Slavic languages, and therefore share many linguistic features, they are also relatively distinct, with Slovene also sharing many typological features with Western Slavic languages like Czech and Slovak (Greenberg, 2000).

Therefore, Ex-Yu migrants arriving in Slovenia were able to some extent to rely on mutual intelligibility between their first language and the dominant language of their surroundings when engaging in communication. This was aided by further sociolinguistic factors, in particular the fact that at the time in Slovenia, Serbo-Croat had the status of a second language associated both with official functions as well as high-prestige domains such as culture, science and business (Stabej, 2007) and was thus acquired by the majority of the population passively, through regular contact, despite having only a nominal presence in the Slovene educational system (Požgaj-Hadži & Balažic-Bulc, 2005). In the rest of the federation, Slovene had no comparable role or status and was therefore not spoken widely outside Slovenia. This meant that arriving migrants likely had little or no competence in Slovene, and since almost all Slovenes were either able to communicate in Serbo-Croat or get by with the partial mutual intelligibility between the languages, there was little motivation for migrants to learn Slovene to fulfil their immediate communicative needs. Additionally, evidence from Mežnarić's (1986) study of Bosnian migrant workers in Slovenia suggests that there was often little social contact among the different ethnic communities at the time, a divide that was presumably compounded to some extent by rising nationalism in this period as well as by the disparity between the social classes that the members of different communities belonged to.

These linguistic and sociolinguistic factors set the Slovene context apart from many others (see, e.g., Capstick and Or & Shohamy, this volume) and had major implications for the linguistic repertoires of the first generation of Ex-Yu migrants in Slovenia. This group, having arrived as adults for the express purpose of filling vacant skilled labour positions, was able to largely rely on Serbo-Croat to fulfil their daily communicative needs. Additionally, as they had no contact with Slovene formal education, any language learning likely occurred passively, through social contact with L1 Slovene speakers and L1 Slovene cultural production (TV, radio, newspapers). While this was to a large extent facilitated by the proximity between the two languages, which allowed many features of Serbo-Croat to be transferred in the process of acquiring Slovene, evidence gathered by Balažic-Bulc (2004) also suggests that the combination of proximity and mutual intelligibility (and likely the lack of explicit instruction) meant that many lexico-grammatical features were overgeneralized as part of this transfer. In terms of second language acquisition, while the proximity of the two languages increased the likelihood of positive transfer where the two systems display significant macro-parametric parallels (e.g. Bardovi-Harlig & Sprouse, 2017;

Ringbom, 2007), it also greatly increases the potential for negative transfer in cases where differences exist at the micro-parametric level (Liceras & de la Fuente, 2015). Table 2.2 summarizes some specific differences between Slovene and Serbo-Croat which may cause negative transfer for learners.

The linguistic repertoires of the first generation of Serbo-Croat-speaking migrants in Slovenia, while disparate and dependent upon a series of local contextual factors, can therefore broadly be described through the continued centrality of the L1. Serbo-Croat, being the dominant language of the Yugoslav federation as a whole and a prestigious second language in Slovenia, continued to be the dominant language of communication for this group, while their linguistic repertoires were supplemented with elements of Slovene where needed. Over time, as they acquired more Slovene, Serbo-Croat L1 migrants can be described as gradually developing an interlanguage, one which contained features of both the L1 and L2, and which, being sufficient for their communicative needs, slowly stabilized (Long, 2003) and became a more permanent part of their linguistic repertoire, with transfer also occurring from L2 to L1 (Mežnarić, 1986; for bidirectional transfer see Pavlenko & Jarvis, 2002). As indicated by various studies (e.g. Baltić, 2006; Bučar Ručman, 2014; Mežnarić, 1986), this drift away from the L1 is likely to have been stimulated by the fact that most migrants received negative feedback from ethnic Slovenes, in either implicit or explicit forms, when using their L1 in public in Slovenia, owing to the increasingly negative attitudes towards it since the 1980s.

Ex-Yu Communities in 1990s Independent Slovenia

Key social and political debates

While Slovene independence was in part motivated by economic and political conditions in other Yugoslav republics – underdevelopment, rise of totalitarianism and nationalism – it was also largely sparked by the reappearance in public discourse of conservative nationalist voices which had largely been silenced since the establishment of socialist Yugoslavia. As described by Močnik (1995; see also Krašovec & Žagar, 2011), the postwar order in the Slovene public sphere was based on an implicit compromise, which allowed the remnants of the conservative middle class to retain their dominance over the fields of culture and education in exchange for their surrender of political and economic power to the new communist bureaucratic elite (see also Savski, 2018a). With the

Table 2.2 Examples of features which (may) cause negative transfer for L1 Serbo-Croat learners of Slovene (summarized from Balažic-Bulc, 2004; Požgaj-Hadži & Ferbežar, 2001; Sussex & Cubberley, 2006).

			Examples of transfer	
Level	Description of difference (examples)	Serbo-Croat	Slovene	Examples of interlanguage[3]
Morphology	Slovene has retained the dual number as an inflectional category while Serbo-Croat has not.	(a) jedna ruka, (b) dve/tri ruke (Eng. (a) one hand, (b) two/three hands)	(a) ena roka, (b) dve roki, (c) tri roke (Eng. (a) one hand, (b) two hands, (c) three hands)	(a) ena roka, (b) dve/tri roke
Syntax	Noun morphology (case) establishes key relationships between clause elements (valency), but the case type used for the same relationship often differs between the two languages.	raditi rukama (Eng. to work with your hands)	delati z rokami (NB: use of preposition)	delati rukama or delati rukami or delati z rukama etc.
Phonology	Both languages have tonal systems for vowel stress, but the systems differ both in pitch and location.	Ekav. [ˈsêːno] or ljekav. [ˈsiêːno] (Eng. hay)	[seˈˌnòː] (tonal) or [seˌ noːˑ] (non-tonal)	[ˈsêːno]
	Certain vowels and consonants are pronounced with slight differences in manner or place of articulation (e.g. Slovene clear [l] differs from the typical Serbo-Croat velarised dark [ɫ]).	[ˈɫɔnats] (Eng. pot)	[ˈlɔ̂ːnəts] (tonal) or [ˈlɔːnəts] (non-tonal)	[ˈɫɔ̂nəts] or [ˈɫɔːnəts]

death of Tito and the subsequent weakening of communist power, open criticism of state power began to be possible from both liberal left-wing voices, in many cases emanating from youth organizations affiliated with the League of Communists, and conservative right-wing voices, mainly promoted by figures from the field of culture. In 1987, the intellectual journal *Nova revija* published a special issue devoted to formulating a 'national programme', with articles written by academic and cultural figures arguing for Slovene independence from Yugoslavia.

The basis for such calls was, in line with the fields from which they emanated, often cultural, based on an entrenched nationalist discourse stemming from the 19th century. Promoted by an upwardly mobile Slovene-speaking petite bourgeoisie locked in competition with the local German-speaking elite of Habsburg times, this discourse combined aspirations for national independence and development with fears of subjugation by external forces (Savski, 2018a). This created a paradox, as larger and more developed Western nations were at the same time constructed as both threats to the existence of the Slovene nation and as ideals of organization and development to which Slovenes should aspire (Vezovnik, 2010; Žižek, 1984). However, while this paradox continues to exist in Slovene public discourse, the predominant representations of the West during the 1980s and 1990s were without doubt positive, to the extent that when the Slovene League of Communists rebranded itself as the more moderate Democratic Renewal Party before the 1990 election, it switched its traditional red colour for the blue associated with the European Community. In contrast, representations of the East, and with it the rest of Yugoslavia, were predominantly negative, associated with underdevelopment, war and political instability (Vezovnik, 2010). The resulting dichotomy was actively perpetuated to justify decisions which worsened the status of Ex-Yu communities in Slovenia.

The most notable of such policies was the case now referred to as 'the Erased' (Sl. *izbrisani*), which refers to approximately 25,000 citizens of other Ex-Yu republics whose names were struck from the register of permanent residents of Slovenia in 1992. This move, since found to have had no legal basis by the Slovene Constitutional Court (in 1999) and to have violated fundamental human rights by the European Court of Human Rights (in 2012), affected migrants who had settled in Slovenia but relied on their equal rights as citizens of other Yugoslav republics rather than requesting Slovene citizenship. Following Slovene independence, these individuals were sent documents calling for them to apply for Slovene citizenship within six months. During this period, many either failed to submit the necessary paperwork or were rejected for either substantive or administrative reasons. After the deadline had passed, following instructions given by the Ministry of Internal Affairs, all these individuals immediately lost the rights associated with permanent residence in Slovenia, such as healthcare, employment, ownership of property, education etc. As a result, many of 'the Erased' were subjected to various degrees of hardship in the following decades (see Kogovšek, 2010), a position which largely remained unresolved until 2010, when legislation to this end was passed.

The case of 'the Erased', while extreme, is also an indicator of how negative representation in public discourse (Vezovnik, 2010) legitimated overtly negative policies against Ex-Yu minorities in Slovenia, a state of affairs mirrored by language policy in newly independent Slovenia. As the issue of language had been one of the main themes raised by pro-independence voices in the late 1980s, in particular the perceived threat it faced from Serbo-Croat (see e.g. Stabej, 2007), it is unsurprising that the main focus of post-independence language policy was on safeguarding the dominance of Slovene in the public sphere, as evidenced by the 1991 Constitution and the 2001 Public Use of Slovene Act. Both acts foregrounded the primacy of Slovene while granting full collective rights to two ethno-linguistic minorities located along borders with Italy and Hungary, mirroring the arrangements made in Yugoslavia, but made no mention of EX-Yu communities or their languages. The backing for this decision was the categorization of Italians and Hungarians as indigenous communities who 'have lived in Slovenia for centuries and in a consolidated territory where they do not self-identify as foreigners or immigrants, but justifiably consider themselves as indigenous, aboriginal or native populations, and in some small settlements retain majority status to this day' (Ribičič, 2004: 32).

Therefore, while it had been first noted as a major language in the territory of Slovenia in 1846, when around 20,000 declared it as their first language (Kržišnik-Bukić *et al.*, 2003), and while its speakers constituted a significant proportion of the population of Slovene urban centres, Serbo-Croat and other Ex-Yu languages were considered to be associated with immigrant communities and therefore not granted collective rights (Petković, 2010). In contrast to the Italian and Hungarian communities, speakers of EX-Yu languages therefore enjoy no special cultural protection with regard to education or public administration, despite the fact that their total number greatly exceeds that of the Italian or Hungarian communities. Any special rights which had been available to them in Yugoslavia were rolled back upon independence, most notably the right to first language education (available at one school in Ljubljana until

1992) and the right to use their first language in communication with officials. The unavailability of the latter was likely a contributing cause to failed communication in cases such as 'the Erased'.

These policy debates were accompanied by various demographic changes in the immediate aftermath of independence. Many immigrants left the country to return to other Ex-Yu republics, particularly those who had either disagreed with Slovene independence or had been affiliated with the Yugoslav People's Army and were considered *personae non gratae* on Slovene soil. Official figures suggest that around 12,000 people emigrated from Slovenia to other Ex-Yu countries during 1991–92, although Kržišnik-Bukić *et al.* (2003) argue that these figures are likely to have been overestimated. The 1990s also saw a new push of immigration to Slovenia, this time in the form of refugees fleeing from the wars in Croatia and Bosnia, who caused a considerable spike in immigration figures in the mid-1990s, and conversely an increase in emigration figures in 1997–98, once hostilities in the post-Yugoslav space had definitively subsided. However, many of those who arrived in this period became long-term residents of Slovenia, as evidenced by the results of the 2002 Census. This adds a further level of complexity when considering Ex-Yu communities in Slovenia, as the different waves were sparked by different motivations and occurred in radically different political environments in Slovenia and their republics of origin.

From interlanguage to sociolect?

On the sociolinguistic side, the 1990s saw a transformation of the linguistic market (Bourdieu, 1991) in Slovenia. While Slovene had been the dominant code within the country during the Yugoslav period, its market value was tempered throughout this period by the higher value that Serbo-Croat gained through its dominance in high-prestige domains, such as federal-level politics, the military, business, academia, as well as popular culture (Stabej, 2007). In the 1990s, however, Serbo-Croat lost most of these markers of prestige while acquiring an increasing number of negative connotations in the public sphere, linked both to the armed conflicts surrounding the breakup of Yugoslavia and to the broadly low socio-economic status of its L1 speakers in Slovenia, who had traditionally occupied positions of employment associated with lower social strata (e.g. manual labourers in construction, cleaners). This combination of factors caused its value on the linguistic market to drop sharply, and as a result its use in the public sphere became rare (Požgaj-Hadži *et al.*, 2009), while other languages symbolic of Western culture, particularly English, began to play a more important role in high-prestige domains alongside Slovene.

For L1 speakers of Serbo-Croat who resided in Slovenia and who had acquired Slovene as a second language, this shift also had other consequences. As described above, the acquisition of Slovene for these individuals, as adult first-generation migrants, predominantly occurred informally, in response to daily communicative needs, and was both enabled and limited by the proximity between the two languages. For these reasons, their acquisition of Slovene as a second language often remained at the level of a stabilized interlanguage, which integrated elements of both languages to different degrees. In the Slovene public sphere, which has traditionally been dominated by a monolingual and prescriptivist language ideology intolerant towards non-standard usage of any kind (Savski, 2018a), this left many first-generation migrants at a serious social disadvantage. Evidence presented by Pirih-Svetina and Ferbežar (2005), who presented authentic samples of L2 Slovene writing to L1 speakers and asked them to correct and rate the texts, indicates that errors in L2 writing are in general poorly received by L1 Slovene speakers, who were generally hesitant in labelling such writing as Slovene. Notably, the extract displaying recognizable signs of negative transfer from Serbo-Croat was given the poorest overall rating by the L1 raters participating in this study (Pirih-Svetina & Ferbežar, 2005).

The 1990s was also a time of growing complexity with regard to ethnic structure in Slovenia, as a second generation of Ex-Yu migrants began to forge its own identity. This growing group, while retaining links to their parents' country of origin, grew up in Slovenia, mostly in apartment blocks newly built to accommodate the expanding population of cities during the 1970s and 1980s. In these areas, families of different Ex-Yu ethnicities reside in close proximity and mixed marriages are common, leading to a blurring of boundaries between ethnic Serbs, Croats, Bosnians, Montenegrins and Macedonians (e.g. Razpotnik *et al.*, 2012). This blurring was also fuelled by the way in which members of Ex-Yu communities were positioned in discourse by the in-group, ethnic Slovenes, where umbrella terms like 'worker' were used in formal situations, while more pejorative expressions prevailed in everyday communication, particularly 'bosanec' (Bosniak, referring to all Ex-Yu ethnicities collectively), 'južnjak' (Southerner) or 'jugović' (a play on the ethnonym 'jugoslovan' [Yugoslav] in which the suffix '-ić' mirrors the common pattern of surnames in the Serbo-Croat-speaking area). In the late 1990s and early 2000s, these pejorative terms were complemented with 'čefur', a term whose recent roots are not clear but which has been hypothesized to have been derived from a historical anti-Semitic slur (Snoj, 2003).

The word 'čefur' has since acquired a variety of new meanings, many of which are no longer directly related to the ethnic affiliation of a group or individual. The term has become synonymous with the Ex-Yu community in the sense that it mediates both negative representation by others while also being used for a type of resistant positive self-representation, as is often the case with ethnic and racial slurs (Bianchi, 2014). Through its association with this type of resistance against in-group discourse, 'čefur' has also become a signifier for a broader youth subculture centred around subversion, one which continues to be associated with Ex-Yu ethnic affiliation, but where such an affiliation is no longer a condition of membership. Instead, Bajić and Protner (2012) argue that the 'čefur' identity is built around a variety of ethnicity-independent characteristics. Among these are features commonly associated with out-groups, such as sociolect (see below), antisocial practices (crime), socio-economic status and class (working-class, blue-collar professions). However, many features are also highly context-specific, in particular those related to visual appearance, where the archetypal 'čefur' is, for instance, associated with particular items of clothing, such as tracksuits and branded items, as well as particular accessories and styling practices (Bajić & Protner, 2012), all of which underlines the partial detachment of the identity of this subculture from ethnicity.

While such visual aspects of 'čefur' identity are difficult to link to particular ethnicities, the language associated with this subculture retains some links to the heritage languages of the Ex-Yu communities. In particular, it is associated with the language use of the second generation of Ex-Yu migrants, which is generally bilingual, having acquired their parents' first language in parallel with the dominant language of the country they live in. Ex-Yu migrants settled predominantly in urban areas, and the contemporary sociolinguistics of Slovene urban centres mirrors that of many European cities, where distinct language varieties have emerged from the innovation of younger members of migrant communities (e.g. Wiese, 2009). The language practices of second-generation Ex-Yu migrants in Slovene cities indicate the emergence of a distinct sociolect, which is clearly a sub-variety of Slovene in terms of lexical and grammatical structure but is at the same time also characterized by the presence of several features rooted in Serbo-Croat. Overall, however, these features are significantly lower in number when compared to the interlanguage of the first generation (see Table 2.2). Examples of such features on the phonological level are the replacement of Slovene phoneme /l/ with its velarised Serbo-Croat equivalent /ł/ and the replacement of the Slovene postalveolar consonants /ʃ, ʒ, tʃ, dʒ/ with the retroflex consonants /ʂ, ʐ, tʂ, dʐ/ characteristic of Shtokavian varieties of Serbo-Croat.

This sociolect gained particular recognition with the publication of the novel Čefurji raus! (Southerners Out!) by author Goran Vojnović in 2008. The main focus of this work, which became a bestseller in Slovenia, is the complex everyday life of a group of young second-generation Ex-Yu migrants, with questions of belonging (such as those highlighted by Angouri et al., this volume) being particularly highlighted. One of the notable elements of this novel is its language, as the narration switches between different varieties of Slovene and Serbo-Croat, with the main characters' sociolect being the dominant code. This signalled a significant departure from the Slovene literary tradition, which generally conforms to the historically negative valuation of non-standard language varieties (Savski, 2018a) by using standard Slovene as the dominant code. With Čefurji raus!, Vojnović challenged this established balance of powers on the linguistic market by elevating the sociolect to the level of literary discourse, and it is significant that the novel became a bestseller while also receiving multiple awards from the Slovene literary establishment.

This acceptance can be seen as an indication of ongoing changes in Slovene society, particularly with regard to the socioeconomic status of Ex-Yu migrants, their visibility in the public sphere and an ongoing revaluation of history. As discussed above, upon their arrival in Slovenia, the first generation of Ex-Yu migrants occupied low-status positions of employment in sectors like industry and construction. However, by the mid-2000s, upward mobility had gradually raised the educational profile of members of the Ex-Yu community, particularly of the second generation (Medvešek, 2007). At the same time, the appearance of public figures representing the community has increased its overall visibility and has, to an extent, improved the level of social and cultural capital of its members. A notable example is Ljubljana mayor Zoran Janković, born in Serbia and previously CEO of the largest Slovene supermarket chain Mercator, who in 2011 formed a national political party and secured the largest share of the vote in the parliamentary election only months later. Finally, improvement of Ex-Yu migrants' cultural capital has also been facilitated by trends in pop culture, for instance the appearance of Yugo-nostalgia, a positive revaluation of the former state's cultural legacy which has grown in popularity across the post-Yugoslav space (e.g. Volčič, 2007).

Ex-Yu Communities in 21st-Century Slovenia: Drafting and Debating Language Policy

Language policy is a particular area where the existence both of a shift in attitudes towards Ex-Yu communities and of resistance to it may be observed. An example of this is the Resolution for a National Language Policy Programme 2014–2018 (below: RLP-14), adopted by the Slovene parliament in July 2013 and intended to set a common agenda for state institutions in the area of language policy. This document went through several stages of development during a turbulent political period, which also saw significant debate regarding the status of different minorities in Slovenia, in many cases explicitly or implicitly in relation to the Ex-Yu communities. This section reports on the findings of a broader study concerning the development and implementation of this policy, featuring analyses of key documents, media discourse and interviews with key actors (see also Savski, 2016a, 2016b, 2017, 2018b). Extracts presented below are drawn from the data used in this research.

The first stages in the development of this policy, its planning and drafting, while coordinated by parts of the Slovene government, were largely delegated to various expert committees, consisting mainly of linguists. As described elsewhere (Savski, 2017), this period was marked both by political instability and by struggles between different interest groups to dominate the agenda in language policy. Different groups of linguists aligned themselves with different political parties, and as governments changed, so did the access of different actors to the drafting process, which ultimately meant that several different draft versions of the policy were produced. While the central focus of these struggles was often the issue of which areas would secure research funding through the policy (Savski, 2017), the surrounding debates also involved significant clashes between different language ideologies and therefore also between different visions of minority language policy. An example of such struggles can be seen in the following two versions of a part of the section entitled 'Languages of minorities and immigrants in Slovenia'[4]:

> One of the important goals to which Slovenia is bound by EU principles is therefore to ensure to all speakers whose L1 is not Slovene (including members of indigenous communities, the Roma community and all others) the right to maintain and/or revitalise their own language and culture. Some goals and measures to this end are proposed by the White paper for education (2011), for instance the systemic teaching of mother tongues (and respective cultures), the formation of suitable curricula and

teacher training. However, the solutions and recommendations of the 2011 White paper must be expanded with the following measures:

- Language training for public officials for communication in Hungarian and Italian, and Romani in the areas settled by the Roma community.
- Training public officials to work with speakers whose first language is not Slovene (including accommodation to speakers by using their language or a third (common) language if needed).
- Training translators and interpreters for languages where shortages may occur (as required by community interpreting).
- Ensuring suitable space in the public media in the languages of speakers whose first language is not Slovene and who have no space thus far and who wish to have such a media presence.

When comparing this initial version (published April 2012) to its later revision (published January 2013), there is clear evidence of a shift in influence with regard to language ideology:

The starting principle of language policy in this area in the following period is that all speakers whose first language is not Slovene have, in line with human rights and EU principles, the right to maintain and develop their first language and culture. To this end, the Sub-programme for language education must include measures which will also ensure better opportunities at a systemic level for first/mother tongue learning to other immigrants and minority communities in those areas, where this need is detected by the state or local communities. Such provisions shall be systemically conditioned by parallel learning of Slovene as a second or foreign language.

In addition to the measures to be specified by the Sub-programme, the following measures shall be implemented:

- Language training for public officials for communication in official minority languages.
- Training translators and interpreters for languages where shortages may occur (as required by community interpreting).

The transformations made during the redrafting can be observed in both parts of this extract. The first is the paragraph which provides a rationale for policy in this area: whereas the initial version placed great focus on the need to expand existing provisions, the revised text mitigates this claim by adding two statements, one conditioning the implementation of the policy with a 'need [being] detected by the state or local communities' and another conditioning it with 'parallel learning of Slovene'. The second set of changes occurred in the part enumerating the specific measures, whose number was significantly reduced in the revised version, in particular with the deletion of measures regarding officials' use of other languages and in terms of providing media space for minorities. These changes followed a broader pattern, stemming from the fact that the writers of the original text had significantly different views on minority language policy compared to the writers charged with its revision (Savski, 2017). This disparity is confirmed by one of the original writers' memory of a meeting which occurred after the first version was complete but before the revisions were made and which included figures from both sides:

> **Stabej:** At this only meeting there was a lot of discourse about how, while there are many good solutions [in the policy], there are also many cases where we had gone too far, and these may endanger the good solutions. I don't know what was meant by good solutions, but out of the bad ones there was this idea that we had offered far too much to the non-indigenous minorities, where I personally had had the feeling that we had remained at the level of political correctness. [...] For example I heard comments that, well, a couple of Vietnamese could just set up their own school [based on our policy], that sort of stuff.

This narrative from linguist Marko Stabej (University of Ljubljana), leader of the team which had written the first version of the policy, provides insight into one of the key debates surrounding the creation of the policy. As discussed above, previous language policies in Slovenia had invariably followed the criterion of indigeneity (Sl. *avtohtonost*) by drawing clear distinctions between the Italian- and Hungarian-speaking communities and all other groups. This dichotomous approach had been challenged to an extent by awarding limited rights to the Roma community in 2007 (Rončević, 2005), but there had previously been little deviation from it in the case of Ex-Yu minorities. The first version of the policy made clear moves toward shifting this policy and extending several rights to non-indigenous communities, including the rights to representation in the media and to communication with public officials using the community's L1, both of which had previously only been granted to the Italian and Hungarian communities, and to the Roma in some cases. The second version, while retaining some of the language which had been used to support these changes, saw the deletion of the concrete measures proposed.

The tension between these two visions continued to be apparent as the proposed policy was discussed in the Slovene parliament, which was due to formally adopt it as a resolution. In the Slovene National Assembly, the main legislative body, RLP-14 was debated twice at the committee level, once by the Committee for Culture and once by the Commission for National Communities. The latter is the main locus for political representation of the Italian and Hungarian minorities, each of which has one deputy out of a total of 90 in the National Assembly, whereas other minorities have no formal representation. In the case of RLP-14, the Committee for Culture was designated as the parent committee and was therefore the site where concrete amendments could be debated, whereas the Commission for National Communities was an interested body which could debate the policy but had to submit any proposed amendments to the Committee for Culture.

The dynamics of the different debates about RLP-14 were heavily influenced by the formal composition of the National Assembly. Most notably, the Italian and Hungarian deputies were able to make concrete proposals for the document to be changed, most specifically to divide the section on minority languages analysed above into two parts, one referring specifically to the Italian and Hungarian language, and another covering all other minority languages. This expanded section contained a number of measures aimed at 'securing the conditions for equal private and public use of the Italian and Hungarian languages', and though it was ultimately not included in the final version of the policy, several of its elements were integrated into the text. Another influence on the debates was the background of the different deputies involved, which allowed a number of different agendas to be pushed to the foreground. For instance, the position of Slovene Sign Language in RLP-14 was greatly enhanced due to the background and personal negotiating efforts of deputy Jani Möderndorfer, leader of the largest political group in the National Assembly and previously a sign language interpreter.

Debates surrounding Ex-Yu minorities saw much less explicit advocacy. While further changes had been made to the policy before it was submitted to the National Assembly, with the newly incumbent centre-left government reversing several of the deletions made by the second drafting team (see above), no changes were proposed in the parliamentary debates on behalf of the Ex-Yu communities. The only debate in which the communities were explicitly mentioned occurred not at the Commission for National Communities but at the Committee for Culture, where right-wing deputy Jožef Jerovšek questioned the terminology used in the proposed text. Specifically, he argued that the term 'minorities' should not be used in reference to immigrant communities, since that would establish a legal precedent and serve as a basis for demands to expand the rights of Ex-Yu communities:

> Jerovšek: Well, I don't want to create a precedent, but there have been different types of demands that we have to grant the status of indigenous minorities or minorities with equal constitutional rights to other immigrant communities. But this means a complete change of our constitution, the number of deputies will change, everything, all other stuff. And to make a precedent about things through this law I think is incorrect. This is a precedent which they will of course quickly be happy about and lean on. [...] And of course, if you give some community the status of a minority, it will then for example sooner or later demand to have bilingual signs in Cyrillic script, which were there at railway stations under another regime in Slovenia for a long time, but they have all the right to demand even this if they get the status of a minority.

As can be seen, Jerovšek's claims mainly relied on the slippery slope argument, i.e. suggesting that the wording used in RLP-14 might establish a precedent which would then allow the Ex-Yu communities to demand much greater rights. Also of interest is his use of historical narrative in this extract, specifically his veiled reference to communist Yugoslavia ('another regime'), which indicates a continued association between Ex-Yu communities and the former state, particularly in right-wing rhetoric. Jerovšek's arguments, though ultimately having no consequence for the wording of RLP-14, also highlight the effects of the lack of representation of Ex-Yu communities in the Slovene parliament. Whereas the Italian and Hungarian minorities could rely both on their own deputies and on an established locus for debates relevant to them (the Commission for National Communities), and Slovene Sign Language users could rely on the efforts of an interested deputy, the Ex-Yu communities could avail themselves of no such possibility, and were therefore left largely without a voice in this debate.

Conclusions: When Does a Migrant Become Indigenous?

This chapter has focused on the past and present status and identity of communities which developed largely during the existence of socialist Yugoslavia through migration to Slovenia from its other parts. As discussed, the motivation for this migration was largely economic, as a combination of emigration and social development had led to a shortage of blue-collar workers in Slovenia. However, this movement can also be attributed to a secondary driving factor, namely the integrative policy of the Yugoslav state, which sought to alleviate the ethnic divisions that had previously caused conflict between its nations. The migration happened in several waves, the first of which occurred in the 1960s and the last in the early 1980s, with the economic downturn that followed the death of President Tito also causing a slowdown in employment opportunities in Slovenia. A further wave of migration, although less significant in number, came after the dissolution of the federation as a direct result of the Yugoslav wars, the new arrivals being refugees rather than economic migrants.

While citizens of other Yugoslav republics enjoyed some linguistic rights for as long as the federation existed, a review of Slovene language policy since independence indicates that little attention was paid to the needs and rights of the Ex-Yu communities. This approach was backed by the concept of indigeneity, which promoted minorities that occupy a consolidated territory and have done so for a considerable period of time (Ribičič, 2004). This criterion established a clear differentiation between the Hungarian and Italian minorities on the one hand, which are afforded collective linguistic rights, and the Ex-Yu communities on the other, which are treated as immigrant communities and granted no collective rights. Such a clear distinction has also been supported by a clear pattern of negative representation of Ex-Yu communities in public discourse, a consequence mainly of inter-ethnic conflicts stemming from the end of the Yugoslav period, and by the relatively low socioeconomic status of most members of the communities.

This asymmetric approach to minority rights in Slovenia should be seen as an example of continuity in language policy, as the arrangement has largely remained unchanged since the Yugoslav period (Ribičič, 2004). It should at this point be noted that this policy has largely been facilitated by the continued active engagement of the Italian and Hungarian states on behalf of each minority, both through financial support and advocacy through diplomatic channels, justified through the relatively recent dates when each minority came to be part of the territory of Yugoslavia or Slovenia rather than their respective nation states (Hungarians: 1919, Italians: 1945). With this in mind, their situation contrasts sharply with that of other communities. For instance, the German-speaking minority in Slovenia, while greatly diminished in number due to mass emigration after its members had been branded as aggressors in the aftermath of World War II, remained anchored in the history of a number of Slovene regions but failed to secure collective linguistic rights as a result of relative disinterest from the newly formed Republic of Austria. Similarly, Ex-Yu minorities could hardly count on the advocacy of newly formed nation states during the 1990s, when the states themselves were either engaged in or recovering from the Yugoslav wars. Therefore, while the indigenous versus non-indigenous dichotomy appears to be grounded in empirical evidence, this is in fact a highly subjective criterion in the Slovene context, influenced as much by the geopolitical balance of powers in the present as it was in history.

The positioning of Ex-Yu communities as non-indigenous in Slovenia is further challenged by their ambiguous position with regard to the concepts underlying this categorization of minorities. Fundamentally, the Slovene understanding of the distinction relies on a differentiation between communities as either active or passive actors in historical processes, with indigenous communities seen as passive bystanders in the process of breaking up multi-ethnic states and non-indigenous communities seen as active movers who cross political and ethnic boundaries with economic motivation. While this distinction appears clear-cut, it is in truth far from that, as Ex-Yu minorities could conceivably be positioned in either category, having on the one hand migrated to Slovenia driven by economic motivation, but on the other hand having done so within the territory of what was then a single state. Crucially, these communities have also ended up on the territory of independent Slovenia as a result of its secession from Yugoslavia. This underlines the complexity of Ex-Yu migrants' present-day status in Slovenia, where they alternately play various roles, ranging from that of a dangerous Other to that of an outlet for the development of youth subculture.

Notes

(1) I wish to thank Dr Robert Grošelj for his input on Table 2.2, though any inaccuracies in any part of the chapter are of course my own responsibility.
(2) For the purposes of this chapter, Serbo-Croat will be used as an umbrella term to refer to all standard and non-standard historical and present-day varieties of Serbian, Croatian, Bosnian and Montenegrin.
(3) It should be noted that the comparison here is between Shtokavian (Ekavian and Ijekavian) Serbo-Croat and standard Slovene, which differs significantly from informal spoken Slovene. For instance, while the dual is a key component of standard Slovene, its use in spoken language may vary. Additionally, while standard Slovene is nominally tonal, in line with dialects spoken in the north-western and central areas of the country (including the surroundings of the capital Ljubljana), the majority of other dialects are not tonal, and realizations of standard speech can be assumed to vary greatly between these two possibilities.
(4) All translations of policy documents, interview extracts and parliamentary records by the author.

References

Bajić, B. and Protner, B. (2012) 'Trenirke' in 'oranžne face' – 'vidiš ga pa veš': Diskurz o zunanji podobi čefurja. *Etnolog* 22, 93–110.

Balažic-Bulc, T. (2004) Jezikovni prenos pri učenju sorodnih jezikov (na primeru slovenščine in srbohrvaščine). *Jezik in slovstvo* 49 (3–4), 77–89.

Baltić, A. (2006) *Diskriminacija na osnovi etnične pripadnosti z vidika Albancev, Bošnjakov, Črnogorcev, Hrvatov, Makedoncev in Srbov: poročilo o raziskavi.* Ljubljana: Mirovni Inštitut.

Bardovi-Harlig, K. and Sprouse, R. (2017) Negative versus positive transfer. In J. Liontas (ed.) *The TESOL Encyclopedia of English Language Teaching.* Hoboken, NJ: Wiley. See https://doi.org/10.1002/9781118784235.eelt0084 (accessed 11 October 2019).

Bianchi, C. (2014) Slurs and appropriation: An echoic account. *Journal of Pragmatics* 66, 35–44.

Bourdieu, P. (1991) *Language and Symbolic Power.* Cambridge, MA: Polity Press.

Bučar Ručman, A. (2014) *Migracije in kriminaliteta. Pogled čez meje stereotipov in predsodkov.* Ljubljana: ZRC SAZU.

Bugarski, R. (2012) Language, identity and borders in the former Serbo-Croatian area. *Journal of Multilingual and Multicultural Development* 33 (3), 219–235.

Constitution of the Socialist Federal Republic of Yugoslavia (1974), Ustava Socialistične federativne republike Jugoslavije (1974). See https://sl.wikisource.org/wiki/Ustava_Socialistične_federativne_republike_Jugoslavije_(1974) (accessed 13 November 2017).

Greenberg, M.L. (2000) *A Historical Phonology of the Slovene Language.* Heidelberg: Universitätsverlag C. Winter.

Kogovšek, N. (2010) Izbrisani včeraj, danes, jutri – spodkopani stereotipi in nepovrnljiva pot k popravi krivic. In N. Kogovšek and B. Petković (eds) *Brazgotine izbrisa: prispevek k kritičnemu razumevanju izbrisa iz registra stalnih prebivalcev Republike Slovenije* (pp. 219–244). Ljubljana: Mirovni inštitut.

Krašovec, P. and Žagar, I. (2011) *Evropa med socializmom in neoliberalizmom: Evropa v slovenskih medijih.* Ljubljana: Pedagoški inštitut.

Kržišnik-Bukić, V., Komac, M. and Klopčič, V. (2003) *Položaj in status pripadnikov narodov nekdanje Jugoslavije v Sloveniji.* Ljubljana: Inštitut za narodnostna vprašanja.

Liceras, J.M. and de la Fuente, A.A. (2015) Typological proximity in L2 acquisition: The Spanish non-native grammar of French speakers. In T. Judy and S. Perpiñán (eds) *The Acquisition of Spanish in Understudied Language Pairings* (pp. 329–358). Amsterdam: John Benjamins.

Long, M. (2003) Stabilization and fossilization in interlanguage. In C. Doughty and M. Long (eds) *The Handbook of Second Language Acquisition* (pp. 487–536). Oxford: Blackwell.

Medvešek, M. (2007) Kdo so potomci priseljencev z območja nekdanje Jugoslavije? *Razprave in gradivo* 53–54, 28–67.

Mežnarić, S. (1986) *Bosanci. A kuda idejo Slovenci nedeljom?* Ljubljana: Krt.

Močnik, R. (1995) *Ekstravagantia II: koliko fašizma.* Ljubljana: ISH – Institutum studiorum humanitatis.

Pavlenko, A. and Jarvis, S. (2002) Bidirectional transfer. *Applied Linguistics* 23, 190–214.

Petković, B. (2010) Izbrisani jezik. In N. Kogovšek and B. Petković (eds) *Brazgotine izbrisa: prispevek k kritičnemu razumevanju izbrisa iz registra stalnih prebivalcev Republike Slovenije* (pp. 219–244). Ljubljana: Mirovni Inštitut.

Pirih-Svetina, N. and Ferbežar, I. (2005) Slovenščine tujejezičnih govorcev. *Jezik in slovstvo* 50 (6), 3–15.
Požgaj-Hadži, V. and Ferbežar, I. (2001) Tudi to je slovenščina. In I. Orel (ed.) *37. seminar slovenskega jezika, literature in kulture* /.../ (pp. 57–68). Ljubljana: Center za slovenščino kot drugi/tuji jezik.
Požgaj-Hadži, V. and Balažic-Bulc, T. (2005) Kam je izginila srbohrvaščina? Status jezika nekoč in danes. In M. Stabej (ed.) *41. seminar slovenskega jezika, kulture in literature* /.../ (pp. 30–39). Ljubljana: Center za slovenščino kot drugi/tuji jezik.
Požgaj-Hadži, V., Balažic Bulc, T. and Miheljak, V. (2009) Srbohrvaščina v Sloveniji: nekoč in danes. In V. Požgaj-Hadži, T. Balažic Bulc, V. Gorjanc (eds) *Med politiko in stvarnostjo: jezikovna sitaucija v novonastalih državah bivše Jugoslavije* (pp. 27–40). Ljubljana: Znanstvena založba Filozofske fakultete.
Razpotnik, Š., Dekleva, B. and Uzelac, M. (2012) Konec koncev vsaj ni(h)če v moški kulturi. In B. Dekleva and Š. Razpotnik (eds) Čefurji so bili rojeni tu: Življenje mladih priseljencev druge generacije v Ljubljani (pp. 203–258). Ljubljana: Pedagoška fakulteta.
Ribičič, C. (2004) Ustavnopravno varstvo manjšinskih narodnih skupnosti v Sloveniji. *Revus* 2, 29–43.
Ringbom, H. (2007) *Cross-Linguistic Similarity in Foreign Language Learning*. Bristol: Multilingual Matters.
Rončević, B. (2005) Education of ethnic minorities in Slovenia: An element of or an obstacle to development? In N. Genov (ed.) *Ethnicity and Educational Policies in South Eastern Europe*. Berlin & Sofia: Free University Institute of Eastern European Studies.
Savski, K. (2016a) State language policy in time and space: Meaning, transformation, recontextualisation. In E. Barakos and J.W. Unger (eds) *Discursive Approaches to Language Policy* (pp. 51–70). Basingstoke: Palgrave.
Savski, K. (2016b) Analysing voice in language policy: Plurality and conflict in Slovene government documents. *Language Policy* 15 (4), 505–524.
Savski, K. (2017) Language policy at times of instability and struggle: The impact of fluctuating will and competing agendas on a Slovene language strategy. *Current Issues in Language Planning* 18 (3), 283–302.
Savski, K. (2018a) Monolingualism and prescriptivism: The ecology of Slovene in the 20th century. *Journal of Multilingual and Multicultural Development* 39 (2), 124–136.
Savski, K. (2018b) The roles of field and capital in negotiating language policy in the Slovene parliament. *Journal of Language and Politics* 17 (1), 24–45.
Snoj, M. (2003) *Etimološki slovar*. Ljubljana: Modrijan.
Stabej, M. (2007) Size isn't everything: The relation between Slovenian and Serbo-Croatian in Slovenia. *International Journal of the Sociology of Language* 183, 13–30.
Statistical Office of the Republic of Slovenia (2002) *Population Census*. See https://www.stat.si/popis2002/si/default.htm (accessed 13 May 2019).
Sussex, R. and Cubberley, P. (2006) *The Slavic Languages*. Cambridge: Cambridge University Press.
Tollefson, J. (1981) *The Language Situation and Language Policy in Slovenia*. Washington: University Press of America.
Vezovnik, A. (2010) Kritična analiza političnih diskurzov o izbrisanih v žanrih mnenjske zvrsti. *Družboslovne razprave* 64, 45–62.
Volčič, Z. (2007) Yugo-Nostalgia: Cultural memory and media in the former Yugoslavia. *Critical Studies in Media Communication* 24 (1), 21–38.

Wiese, H. (2009) Grammatical innovation in multiethnic urban Europe: New linguistic practices among adolescents. *Lingua* 119 (5), 782–806.

Žižek, S. (1984) Krekovstvo. *Družboslovne razprave* 1 (1), 147–164.

Zorn, J. (2010) Vpisani kot delavci, izbrisani kot Neslovenci: pogled izbrisanih na obdobje tranzicije. In N. Kogovšek and B. Petković (eds) *Brazgotine izbrisa: prispevek k kritičnemu razumevanju izbrisa iz registra stalnih prebivalcev Republike Slovenije* (pp. 19–45). Ljubljana: Mirovni Inštitut.

3 Resisting Discriminatory Immigration Procedures and Practices in the UK and Pakistan: A Discourse-Ethnographic Approach to Exploring Migration Literacies

Tony Capstick

Introduction

The central theme running through this volume is discrimination and the myriad ways language provides opportunities to resist or subvert it. This chapter contributes to this discussion of migrants' opportunities to counter discriminatory discourses by exploring non-institutional contexts and touching on informal sectors of the economy. How migrants negotiate resistance at the family level has received little attention, particularly migrant families' practices before and after migration. This chapter explores one family's attempts to resist and subvert the UK's discriminatory immigration procedures and practices by examining their access to literacy in a range of sites and how this access presents opportunities to contest discrimination, e.g. in the workplace. Settings addressed in this contribution include migrants' homes in Pakistan and the UK, a solicitor's office, a take-away restaurant and taxi office in Lancashire UK, and the online spaces of Facebook which connect family members and friends with each other in these settings and beyond. The chapter draws on work developed by Duchêne et al. (2013), exploring migration and social inequalities by focusing in particular on concepts introduced by Ahearn (2012: 278) and the socioculturally mediated capacity to act by exploring the strategies that migrants use to resist discriminatory discourses. By drawing on work in the Discourse Historical Approach (DHA) in Critical Discourse Studies (CDS) on literacy as social practice, literacy practices are understood as sites of resistance and 'the varying opportunities migrants have to negotiate position, agency, and resistance through language' (Duchêne et al., 2013: 10).

Literacy in this study is seen as social practice, applied in different contexts to meet different purposes. In the vignettes which follow, each of which engages closely with data collected during the study to illustrate key findings, these varied contexts and purposes are all related to migration. Taking the approach outlined above meant exploring different activities involving reading and writing in the everyday lives of family members and relating these practices to individuals' migrations. These literacy practices are embedded in the histories of families connected by chain migration between Pakistan and the UK as well as in the contingent and ever-changing context of immigration policies in the UK. An important aspect to the ethnographic perspective adopted here is participant observation. This approach to data collection necessitated taking part in activities with family members in Pakistan (Mirpur) and the UK (Lancashire) as well as observing activities and asking about individuals' migrations in interviews. As a result, an extensive range of data was generated from many different locations in Mirpur and Lancashire. The combination of the social practices approach to the study of literacy with the DHA adopted here lends itself to working with such large data sets. The insider perspective, which is a central aim of any literacy practices approach, was integrated with the DHA's critical perspective on society. This meant that the framework was used to analyse social situations in which conflicts related to literacy and migration arise.

The scope of this study thus goes beyond an analysis of the texts of immigration to include language use in the workplace as well as the literacy practices that link texts with institutions, social structures and discourses about migration. This approach was taken because, for migrants arriving in a new location, knowledge of the language practices as well as of the appropriate interactional and interpretive strategies is key to negotiating access to work and the organization of family life. The interviews and participant observation carried out in homes and workplaces in Pakistan and the UK were analysed using primarily discourse analysis in order to identify the linguistic resources migrants use to subvert the control of powerful social agents, i.e. both members of the Mirpuri community and the bureaucratic agencies which regulate immigration in the target country, in this case the UK. In Ahearn's (2012: 278) terms, this study traces the 'socioculturally mediated capacity to act, along with strategies to contest and resist'.

Mirpuris in Britain

The term 'community cohesion' emerged out of the Cantle report (Home Office, 2001) in the UK. This report was written in response to the May 2001 'riots', which saw young white men fighting young Pakistani and Bangladeshi men in East Lancashire, West Yorkshire and the Greater Manchester metropolitan area. It is in East Lancashire that Usman, the key respondent in this study, now lives. Since the 2001 'riots' in the northern mill towns, the terror attacks in the US on 11 September 2001 ('9/11') and in the UK on 7 July 2005 ('7/7'), British Muslims have experienced intense scrutiny from both media and politicians. This negative attitude has become central to public debates about Pakistani Muslims in the UK, often focusing on their alleged lack of desire or ability to cohere with their Anglo neighbours. The Cantle report introduced the concept of 'parallel lives' into the debate and the subsequent chain of discourse which, Blackledge (2005) argues, began with the riots. In 2004, David Goodhart argued that 17 of Britain's 20 most segregated towns are in the north and north-west of England, in particular the Pennine towns of East Lancashire and West Yorkshire – in other words, the towns in which the research participants in this study live.

Blackledge (2005) has traced how this portrayal of minority groups links minority languages with threats to democracy, civil disorder and notions of citizenship and nationhood. He argues that these arguments travel along chains of discourse until they gain the legitimacy of the state and are normalized in laws such as the Nationality, Immigration and Asylum Act (2002), which Blackledge links discursively to the riots in 2001. Although such legitimation is granted by the state, it is then taken up in non-institutional as well as institutional settings and sets in motion particular ways of speaking about migrants, ways which are in turn taken up by migrants as well as non-migrants. Until the Nationality, Immigration and Asylum Act (2002), spouses were exempt from the requirement for British citizenship applicants to have 'sufficient knowledge of the English, Welsh or Scottish Gaelic language', which was introduced in the British Nationality Act 1981 (Blackledge, 2005). The 2002 Act extended this requirement to people applying for naturalization on the basis of marriage and introduced a requirement that applicants should demonstrate knowledge about life in the UK. In 2005, the

'Life in the UK Test' became a requirement for those applying for British Citizenship; then, in 2007, this requirement was extended to applicants for indefinite leave to remain in the UK. However, it was not until legislation introduced in November 2010 that visa applicants from non-European Economic Authority countries had to provide evidence of having passed an English language test prior to applying for a visa to the UK. These tests discriminate against the many applicants who do not have access to quality English language courses or test preparation courses in their home countries (Capstick, 2011).

Many young British Pakistanis marrying into Mirpuri families are among those most affected by this legislation. Overall, migrants from the Mirpur district make up the majority of the Pakistani community in England. Indeed, a report produced for the Department for Communities and Local Government in 2009 stated that '[t]here are no accurate figures available but it is estimated that 60 per cent of the Pakistani population is from the Mirpur District' (2009: 6).

In a previous study, Shaw (1988) argues that transnational marriage enables these young British men and women to meet kinship responsibilities through the diversification of assets, such as links to property in Pakistan as well as the UK. In his study of migration and the Mirpuri economy, Ballard (2008) argues that it is economic remittances that have had the greatest impact on Mirpuri society, given the many millions of pounds that have been remitted to the area over the last 60 years. However, Bolognani (2014) argues that British Mirpuris' relationship with Mirpur has shifted over the past 10 years towards the idea that 'back home' offers the potential for social or economic gain and a highly traditional relationship.

In their recent work, Charsley and Bolognani (2017: 45) suggest that the negative portrayal of the marriage migrant or 'freshie' represents an attempt by British-born Pakistanis to clarify cultural boundaries and assertions of belonging by distancing themselves from 'fresh' arrivals. In these representations constructed by British-born Pakistanis, distancing of British Pakistanis from their counterparts from South Asia is made all the more tense by close kinship ties and the ongoing practice of transnational marriage insofar as these counter a clear division between the two constructed groups of 'us', the British-born, and 'them', the 'fresh' migrants. The authors argue that intra-ethnic discrimination of this kind is not unique to British Pakistanis. In their analysis of YouTube comedy videos mocking recent arrivals from Pakistan, the authors demonstrate how the interpretations of the 'freshie' centre on 'internalized racism, displacing of stigma and attempts to negotiate local hierarchies of belonging' (2017: 45).

Others have documented the category of 'fresh off the boat' (see Pyke & Dang, 2003; Shankar, 2008), while McAuliffe (2008) has shown how those in this category often lack fluency in the language of the country to which they are migrating. Realigned gender hierarchies in the UK homes of new migrants mean that male migrants may not necessarily look forward to becoming heads of households in Britain, whilst those arriving as husbands of British Pakistani women may find themselves in subordinate positions in domestic relations of power (Charsley, 2005). Moreover, the contrast with the 'freshie's' supposed dubious immigration status emphasizes British Pakistanis' own ambiguous entitlement to British citizenship. Amid the heightened problematization of British Muslim identities in the wake of 9/11 and the 2001 'riots', and with British national identity increasingly marked as white, British Pakistanis place increasing emphasis on citizenship as a form of identity and belonging (Hussain & Bagguley, 2005).

Theoretical Orientations

The theoretical framework for this chapter draws on literacy studies and Critical Discourse Studies (CDS). This is because both traditions have an interest in the ways in which power dominates spaces and institutions and in how resistance is linked to processes of both regulation and contestation. Issues of power and resistance are explored here in the discourses of immigration produced by migrants themselves, rather than in the discourses of the social actors who discriminate against them. This study is thus part of the recent move towards critical sociolinguistic studies (Blommaert, 2012; Coupland, 2010; Heller, 2010) and shares the view that the settings under investigation are made up of permeable boundaries, shaped by activities, individuals, institutions and discourses which provide countless opportunities to remain open and flexible (Duchêne et al., 2013; Marcus, 2005). Furthermore, following Duchêne et al. (2013), single-site settings and institutional interactions in those settings are not seen as autonomous events with contextual information merely added on; rather, the approach I take looks across these settings, activities and individuals by investigating the ways in which discourses circulate and are recontextualized (Bauman & Briggs, 1990; Duchêne et al., 2013).

Recontextualization is also of significance in Blackledge's (2005) analysis of the connections that were made between civil unrest in towns in northern England in 2001 and, at the end of the following year, the introduction of the Nationality, Immigration and Asylum Act by the UK government. This new legislation meant that the spouses of British citizens had to demonstrate proficiency in English if they wished to apply for British citizenship. Blackledge identified complex chains of discourse, thereby revealing that political actors' attitudes towards the violence in the northern towns reflected their view that some Asian residents' inability to speak English contributed to the violence. Minority language use in this part of the UK and its links to the Mirpur division of Azad Kashmir in Pakistan was a significant theme in work I carried out for my PhD, which explored the language and literacy practices which bind together specific parts of Pakistan and the UK (Capstick, 2016). I will refer to this work as 'the broader study' in this chapter. Data from the broader study as well as new data are analysed here in order to examine in greater depth how migrants counter discriminatory discourses in their literacy practices. When the key respondent in this study, Usman, started work in a take-away restaurant two months after his arrival in the UK, he told me that there was conflict between the men he described as 'Britishborns' – men of Pakistani heritage born and raised in the UK – and those born in Pakistan. It is the linguistic dimension of this discrimination on which the following vignettes focus.

Resistance in Language and Literacy Resources

Research on resistance, language and literacy is brought together here to understand how migrants counter discourses and construct alternative identities to those portrayed in the discriminatory discourses mentioned above. Holly and Meinhof's (2013) work pays attention to what it means to claim a language as a resource. Resistance is linked to the different aspects in which language operates as a means of countering domination. In their study, this approach foregrounds the contestation that social actors in Germany take to dominant discourses of integration which are common in public spaces. Their findings demonstrate how these discourses on immigration have become the object of positioning for migrant communities that often distance themselves by criticizing them and contesting their ideological foundation, but they also tend to adopt some more subtle stance taking which embraces the dominant discourse. Thus, resistance takes the form of counter-discourses which nuance and reconfigure the official and dominant discourse on integration (Holly & Meinhof, 2013).

In the vignettes which follow, I begin by looking at how new migrants counter intra-ethnic discrimination at work. This is followed by an analysis of how family members also seek to counter discriminatory discourses when they appropriate the discourses of the visa application system. I see this as a contribution to what Holly and Meinhof describe as resistance as action through language (2013: 17). This approach has been taken up across different studies as a means to understand the role of language in relation to migration, institutions and work. For example, Holly and Meinhof (2013) focus on how action can be seen in discursive terms, where speaking out and taking a stance vis-à-vis integration is seen as a way of resisting political correctness. They show how taking a stance in this way is a way of 'exercising one's own agency by positioning oneself and creating new forms of allegiance'. In the following vignettes the forms of allegiance Usman develops in the months before and after his migration to the UK are identified. Social networks in the UK as well as in Pakistan are all made up of significant allegiances for Usman, his friends and family in the transnational network.

In order to understand how Usman and his family members exercise their agency, I analyse Usman's workplace practices and the texts of their everyday life as well as the institutional texts of immigration. Work in literacy studies takes practices as the central focus in the study of texts, 'encompassing what people do with texts and what these activities mean to them' (Barton & Hamilton, 2000: 9). However, Barton and Hamilton (2000) claim that practices are neither accidental nor random but are given their structure by institutions. This includes social institutions, such as the family, education and religion. Bureaucratic institutions, which are more formally structured through rules and procedures, documentation and penalties, are also part of this investigation as migrants regularly come into contact with these institutions when attempting to migrate to the UK from Pakistan. Consequently, an important focus of the study was the extent to which institutions, with the power to shape literacy, supported dominant literacy practices while suppressing vernacular literacy practices. Vernacular here refers to the self-supported and self-sponsored literacies which are less about formal institutional practices than about what individuals and communities do with literacy away from formal settings. Vernacular literacies may well be less visible but are still a significant aspect of the reading and writing that occur when migrants migrate.

In this study, these vernacular literacies were primarily related to Facebook postings, as these are the contexts in which Usman orients to discourses and constructs identities which counter the discriminatory discourses of 'sham' marriages. The focus was therefore not on the discrimination itself but rather on the means by which Usman and his family resist this discrimination as part of their everyday vernacular practices. Resisting discriminatory immigration practices through the appropriation of dominant literacies for getting a visa highlights the role of language in relation to migration and institutional power.

In the vignettes which follow I examine how migrants successfully appropriate the literacies that make their migration, even if they do not go as far as challenging the power relations that make their migration from Azad Kashmir to Lancashire difficult. I do this by analysing how migrants negotiate what Wodak describes as the 'gulfs that separate insiders from outsiders' (1996: 1–2) as migrants use their literacy practices to favour their will over that of the empowered actors, i.e. different bureaucracies, institutions and so forth.

Methodology

The data analysed for the broader study were obtained over an extensive period of fieldwork involving participant observation that was carried out between 2008 and 2012, but the interview data and Facebook postings presented in this chapter cover a six-month period from January to April 2012. The following vignette focuses on interviews carried out during this period. The interviews are marked by Usman's arrival in the UK, through an initial low period where he had little to do, his getting to know his new family, and his starting work. During the first stage of the analysis, I broke down the ethnographic data collected during this period into a series of strips of approximate timescales (Kell, 2009) in order to capture the complexity of movement in time and space in the crucial few months after his arrival. I did this to link what Usman was telling me about his literacy practices to what he was telling me about his 'new' life. In Stage 2, I transcribed these four two-hour-long interviews soon after they took place and used those transcriptions to plan the next field visit to Usman and his family in Lancashire. The Facebook postings were all in response to a total of 16 uploaded photographs. The comments made underneath these photographs were made in Urdu, Mirpuri Punjabi (which Mirpuris refer to as Pahari), English, Arabic and Pashto.

After the fieldwork and transcription described above, in Stage 3 I selected textual material from the interviews for the analysis. I did this by identifying segments in which the participants talked about 'discourse topics' related to migration, i.e. salient themes that underlie the meaning of a series of sentences. As the selected interviews were primarily framed by questions about the participants' literacy practices related to their migration, all the discourse topics relate to migration as macro-topic. This macro-topic, realized as discourse, includes various sub-topics (Reisigl & Wodak, 2009). The interviews were analysed quantitatively by looking at references to migration, then by identifying sub-topics 'put forth by the participants themselves' (Krzyżanowski, 2008: 174). This analysis identified four discourse sub-topics, i.e. work, kinship, settlement and leaving. In Stage 4 I coded the interview transcripts using the four sub-topics as categories for data selection. This allowed me to narrow down the data and focus on those sections related to migration. The first vignette in the analysis which follows was selected because it relates to all four discourse sub-topics and deals with an incident Usman faced in the workplace. It demonstrates how Usman resists the 'freshie' identity by claiming spoken English as a resource. The subsequent analyses of Vignettes 2 and 3 focus on the dominant and vernacular literacies which are part of the families' wider migration literacies.

Analysis

Vignette 1: Resisting the 'freshie' identity at work by claiming English as a resource among British-born Mirpuris

This vignette draws on participant observation and interviews carried out with Usman in a take-away restaurant, taxi office and family home in the UK after he had arrived in the UK. The vignette highlights the types of intra-ethnic discrimination migrants face at work, as elaborated above. In doing so, I draw on the work of Charsley and Bolognani (2017) discussed earlier, in which the authors identify the types of cultural capital that the 'freshies' in their study lack. Firstly, it is their inability to be 'cool' that characterizes their portrayal. The authors argue that this lack of dominant cultural capital confines their prospects to both low-status and low-paid work in what they call the ethnic economy. Moreover, they argue that the 'freshie' also lacks the 'tastes and preferences' which would provide them with cultural status in the eyes of young British Pakistanis (Charsley & Bolognani, 2017).

The text extracts illustrate intra-ethnic discrimination and highlight how Usman, a recent migrant, resists discriminatory discourses from within the Mirpuri community. The analysis begins with an extract from an interview with Usman carried out in the seating area of Pizza Place, his workplace in Lancashire, on 23 April 2014. This was one month before he posted the photograph and comments which will be discussed in the subsequent section. Prior to this part of the interview, Usman and I had been talking about how he was settling into life in Lancashire now that he had started work. Usman was just finishing telling me about working at the taxi office and the positive, yet fledgling, allegiances he was developing with some of the older drivers there.

Tony: And so would you say that in terms of how migration has changed, would you say that some of the guys your age or similar to you in age and more recently arrived, do they have different education than the others or are they the same?

Usman: I don't know, there is er, I don't know the person that I've been talking to you who talks in Urdu from Gujranwala he has a good degree from FFCA you know he has went to good colleges but he doesn't even know one word of English.

Tony: Ah really.

Usman: Yeah cos you know...

Tony: And what's he doing at Pizza Place?

Usman: He does the ... he does the ... he does the stuff in the basement like making the pizza bases, making the tomato puree, and marinade the chicken and beef and all that stuff. Making the raw, he does the cooking and the things which is, you know, he makes the things.

Tony: And do you get the feeling that he wants to learn English?

Usman: I don't know, he never mention anything.

Tony: He doesn't really?

Usman: I tell him just take this newspaper home, just try to read it and just try to watch some of the movies. Just work on the accent, you know, and he says [unclear]. He's not really bothered, not everybody's bothered. We've got three workers who are British-borns so I don't like 'em. They just they just use English every time, you know. They can speak Urdu, you know, but don't speak Urdu. They just use English every time.

Tony: Sorry what do you mean with each other they just use?

Usman: With each other they just use English.

Tony: Why do you think they do that?

Usman: Oh I don't know maybe they just brag, you know, we [the Mirpuris] don't know English, with me they do English but not with other people.

Tony: Would you say that the people who are born here. Do some of them keep themselves separate to the others?

Usman: No they don't keep it separate, they are good, they are not like they don't talk to us. But they are some politics in politics going on everywhere, but it's just like they are normally good. Some of them are very good and some of them are, I, er ... The person who I had a fight with he was just, he was making, you know, fun of me, and I was completely cool with it. But then when I made fun of him he just go bezerk and I just slapped him twice and thrice.

Tony: So he was looking for something, was he looking for something to wind you up do you think?

Usman: I don't know, but he ... he was making, what was he saying ... I was on the chips and he was [unclear] and he was saying you've just gone out of your mind and this and that. When the work was a bit steady I just asked him, you know, why did you say to me, that I was, you know, that I was er ... you know, that I'm out of my mind? I just ask a bit roughly and then you know, he's just gone bezerk, he was swearing at me properly you know.

Tony: What language was he swearing in?

Usman: Yeah he was swearing in Pahari, yeah. He knows so as long as he did not swear I was alright but as long as he swears, you know, I got hold of his shirt and I just tear the shirt right in half and then I took a slap and two or three kicks and he was just on the ground. But then he was not stopping he was doing the same swearing and all that you know and they just took it [him] away and then, you know, then they fire him. He's not there any more.

Tony: Do you think he had a problem with you personally or he had a problem generally with...?

Usman: But sometimes when there is a lot of work some workers they just can't cope with the work, you know, they are just like ...

Tony: You mean they don't want to work or they are stressed?

Usman: No, but he's from Britain. His mum and dad are well-off but they said to him go to a workplace, but ... but ... but ... he is the boss's nephew so he said that, you know, he owns the place but that's not the way, you know, if you are a worker you are a worker.

Tony: But they obviously think quite a lot of you?

Usman: Yeah that's why they just fire him. He does this every now and then with everybody but everybody say to him, he's just a nut job, but to me he just provoke me. Nobody ever fights with him because they say he is a kick-boxer but he was nothing.

Tony: Would you say that the guys that have come from Mirpur have been more helpful?
Usman: Yeah the guys that who have been from ... the ... from the, how would you say, that have led a low life er ... not a low life as a personality but low life as a financially, like me, 'cos we were average and everyone else is average and so they know what's the problem of an average man. They don't want any kind of upsets in their life so they all are understanding ... er, but the person who come from a big family and all of that they don't care for ... they don't care about [unclear] they just need to do the things to be happen by their life, so I don't know, there's just a bit ... but mainly you can live with that kind of person as well as if that person doesn't cross the limits.

The discursive construction of individuals and groups within the Mirpuri community: Resisting intra-ethnic discrimination at work

In the following analysis I explore how discursive strategies are employed in the interview above the individuals and groups that Usman came into contact with at work to see which allegiances he was able to develop, and those he felt he could not develop due to discrimination. I also analyse the hierarchies at work and how these were influenced by intra-ethnic discrimination.

'He doesn't even know one word of English'

Usman's co-worker at Pizza Place from Gujaranwala is described as having good qualifications from Pakistan but, in a referential strategy which aligns good qualifications with being a good speaker of English, 'he doesn't even know one word of English': an unlikely claim given that Pakistanis code-switch with English words regularly. The intensification strategy of 'making things' positions this man's work 'in the basement' as more menial to Usman's, even though he does not evaluate this negatively. Usman indulges in positive self-presentation when he describes his attempts to help the man learn English. Collectivization is a salient strategy here as Usman explains 'He's not really bothered, not everybody's bothered', which suggests that there is a group of workers who are not interested in learning English.

'They just use English every time'

From the evaluative statement 'not everybody's bothered', Usman immediately introduces a new out-group: 'We've got three workers who are British-borns so I don't like 'em. They just [...] use English every time, you know. They can speak Urdu, you know, but don't speak Urdu. They just use English every time.' In the two years that I had known Usman I had never known him to tell me he did not like someone. Again, Usman draws on collectivization to describe a group of people who, different to the deictic 'we' which I assume is the rest of the staff at Pizza Place, only use English when they could use Urdu. When I probe Usman for the reasons, he adds 'maybe they just brag, you know, we don't know English'. In this, I take the 'we' to mean newly arrived migrants (possibly through marriage migration, from Mirpur) who would fit the 'freshie' persona described by Charsley and Bolognani (2017). Usman uses a nomination strategy I had not heard him use before, 'British-born', linking nationality to the attributes which sets this group apart.

'He just go bezerk'

Usman's description of events puts the other man firmly in the wrong, suggesting with a predicational strategy that Usman himself had been 'completely cool' with the other man making fun of him. He draws on non-standard varieties of English 'bezerk', a common expression in Lancashire meaning out of control, and the Pakistani English 'I just slapped him twice and thrice' to construct his role in the fight positively. 'Swearing in Pahari' is given as the reason for Usman's violent response. That the man was fired may suggest that Usman was right to stand up for himself, as it would seem from the following section that the man had acted violently before.

'If you are a worker you are a worker'

The salient part of this section and the next is Usman's construction of a group of workers in Pizza Place which is predicated on socio-economic class and its intersection with being born in the UK. Usman describes his violent co-worker as 'from Britain', with 'well-off' parents and as the 'boss's nephew', which, when taken together, attribute a privileged status to the man. Usman next creates a dichotomy when he takes the view 'if you are a worker you are a worker', which juxtaposes being 'well-off' with being 'a worker'.

'Low life as a financially, like me, 'cos we were average'

Usman continues with the discursive construction of an in-group of workers, using the deictic 'we', who are not privileged in opposition to the out-group, in his terms, of the group he described above. He attributes 'low life' meaning low income (which he refers to as 'financially') and 'like me 'cos we were average' to these men. The phrase 'so they know what's the problem of an average man' characterizes these men as having experience and knowledge of life that would set them apart from the privileged group. This in-group 'don't want any kind of upsets', which may well be a euphemism for not wanting to risk their new status in the UK. 'Family' is again salient, as in the close-knit community of Mirpuris family connections are central to negotiating work, marriage and stability.

Resistance through English is linked to workplace relations and negotiations of belonging in which language operates as a means of countering power and critique. In this extract, resistance takes the form of counter-discourses when Usman explains what it means to be from an 'average' Mirpuri family (in contrast to the 'well-off' family) which nuance and reconfigure intra-ethnic discrimination among the workers in the restaurant. Thus, the counter-discourse about being from an ordinary family is constructed with reference to proficiency in English and can be seen as a part of Usman's construction of his new identity in the UK. In contrast, the following vignette shifts the analytical lens to the family's migration literacies as a means of countering discriminatory discourses when face-to-face resistance is not an option.

Vignette 2: Resisting the sham marriage discourse by appropriating bureaucratic literacies to get a visa

This section draws on interview data collected in Pakistan with Usman and interview data collected in the UK with Nadia. When Usman received the letter from the UK Border Agency (UKBA) informing him that his first visa application was unsuccessful, he was given two reasons. The first reason was that the Entry Clearance Officer felt that Nadia was not earning enough money to be able to support Usman if he was unable to find work. The second was that insufficient documentary evidence had been provided to demonstrate that Nadia and her first husband Zeeshan were divorced. Therefore, for the second visa application, Nadia and Usman wanted to 'leave nothing to chance'. The papers were physically carried from Mirpur to Lancashire by a visiting relative and passed to Nadia who employed an immigration solicitor, Fatima, to advise them. Fatima is British Mirpuri and was recommended to Nadia by her brother-in-law in the UK. Although she worked in a town approximately 20 miles from Nadia's home, it was agreed within the family that this was what was needed to get Usman his visa. This is an allegiance that Nadia and other family members developed from within the Mirpuri community. Being able to ask friends of relatives to bring the papers by hand to the UK from Mirpur was further evidence of allegiances within the Mirpuri community.

When I asked Nadia what kind of help she wanted from Fatima, she told me that it was making sure that what Nadia had written about her job and the house fitted with what Fatima knew about a 'good' application. One example of how they drew on Fatima's expertise was when the solicitor told Nadia they must avoid the marriage sounding like, in Fatima's words, 'a sham'. This relates to the dominant discourse in the UK about marriages which are arranged, predominantly between South Asian couples, as a way of maintaining transnational migration. Nadia told Fatima on the phone that she lived with Usman in Mirpur for one month, which Fatima recontextualized and wrote on the form in the voice of Usman as 'we have been co-habiting together and as a result my wife is pregnant. We are committed to remain as a married couple forever'. Fatima felt that this would prove to the UKBA that Nadia and Usman's marriage was not a sham. Access to the bureaucratic literacies of immigration can be seen as resistance through language here as, in Usman and Nadia's case, their marriage is not a sham.

Fatima was able to translate the discourse about a 'sham' marriage and provide her clients with access to the register, e.g. 'co-habiting', related to this discourse. The wording was changed to fit the new context. In the first context, Nadia responded orally to the solicitor's questions on the phone and Fatima recast these words when she wrote them down herself on the visa application form, the second context. The immigration solicitor had access to this register because of her knowledge of immigration law, but it was the allegiances among the Mirpuri community that Nadia and Usman tapped into that transformed Nadia's oral descriptions in English, a process known as register-switching (Baynham & Masing, 2000; Baynham, 1995). This switching involved Fatima following the conventions of official forms but also invoking the dominant discourses about employment in the first example and about sham marriages in the second. Fairclough (1992) refers to this as (re)formulation, as the immigration solicitor presented an interpretation of the family's earnings in which Nadia is recast as a working mother with a home of her own, unlike in the first visa application which portrayed Nadia as an unemployed mother without property.

Nadia's network allowed her to use literacy as a shared resource drawn on from multiple sources including immigration solicitors, thereby counteracting the institutional control of bureaucratic encounters (Sarangi & Roberts, 1999). These literacy practices can therefore be seen as spaces for the appropriation and subversion of the institutional order (Capstick, 2016; Sarangi & Roberts, 1999). Vignette 2 provides a productive way of understanding resistance as action. Nadia and Fatima's attempts to recontextualize the wording on the visa forms allow resistance to forms of regulation imposed by the state, in this case, in the matter of immigration. In the following vignette, the setting shifts from institutional to non-institutional settings.

Vignette 3: Vernacular literacy as resistance to intra-ethnic discrimination and dominant discourses of 'sham' marriage

The data included in this vignette were taken from interviews with Usman which were carried out in front of his laptop while looking at Facebook postings. These self-report interviews involved Usman describing language use in the postings as well as how these postings related to his family relationships, friendships and migration. The analysis turns to Usman's literacy practices on Facebook to examine in detail the way he uses language as resistance to discriminatory portrayals of him as a 'freshie' or in a 'sham' marriage by looking at how he represents himself on Facebook within the Mirpuri community online. This is an example of how Usman used his online vernacular writing to construct the identity of caregiver to Oman, his son. As noted earlier, not all communicative resources are the same; they depend on the language modalities (oral and written), for whom a given language constitutes a resource, and what gets accomplished through the communicative act. Thus, I look at Usman's use of literacy in English to explore how he uses language to construct positive identities related to his family. I do this by analysing the communicative resources that Usman and his Facebook friends draw on.

Usman explained in the self-report interview that the photograph was taken in the street outside his home in Lancashire. The photograph is not reproduced here as it identifies the street in which Usman lives. It

Table 3.1 'Poor Noor' Facebook comments

Zara Begum	28 May	5.09pm	Wats happened to poor Noor!!!!!
Fahd Tenacious	28 May	6.06pm	My little dude, hi.
Usman	28 May	6.50pm	He slipped while walking and broke his arm
Zara Begum	28 May	7.54pm	Aw bless him.hpe he gets better.
Usman	28 May	11.18pm	He is better now been through operation he is good now
Kamran	28 May	11.19pm	nice picture....
Zahir	29 May	8.56am	mashallah!!!nice photo bhai
Fahd Tenacious	1 June	1.21pm	Father take care of him ok nae to....

shows Usman holding his son, Oman. Standing next to them is Usman's stepson, Noor, whose arm is in a bandage. Usman explained to me that Noor had fallen and injured his arm playing cricket. Usman had taken him to the doctor but the doctor had said that Noor's injury would heal. Zara is Usman's wife's cousin and so a close blood relative to Noor. Zahir is Usman's brother in Mirpur. Fahd and Kamran are friends of Usman's in other parts of Pakistan. By this time Usman also had made friends with over 30 'British-born' Pakistani men and women who were either relatives or friends of Nadia's. Usman, I argue, is aware of this audience as much as he is writing in response to each individual post.

Resistance as Action Through Vernacular Literacy

In the third line, Usman addresses Zara's question in standard British English and continues with English throughout the interaction, though not always British English. In his next posting, Usman moves between standard British English and Pakistani English. Despite the powerful ideology of Standard British English language proficiency, Usman draws from the Pakistani variety of English. I found that the English that is used by first-generation Mirpuri migrants is often looked down on by the non-Mirpuri British Pakistanis interviewed for the broader study. Mirpuri migrants' English, like Mirpuris themselves, was described as low class and rough by non-Mirpuri Pakistani interviewees in the broader study (Capstick, 2016). British Mirpuris' use of Pakistani English is not one of the language practices associated with immigrant groups who 'no longer represent backward looking traditions' (Blackledge & Creese, 2010: 28) but rather marks the recent migrant as a 'freshie'.

Usman's brother, Zahir, in contrast to the previous monolingual English practices, posts a comment which draws from standard Arabic, English and Urdu. This contrast is intensified by the topic of his posting, which thanks God, presumably not for Noor's injury, but most likely for the blessing of a new-born son for Usman. Zahir and Zara are drawn to different people in the photograph and they draw from their different language experiences to signal this. While 'Thanks be to God!' is written in Arabic, Zahir uses English to comment 'nice photo', and Urdu to address his brother respectfully. As with many of the findings from Blackledge and Creese's study of multilingualism in the homes of the students of the complementary schools they were researching, this is the usual unmarked multilingualism of English, Arabic and the first language. In their study they found that these languages 'enjoy a flexible and non-conflictual co-existence' (2010: 33), as evidenced here by Zahir.

For the posting by Fahd Tenacious, Usman's friend, Usman felt that the 'little dude' he was referring to was Oman, not Noor. This would have meant that Fahd Tenacious, like Zahir, had chosen neither to comment on the image of Noor with his arm in a sling nor to respond to Zara's exclamatory statement in the opening line. Responding to Zara online, Usman explained that Noor had 'slipped while walking and broke his arm'. Perhaps Usman's priority is to ease Zara's concern, which it does. Her deviant spelling 'hpe he gets better' is the second example of her drawing from abbreviated spelling in British English. Kamran, Usman's youngest brother's karate teacher, posts from his home in Azad Kashmir 'nice picture', drawing from his English language practices. This would again suggest a response to the photograph's inclusion of Oman rather than a reference to Noor's arm, which would not warrant the words 'nice picture'.

The posts end, Usman felt, with Fahd Tenacious referring to Usman as a father. Fahd Tenacious posts in English 'take care of him' and then 'ok nae to' in Urdu, which means 'or else...'. This is the most direct reference to Usman's identity as a father in the online data. Fahd, in Mirpur, chooses to use both English and Urdu here. English may signal Usman's identity as the father of a British English-speaking son but it is unclear why Fahd would then turn to Urdu to issue his warning; perhaps it signals Usman's Pakistani identity alongside his new identity as a father.

Usman's Facebook writing here, I argue, comes at a significant stage in the negotiation of his identities as a father, husband and stepfather. It is important not to lose sight of the photograph to which these comments relate. Having looked through his other profile pictures, this appeared to be the first picture including Noor posted by Usman, and thus it may well have been the first time he went public with his stepson online, a further negotiation of his new identity as stepfather. Both photograph and language choice help Usman express how he wants to be seen by his Facebook 'friends' in Lancashire, Mirpur and beyond – specifically, when he responds in British Standard English to Zara's question with the declarative 'He slipped while walking and broke his arm.' Here, Usman, having already positioned himself as a caregiver by posting a photograph with his sons, emphasizes this identity by responding with an explanation of how Noor had the accident. Usman's writing displays a high level of grammatical competence. The clause structure, which is made up of three verbal groups followed by one nominal group, is clear and demonstrates a clear position on the issue of what happened. Highlighting Usman's competence here is important, as his careful grammatical construction of the line, I argue, illustrates his desire to belong to the collective of British Mirpuris, like Zara, who are fluent in British English.

Usman takes up Zara's point about Noor getting better and assures her that 'He is better now been through operation he is good now.' Although he chooses not to use punctuation between clauses, his arguments are effectively grouped together and respond to Zara's initial concern by emphasising that Noor is well again. Usman omits the auxiliary verb 'has' and the indefinite article 'an' when he explains that Noor has 'been through operation', although he still displays considerable grammatical competence when writing in formal English. The sentence begins with a present tense verbal group which sets up the reference time for the story, but the next verbal group, the embedded clause 'been through operation', uses the perfect tense to describe what occurred in the past, before the final verbal group returns to the present with 'he is good now'. In the language of Usman's inheritance, Pakistani English, the use of the phrasal verb 'been through' collocates with 'operation' rather than 'have an operation' in British English. The narrative is told using present tense forms but with an embedded clause in a past tense. Usman holds back from introducing the operation until the second clause as he manipulates the sequence of events by changing their order to foreground the fact that Noor is better. This, I argue, is central to Usman's goal of convincing Zara he is a responsible stepfather. The choice of verb forms is an important part of this narrative technique whereby Usman positions himself as a caregiver. Here, the past tense establishes two points along a timeline: a time utterance and a time reference. Here, the time utterance is clear, but the reference to time, 'been through', is unclear and is made even less clear by the missing auxiliary verb in order to emphasize that Noor is better. Auxiliaries conventionally accompany lexical verbs in order to provide more information about how the process is to be interpreted, although Usman omits this information about the past and continues to the present point, foregrounding Noor's recovery.

In the exchange analysed above, Usman draws on literacy in different varieties of English to demonstrate that he is a capable stepfather to Noor and a reliable new member of the family. He does this as a response to Zara, who is a blood relative to Noor, while also making these comments available to many of his Facebook friends from across his wife's social network. The discussion here benefits from seeing Usman's literacy practices in the same light as Sabaté i Dalmau sees the migrants in her study articulate bottom-up resistance against discrimination, that these are examples of a 'window into how migrants, through language, mobilise resistance through their own linguistic capital and in their own self-regulated discursive spaces' (2013: 249).

Conclusion

In this chapter my aim was to look across different sites in Pakistan and the UK, both work and family related, to explore what Ahearn has described as the 'socioculturally mediated capacity to act, along with strategies to contest and resist' (2012: 278) when migrants face discrimination from inside and outside their immediate community. I was particularly interested in what it means to claim a language as a resource in these settings and how those resources are taken up in different ways at different times and with different family members. I found that resistance is linked to the different aspects in which language operates as a means of countering domination as different languages and literacies are taken up with different friends, family and workmates. This is because, as Holly and Meinhof have shown, taking a stance is a way of exercising one's own agency by positioning oneself and creating new forms of allegiance (2013). Creating new forms of allegiance was an important orientation, illustrated in the vignettes above, which I identified by studying the forms of allegiance Usman developed in the months before and after his migration to the UK.

The three vignettes above provide a productive way of understanding resistance as action and allegiance. The first vignette highlights the intra-ethnic discrimination some migrants face at work from within their own community. The bottom-up view of ordinary members of those ethnic minorities was explored through interview data where Usman described the ways he countered discriminatory discourses from inside his community. I found that the discursive strategies of migrants, identified by Holly and Meinhof as resistance discourses, appear in the localized context of everyday communicative action and not always at the institutional level of bureaucratic organizations (2013: 172). In the second vignette, the lens shifted to those forms of resistance related to institutional discourses. In the account of Nadia's appropriation of dominant literacies to challenge the sham marriage discourse, the analysis revealed the ways in which language operates as a gatekeeping mechanism to access an immigration visa. Nadia and Fatima's attempts to recontextualize the wording on the visa forms allowed the family to resist the forms of regulation imposed by the state and counter the discriminatory discourses which single out families from non-EEA countries. In the third vignette, resistance was action in the form of the vernacular literacies which migrants employ when generating and maintaining relationships across their extensive family networks online. For the analysis of resistance, the types of cultural capital that the 'freshies' lack was contrasted with Usman's vernacular literacies which provided him with the cultural capital he needed to both sustain old friendships in Mirpur while building new family relationships in Lancashire. Usman used all of the language varieties in his repertoires to reject the identities imposed on him and demonstrated that his marriage was not a 'sham' by constructing new identities as a caregiver and stepfather online.

Methodologically, my analysis reached across multiple settings, activities and individuals by investigating the ways in which discourses circulate and are recontextualized. By focusing on the institutional discourse of official rules and norms through which public bodies, such as the UKBA, articulate migration policies and laws I was able to demonstrate how institutional discourses are appropriated to get a visa. By analysing observational data, interviews and Facebook postings, I demonstrated how Usman constructs strategies which engage with anti-immigration discourses circulating both in his community (related to the 'freshie') and in the wider public sphere (related to 'sham' marriage). The analysis also showed how he moulds specific literacies in English to construct positive identities which resist some of the undesirable identities he faced at work. The findings endorse a critical approach to discourse-ethnographic work on discrimination which focuses attention on the question of what it means to claim a language as a resource and the detailed ways that language and literacy constitute valuable resources for expressing this resistance in online spaces and in the workplace.

References

Ahearn, L. (2012) *Living Language: An Introduction to Linguistic Anthropology*. Oxford: Wiley.
Ballard, R. (2008) The political economy of migration: Pakistan, Britain and the Middle East. In V.S. Kalra (ed.) *Pakistani Diasporas: Culture, Conflict, and Change* (pp. 19–42). Oxford: Oxford University Press.
Barton, D. & Hamilton, M. (2000) Literacy practices. In D. Barton, M. Hamilton and R. Ivanič (eds) *Situated Literacies: Reading and Writing in Context* (pp. 7–15). London: Routledge.
Bauman, R. and Briggs, C. (1990) Poetics and performance as critical perspectives on language and social life. *Annual Review of Anthropology* 19, 59–88.
Baynham, M. (1995) *Literacy Practices*. London and New York: Longman.
Baynham, M. and Masing, H.L. (2000) Mediators and mediation in multilingual literacy events. In K. Jones and M. Martin-Jones (eds) *Multilingual Literacies: Reading and Writing Different Worlds* (pp. 189–208). Amsterdam: John Benjamins.

Blackledge, A. (2005) *Discourse and Power in a Multilingual World.* Amsterdam: John Benjamins.
Blackledge, A. and Creese, A. (2010) *Multilingualism.* London: Continuum.
Blommaert, J. (2012) *The Sociolinguistics of Globalization.* Cambridge: Cambridge University Press.
Bolognani, M. (2014) Visits to the country of origin: How second-generation British Pakistanis shape transnational identity and maintain power asymmetries. *Global Networks* 14 (1), 103–120.
Capstick, T. (2011) Language and migration: The social and economic benefits of learning English in Pakistan. In H. Coleman (ed.) *Dreams and Realities: Developing Countries and the English Language* (pp. 207–228). London: The British Council.
Capstick, T. (2016) *Multilingual Literacies, Identities and Ideologies: Exploring Chain Migration from Pakistan to the UK.* Basingstoke: Palgrave Macmillan.
Charsley, K. (2005) Unhappy husbands: Masculinity and migration in transnational Pakistani marriages. *Journal of the Royal Anthropological Institute* 11, 85–105.
Charsley, K. and Bolognani, M. (2017) Being a freshie is (not) cool: Stigma, capital and disgust in British Pakistani stereotypes of new subcontinental migrants. *Ethnic and Racial Studies* 40 (1), 43–62.
Coupland, N. (ed.) (2010) *Handbook of Language and Globalization.* Malden, MA and Oxford: Wiley Blackwell.
Department for Communities and Local Government (2009) *The Pakistani Muslim Community in England: Understanding Muslim Ethnic Communities.* London: DCLG.
Duchêne, A. Moyer, M. and Roberts, C. (2013) Introduction: Recasting institutions and work in multilingual and transnational spaces. In A. Duchêne, M. Moyer and C. Roberts (eds) *Language, Migration and Social Inequalities: A Critical Perspective on Institutions and Work* (pp. 1–21). Bristol: Multilingual Matters.
Fairclough, N. (1992) *Discourse and Social Change.* Cambridge: Polity Press.
Goodhart, D. (2004) Too diverse? *Prospect Magazine* 95, 30–37.
Kell, C. (2009) Literacy practices, text/s and meaning making across time and space. In M. Baynham and M. Prinsloo (eds) *The Future of Literacy Studies* (pp. 75–99). Basingstoke: Palgrave Macmillan.
Heller, M. (2010) *Paths to Post-Nationalism.* Oxford: Oxford University Press.
Holly, W. and Meinhof, H. (2013) 'Integration hatten wir letztes Jahr'. Official discourses of integration and their uptake by migrants in Germany. In A. Duchêne, M. Moyer and C. Roberts (eds) *Language, Migration and Social Inequalities: A Critical Perspective on Institutions and Work* (pp. 171–195). Bristol: Multilingual Matters.
Home Office (2001) *Control of Immigration: Statistics United Kingdom 2000.* London: The Stationery Office.
Hussain, Y. and Bagguley, P. (2005) Citizenship, ethnicity and identity: British Pakistanis after the 2001 'riots'. *Sociology* 39 (3), 407–425.
Krzyżanowski, M. (2008) Analysing focus group discussions. In R. Wodak and M. Krzyżanowski (eds) *Qualitative Discourse Analysis in the Social Sciences* (pp. 162–181). Basingstoke: Palgrave Macmillan.
Marcus, G. (2005) Ethnography in/of the world system: The emergence of multi-sited ethnography. *Annual Review of Anthropology* 24, 95–117.
McAuliffe, C. (2008) Transnationalism within: Internal diversity in the Iranian diaspora. *Australian Geographer* 39 (1), 63–80.
Pyke, K. and Dang, T. (2003) 'FOB' and 'whitewashed': Identity and internalized racism among second generation Asian Americans. *Qualitative Sociology* 26 (2), 147–172.

Reisigl, M. and Wodak, R. (2009) The discourse-historical approach (DHA). In R. Wodak and M. Meyer (eds) *Methods of Critical Discourse Analysis* (2nd edn) (pp. 87–122). London: Sage.

Sabaté i Dalmau, M. (2013) Fighting exclusion from the margins: Locutorios as sites of social agency and resistance for migrants. In A. Duchêne, M. Moyer and C. Roberts (eds) *Language, Migration and Social Inequalities: A Critical Perspective on Institutions and Work* (pp. 248–271). Bristol: Multilingual Matters.

Sarangi, S. and Roberts, C. (eds) (1999) *Talk, Work and Institutional Order: Discourse in Medical, Mediation and Management Settings*. Berlin: Mouton de Gruyter.

Shankar, S. (2008) *Desi Land*. Durham: Duke University Press.

Shaw, A. (1988) *A Pakistani Community in Britain*. Oxford: Blackwell.

Wodak, R. (1996) *Disorders of Discourse* (Real Language series). London: Longman.

4 Biography as Political Tool: The Case of the Dreamers

Anna De Fina

Our late modern world has seen an intensification of human flows (Appadurai, 1996), principally due to global and local economic policies leading to greater and greater inequality and to increasing violence in many countries as a consequence of wars, conflicts and the redrawing of boundaries between communities. As greater numbers of migrants enter developed countries, anti-immigrant discourses are becoming increasingly mainstream and have come to represent a fundamental element of right-wing populist discourses (Wodak, 2015; Savski, this volume; Rheindorf & Wodak, this volume). In some countries such as the United States, however, the resurgence of anti-immigrant sentiments is not explained by the renewed force of migrant flows, but simply by the popularity of such views popularity among center and right-wing voters. Populism favors simplified versions of reality and it is indeed much easier to point to migrants as the source of social and economic problems than to look for the complex processes that cause their dislocation. Although many sociolinguistic and discourse-analytic studies of mainstream and populist discourses about migration exist, less attention has been devoted to how migrants and other disadvantaged groups react to them (but for an exception see Capstick, this volume).

In this chapter I focus precisely on this issue, taking as an example the case of the Dreamers, young migrants who were taken into the US by their undocumented parents when they were children and who have since remained in the country. More specifically, I study the contribution of biographical narrative to the construction of a collective identity for those youth within the context of their organized struggle for migration reform as well as for recognition of their rights and their dignity. The structure of this chapter is as follows: first I discuss my theoretical-methodological framing. More specifically, I lay out my conception of discourse and of storytelling as well as of the way they shape and are shaped by different contexts. Then I explore the multiple relationships between narrative and identities as well as between narrative and politics. In the following sections I present my corpus and methodology, the analysis of my data and conclusions.

Discourse and Storytelling

A great part of the images and representations of migration and migrants that are formed and negotiated in society emerge within and through discourses, particularly those that Gee calls Capital D Discourses, that is socially accepted associations 'among ways of using language, other symbolic expressions, and artifacts, of thinking, feeling, believing, valuing and acting that can be used to identify oneself as a member of a socially meaningful group or "social network"' (Gee, 1996: 131). Such Discourses, which are circulated and repeated through a variety of semiotic modes and through transmedial connections, in both institutional and non-institutional practices, can be more or less influential, more or less controlled. In Foucault's view (1970) power relations determine the 'order of discourses', that is their importance and influence. Mainstream discourses about migration are usually particularly dominant ones, on the one hand because most modern nation states have set as one of their priorities the control of migration flows, and, on the other hand, because to appeal to national sentiments and national unity against foreigners is an easy way for politicians to evade responsibility for economic and social inequalities and to rally popular consensus. As a consequence, mainstream views of migration are massively circulated through media. Indeed, research on mainstream discourses about migrants in popular media shows that their representations are overwhelmingly stereotypical and negative (see, among many others, Busch & Krzyżanowski, 2012; KhosraviNik, 2009; Baker *et al.*, 2008; Charteris-Black, 2006; Gotsbachner, 2001; Rheindorf & Wodak, this volume). Such representations reflect and shape contexts at different scales, from local political struggles to processes that involve the national and/or the transnational level.

While anti-immigrant stances are widespread and persistent, migrants and advocates have, little by little, been able to open the way to different representations of themselves through activism and through participation in social media and alternative information outlets. Martín Rojo (2013) notes that recent years have seen an increase in the ability of such alternative Discourses to reach wider audiences and to counter prevailing negative images. Thanks to popular movements such as the Arab Spring and Occupy Wall Street, for example, dissenting groups have imposed new ways of communicating with audiences through mobilization within urban spaces and through coordination of online and offline activities. These tactics have become more generalized, as we will see in the case of the Dreamers, and have thus provided migrants and other minorities with the tools for circulating alternative Discourses and therefore to try to modify the hostile political atmosphere and win concrete political battles. In the light of this change, it is important for discourse analysts to examine the strategies and tools used by migrants to create alternative representations of who they are. Indeed, discourses have the ability to change social realities. As I will argue below, in the case of the Dreamers movement, the use of storytelling is in and of itself one of the most important strategies used to combat discrimination and negative stereotyping. Below, I will describe the conception of storytelling that inspires this chapter.

For many decades after the groundbreaking work of Labov and Waletzky (1967) and Labov (1972) on narratives of personal experience, narrative analysis had been focused on the form and function of 'stories', seen in essence as texts defined by certain characteristics: mainly temporal ordering, the organization of events into a meaningful plot, and the embedding in the text of the narrator's point of view through evaluation. In the last 20 years this conception has given way to a very different orientation: an approach to narratives as practices. From this point of view, storytelling should be seen as a discursive and semiotic practice that always takes place and is embedded within other discursive and semiotic practices and establishes relations with a variety of contexts at different scales (see De Fina & Georgakopoulou, 2012). The narrative texts that are produced as an outcome of this activity can take very different shapes and functions. However, the latter cannot be given a priori but need to be investigated in concrete contexts of interaction and communication. And although canonical stories of the kind studied by Labov are a very common genre, there are many other types of stories such as habitual or generic narratives, autobiographical recountings, chronicles and small stories (on this point, see Ochs & Capps, 2001; Riessman, 1991; De Fina & Georgakopoulou, 2012), which present very different structural and functional characteristics.

Narratives are embedded within other discourse genres such as arguments, interviews and legal depositions, and at the same time they are part of semiotic and social practices of different kinds such as institutional gatekeeping encounters, political debates, artistic performances and so forth. In that sense, they cannot be seen as separate from those contexts and from users and audiences. A practice-oriented conception of narratives puts the accent on users and on the way they communicate with each other rather than on the texts themselves and therefore interrogates participants' orientations as an important element to determine whether certain texts are treated as stories or not. In this chapter I use the terms 'stories' and 'narratives' interchangeably and I will refer to autobiographical narratives when the teller of the story is also the protagonist of the events recounted, while I call biographical narratives those where the teller and the protagonist do not coincide.

Storytelling has historically been related to identity in the work of many scholars across the social sciences. Bruner talked about narrative shaping our lives and who we are (1994: 53) to the point that we 'become the autobiographical narratives through which we tell about our lives.' After him, many representatives of the so-called 'narrative turn' have continued to identify narrative with the expression of identity. Particularly in biographically oriented narrative research, there is a tendency to equate the telling of one's own personal story with the process of giving meaning to one's life and unity to one's self (see, for example, McAdams, 1988; McIntyre, 1984). Within this theoretical frame, the study of autobiographical stories has significant cognitive and psychological implications given that storytelling is seen as a fundamental mechanism for self-development (Gregg, 2011: 319), as a way of enhancing a positive sense of self (Smorti, 2011) and even as a tool for coping with difficult life events (Bohlmeijer et al., 2007; Fivush & Sales, 2006).

Sociolinguistic scholarship has taken a very different view of the relationship of narrative and identity, underlining that identities are constructed and shaped in relation to specific contexts of production and reception of stories (see De Fina et al., 2006; De Fina, 2003, 2015), and that autobiographical stories therefore are never unmediated expressions of the self, but rather shaped and reshaped by the interaction of personal agency and social circumstances. This view is particularly significant for the study of personal storytelling in political contexts, since those environments more clearly allow for an appreciation of the constructed nature of identities. The use of stories is widespread in political speeches (see, for example, De Fina, 2018a; Perrino, 2015; Souto-Manning, 2014; Schubert, 2010; Fetzer, 2010; Shenav, 2005). Scholars have shown that politicians use narratives to support their positions through what they present as being everyday experience by everyday people and also to shape their own self-representation in order to appear more informal and closer to ordinary people (Goetsch, 1994). But biographical narrative has been shown to play a particularly significant role as a weapon in the discourse of minorities. Researchers, for instance, have long been interested in the 'testimonio' as a form of political struggle (see Beverly, 2004; Gugelberger & Kearny, 1991; Tierney, 2000) and in storytelling as integral to the fight for recognition (Merino *et al.*, 2016).

A number of other studies have widened the scope of investigation into this issue by looking at identity construction and forms of agency and activism among minority groups such as members of the LGBTQ communities (see Gray, 2009; Jones, 2015) or participants in minority political movements (see García Agustín & Aguirre Díaz, 2014), including online contexts as well. In this research, the telling of stories (particularly of personal experience) has been proven to play an important role both in the creation of alternative and positive identities and in conducting political struggles for the recognition of rights. Such investigations can help to fill a gap in the literature on processes of identity representations by and about migrants that is currently mostly focused either on biographical approaches or on the analyses of mainstream discourses.

My main argument in this chapter is that storytelling constitutes a powerful strategy of political struggle for the Dreamers, and I will be addressing the ways in which it is used and how it contributes to emerging collective identities that are finely tuned to political contingencies. In order to do so, I will attempt to answer the following questions:

(1) What kinds of storytelling practices do Dreamers engage in in the political arena? How do these practices relate to other semiotic and discursive practices endorsed by the movement?
(2) What kinds of narratives do Dreamers produce and circulate?
(3) What kinds of identities do narrators stress and how do these portrayals contribute to collective identities?
(4) Do collective self-representations change in relation to different political contexts?

In order to answer these questions, I will analyze narratives uploaded by the United We Dream (henceforth UWD) movement and by individual Dreamers on the Medium website; I will then compare them with a previously analyzed corpus of narratives uploaded on the UWD website. Before I present my data and the analysis, I will provide some background information on the Dreamers and their political struggle.

The Dreamers Movement

The United We Dream, or Dreamers, movement in the US represents the aspirations and the struggles of those migrants who came to the United States as children with their undocumented parents and who remained in the US therefore becoming undocumented as well. These young people are faced with enormous obstacles, both material and psychological, because of their undocumented status. Most of the time, they cannot continue studying after completing high school and thus cannot attend college; they cannot get a social security number or a driving license. As they live in fear of being deported or seeing their parents deported and of being found out by classmates and friends, they often keep a semi-secret existence. According to Nicholls (2013: 1), the Dreamers movement was born on 17 May 2010, when four undocumented students occupied Senator McCain's office in Arizona in order to demand Senate approval of the so-called DREAM Act, a law that would have provided undocumented students with the right to remain in the United States.

After this occupation, Dreamers started creating a network that led to the formation of a significant organization composed of 55 affiliate groups in 26 states of the US, with a total membership of about 100,000. The movement has since become one of the most influential grass roots organizations in the country and has continued to be very active through occupations, sit-ins, protests on the streets, irruptions into legislative sessions, encounters with undocumented parents near the border, and a variety of other actions through both direct participation and use of social media. Dreamers fight for the reform of the migration system and for a stop to deportations, particularly to avoid the separation of family members. Their mission is described on the UWD website as follows:

> We seek to address the inequities and obstacles faced by immigrant youth and believe that by empowering immigrant youth, we can advance the cause of the entire community—justice for all immigrants. We're driven by and accountable to our thousands of members across the country who make up our sustainable and robust grassroots network. We believe we can build power by organizing at the local, regional, and national levels and aim to provide tools and resources to support our leaders and member organizations, as well as create meaningful alliances with other advocacy organizations. (https://unitedwedream.org/about/our-missions-goals/)

The Dreamers scored one of their most important victories on 15 June 2012, when then-President Barack Obama approved the Deferred Action for Childhood Arrivals Act (DACA) that allows young people who meet certain conditions to avoid deportation and remain in the country for two years, with a possibility of renewal of their visa.

According to recent data (Nakamura & O'Keefe, 2017), about 800,000 individuals have been granted DACA status since 2012. In November 2014, Obama announced changes to DACA which would expand it to include undocumented immigrants who entered the country before 2010, eliminate the requirement that applicants be younger than 31 years old, and lengthen the renewable deferral period to two years. The Pew Research Center estimated that this would have increased the number of eligible people by about 330,000 (Lopez & Krogstad, 2017). The presidential decree that would have allowed for the extension of DACA was blocked by a judge of the District Court in Texas under a legal pretext, and that decision was subsequently upheld by the Supreme Court on 23 June 2016. The Trump administration completely reversed the Obama policies, leaving the Dreamers in danger of deportation. On 5 September 2017, Trump directed the US Department of Homeland Security (DHS) and US Citizenship and Immigration Services (USCIS) to phase out and eventually end DACA over two and half years.

In typical fashion, he expressed conflicting and contradictory views on the Dreamers, for example declaring on the campaign trail that he would end the program and then tweeting messages in which he expressed empathy towards them or referred to them as 'these incredible kids' (Hamilton, 2017). But the reality is that his administration immediately started deporting Dreamers and their families and enforcing extremely anti-immigrant measures that have elicited profound condemnation not only from advocates, but also from the public at large. Indeed, according to a 2017 ABC poll, 'eighty-six percent of people surveyed favors allowing them to permanently remain in the country' (Clement & Nakumara, 2017). Data quoted by Hamilton (2017) reveal that already in May 2017 Trump had deported 'at least 43 former DACA recipients because of alleged criminal activity' and 'another 676 people who were once protected by DACA' were facing deportation. The situation has turned extremely difficult for these youth since at the present moment they are still in limbo, as the elimination of DACA has been blocked by two federal judges, but the Trump administration has appealed their decision and therefore it is highly likely that the final ruling on this case will come once again from the Supreme Court.

Storytelling Practices among the Dreamers

As I mentioned in the introduction, anti-immigrant Discourses occupy a particularly powerful position among mainstream Discourses in many countries. The US is no exception to this trend, as demonstrated by the failure of any legislative attempt at migration reform made in the past 20 years. Mainstream Discourse presents economic migrants as parasites and potential threats to the rights of local people through dehumanizing metaphors evoking animals and natural disasters (see Santa Ana, 1999; Gómez et al., 2017). It also builds on the tropes of terrorism and criminality by circulating images of migrants as gang members, assassins or potential terrorists and therefore creating panic about their presence or arrival among local populations. The latter characterization has constituted a pillar of the campaign through which Trump won his election to the presidency. Trump has focused on a criminalization of immigrants, particularly Mexicans, whom he has called 'bad hombres' and 'animals' and against whom he has started to build a wall. It is important to keep this background in mind when talking about the self-presentation strategies adopted by the Dreamers since, as we will see in the analysis of their stories, in the construction of alternative discourses, they constantly make implicit or explicit reference to these types of stereotypes and negative conceptions about who they are. In the analysis of plural discourses circulated by the Dreamers, it is therefore useful to recognize the important role played by intertextuality. The construct as proposed by Bakhtin (1981) and Kristeva (1986) refers to the incorporation into every text of a plurality of, sometimes heteroglossic, voices and the establishment of a dialogue with them. In particular, Kristeva stated that 'any text is constructed as a mosaic of quotations; any text is the absorption and transformation of another' (1986: 37). An interesting extension of this concept that has found application to discourses and counter-discourses about immigrants and refugees (see Wroe, 2017) has been proposed by Leudar and Nekvapil through their construct of 'dialogical network'. According to these authors a dialogic network presupposes that identity negotiations in situ do not manifest as discrete or isolated events; rather they are 'inter-textual'. Participants orient themselves to the exophoric circumstances of their talk and are 'sometimes involved in two "conversations" at the same time – with those present and those absent' (2004: 248).

Dreamers (like other minorities) seem to be constantly responding to voices that classify immigrants as criminals and parasites, and this is important to understand not only many of the intertextual references present in their stories, but also their adoption of storytelling as a centerpiece of their defensive strategies. As we will see, the movement continuously produces and circulates personal stories: members tell their personal narratives orally during protests and meetings, and UWD publishes a great variety of personal biographical texts and constantly invites migrants to tell stories. Interestingly, so do Dreamers supporters. In a recent meeting with faculty at a large American university, advocates urged sympathizers to write letters on behalf of Dreamers to US senators incorporating personal stories of youngsters that they had been in touch with in order to push for legislation in their favor. Sample letters referenced the biography of specific undocumented students who had attained success at school but were also compassionate and committed to their communities.

Storytelling is regarded as a defining practice of Dreamers in many articles in the press as well. In a piece on the Dreamers' struggle to push for legislation under Trump, the authors assert that the broad support that they enjoy among the American public 'reflects the dreamers' political success in telling their own narrative, a process that began in the final years of the Bush administration amid ramped-up immigration enforcement raids. As Dreamers were caught up in the dragnet, they began to go public with their stories, daring authorities to make them a target' (Nakamura & O'Keefe, 2017).

At the same time, the Dreamers have also been successful in getting the media to publish their stories. For example, on 30 August 2017, the UWD Facebook page shared the comment 'Undocumented youths are sharing their stories online in protest', followed by a link to the *Time* magazine online page featuring video stories told by undocumented youth (Rhodan, 2017). Thus, storytelling appears to be a ubiquitous strategy for circulating alternative discourses on migrants both in their own and in other media.

The same strategy has been widely adopted by other minority movements in the past, particularly by members of the LGBTQ community (Jones, 2015), who have made the telling of the coming out story a centerpiece of their political struggle. The reason for this ubiquitous recourse to storytelling can be seen in the need to counter mainstream dehumanizing metaphors and tropes with a particularization of experience, in other words to highlight the fact that migrants (like other marginalized minorities) are not an amorphous mass of people, but rather are humans with families, with distinct personal lives and experience, highly susceptible to suffering as a consequence of hostile policies.

Data and Methods

In this section I describe the data that I will be analyzing and the methodological tools used for their analysis. As already mentioned I will use the terms 'narratives' and 'stories' interchangeably to refer to recapitulations of personal experiences usually in the past. As we will see, most of these narratives are not canonical stories, but rather hybrid texts that incorporate significant narrative components.

As mentioned in the introduction, my research focuses on the strategies of self-presentations that are apparent in Dreamers' narratives and also on possible evolutions and changes in their construction of collective identities through time. I have been studying the Dreamers since 2015. In that year I analyzed a series of 15 video narratives that they posted on the UWD official website (De Fina, 2018b) on the occasion of a campaign to push President Obama to extend his DACA legislation. Since then, I have been following them on Twitter and Facebook, paying regular visits to these social media sites; I have participated in some of their organized events, and I am a frequent contributor to their campaigns so that I receive messages addressed by the movement to supporters. In spring 2016, I started collecting some further stories posted on different media by the movement or by individual Dreamers. The narratives analyzed here are part of this corpus. They are 13 biographical narratives (12 autobiographical and 1 biographical), posted between March 2016 and March 2017 under the logo United We Dream on the blogging platform Medium.com, that can be accessed on the internet by anyone, but whose authors (both individuals and organizations) are invited contributors.

These stories have been chosen for analysis partly because they appeared in a period that covered Trump's campaign and election, so they could be compared to the narratives analyzed earlier; partly because they all appeared on the same site; and partly because they are mostly autobiographic, as opposed to many of the narratives that I found on Facebook, which are often portraits of Dreamers told in the third person. In the analysis of the narratives I have been looking at the main themes and functions of the stories as can be derived from their internal organization, internal development, endings, the semiotic resources that accompany the texts (photographs, drawings etc.), as well as the intertextual relationships among stories and with other kinds of texts produced by the movement or by other political agents as signaled by links, and repetitions of slogans or phrases. The individuation of themes is partly a holistic process and I have worked together with a research assistant in order to ensure that there was agreement between us. However, I also run the texts of the narratives through the software AntConc in order to obtain a ranking of most frequent words and word concordances. It is important to note that the analysis of these particular narratives runs parallel to regular observation of the political activities that the Dreamers were carrying out in the period in which the narratives were published, particularly as shown in their Facebook postings and communication with sympathizers; of the types of storytelling practices that they were engaging in; and of the other types of stories that they were publishing. I also compared the narratives under analysis with the 15 narratives that I had analyzed in my previous research.

Analysis

The narratives that I analyze here were part of a stream of biographical and autobiographical stories that were either posted on Facebook and other media by the UWD movement or told during their demonstrations in the period between March 2016 and March 2017. This was a period of uncertainty in terms of what the Trump government would eventually do with respect to the Dreamers themselves. However, Trump during his campaign had already announced the construction of a wall to prevent undocumented migrants from entering from Mexico, and after his election immediately attempted to promulgate different versions of a travel ban against immigrants from a certain number of countries; he had also chosen Jeff Sessions, a rabidly anti-immigrant politician as his attorney general, and initiated raids against undocumented migrants in many major cities in the US. In the same period, besides carrying out the practice of 'coming out' for individual Dreamers during interviews and demonstrations, the movement published the following types of narratives on the Facebook site directly or through links that gave access to other media:

(1) First-person autobographical portraits of Dreamers who had achieved important personal goals such as finding a job or completing their course of studies.
(2) Third-person biographical portraits of Dreamers and other undocumented migrants who had been deported or were in danger of being deported.
(3) Third-person biographical portraits of Dreamers who were activists or were involved in advancing the cause of the movement.
(4) Third-person biographical portraits of Dreamers who had achieved DACA status and were now afraid of losing it.
(5) First-person autobiographical videos by specific individuals who had defied prejudices by telling their stories.

All the third-person narratives were written by someone other than the protagonist but incorporated many quotes representing the protagonist's own voice. The narratives appear to be aimed at one or more of the following objectives: raise consciousness about the actions of the government and the present dangers for Dreamers, provide a forum for young migrants to share their fears and receive feedback, strengthen the image of Dreamers as successful individuals who deserve to stay in the country, and provide evidence of the repressive nature of the Trump administration actions. The different nature of these objectives is related to the way communication in digital environments works, since as noted by Marwick (2010), producers of texts embedded in digital environments address imagined audiences rather than known audiences. Although it is natural to suppose that most users of the UWD Facebook page and other outlets will be sympathizers, there will also be users who are not close to the movement. Thus, texts posted online need to reach at the same time different goals that fit this composite audience: the goal of informing, the goal of forming opinion, and the goal of rallying members of the movement around common objectives.

The particular group of narratives on which I am focusing were all posted on Medium, but some were also reposted on Facebook and presented a link to the original texts. In fact, I came across them through the posting of the first of those narratives on Facebook.

As mentioned, all the stories had in common the fact of being autobiographical narratives by young undocumented migrants or DACA recipients. Only one of them (no. 10) is not autobiographical but is a third-person narrative. The themes, starting points and functions of the narratives vary, although there are many ways in which the stories are related to each other. First, there is physical and temporal contiguity that characterizes groups of stories that at the time of my research appeared consecutively on the Medium feed and at temporal proximity to each other in terms of when they were posted. The following groups of narratives exhibited these relations with each other: 1-2-3-4, 5-6, 7-8-9, 10-11-12. There were also other elements of cohesion between different stories. For example, three narratives (7-8-9) are posted under the same hashtag: #udocugrads, and three (10-11-12) appear under the title 'The undocumented Story of + name'. Some narratives repeat the slogan 'heretostay' either as a hashtag or as part of a clause, others repeat the same slogan at the end ('I fight because I have power'), and yet others repeat the adjective 'unafraid'. All these words and hashtags represent part of slogans widely circulated by the UWD movement. These similarities show that most of these narratives were elicited and or spontaneously posted to highlight specific aspects of the UWD political campaigns.

How are these narratives constructed? As in the case of the video stories posted on the UWD website in 2015 (De Fina, 2018b), these narratives are hybrid texts. Sometimes they revolve around the life events that led narrators from crossing the border with their parents to their present situation, highlight their and their families' suffering, and end either in positive personal outcomes or in the present state of anxiety. In other cases, they present a few biographical elements and happenings which are embedded in texts that are substantially argumentative. For example, the narrator of story 1, titled 'Name + Undocumented and Black Story' tells just a few details about her life (the age at which she came to the US and where she came from) but devotes most of the text to describing who she is and what she does now and presenting herself as an advocate for the 'black undocumented immigrants'. Her brief autobiography is used to make the argument that all undocumented migrants need support, not only those who came as children with their parents. Other stories start from a particular moment in time (for example, the night of the election of Trump, the deportation of a parent, the moment of arrival in the US) and the fears or difficulties that followed it as a point from which the narrator's personal life took a particular turn, and use those experiences to motivate a call for activism or the expression of a specific moral stance. This is the case for example with story 2, in which the narrator recounts how she feared the moment she had to call her mother on the phone after Trump's election, and how the frustration and dejection of her community led her to become an activist. She concludes the story with the following:

> I continued to fight for our communities. I fight for the vision and hope of liberation for the undocumented community. My mother and my loved ones deserve a life without fear and with dignity and I will not stop fighting until all of the undocumented community are liberated.
> #HereToStay
> (United We Dream, 2016a)

The stories that are posted under the title 'the undocumented story of + Name' are brief self-portraits in which narrators address the audience directly, by starting with 'Hello, my name is ...', and then tell more or less extended narratives about how and why they came to the US. In this case as well, biographical events are used as a platform to counter negative images of undocumented immigrants, declare pride in wearing the 'illegal' label, and put forth alternative values and dreams for the future. In these stories the narrators explicitly enter into 'a dialogic network' with those who circulate the trope of the immigrant as a criminal alien. For example, the narrator of story 12 recounts how she came from Mexico fleeing violence there and how it was by coming to the US that she discovered what being 'illegal' means. The author then declares

> I am proud of being an immigrant because I'm not taking anything away from this country. I am contributing and I want to contribute even more. I know the struggle – the struggle is real – but it gives me strength to accomplish my goals and show the world that <u>I am not a criminal, I am just a dreamer</u>. [my underlining]

The #undocugrad stories are part of a series of narratives published during the graduation period in American universities and high schools (May–June 2016), and they constitute brief self-portraits by undocumented students that just graduated. The narrators each present a brief story on the many obstacles that they had to overcome in order to get to that point, describe how they received the help of family members or other activists, and conclude with a positive note on how graduating represents a great achievement for them.

As we see, there are many variations among the 13 narratives analyzed: the tone may be more or less optimistic, the objective may be simply putting out a positive self-presentation or also spurring others to action. The amount and type of biographical elements included may vary too, but all the narratives published on Medium have in common the use of the personal story as both a way of presenting narrators as worthy people and people who have suffered and a positive example for others even in the face of difficulties and suffering. This kind of self-presentation (or in one of the cases other-presentation) is achieved sometimes simply through the use of the personal story as a kind of 'testimonio' about suffering and resilience or through the embedding of personal events within argumentative structures. Narrators and authors also use other semiotic elements such as photographs, and other verbal resources such as titles, subtitles and summaries, when the story is embedded through a link, to project positive images of the protagonists. All the narratives are accompanied by photos and these are important to underlining this positive part of the message. In 10 out of the 13 narratives, the protagonist is depicted alone or with family members, but always smiling or engaged in some agentive activity. One picture, for example, portrays a young girl smiling, wearing a graduation gown and proudly holding a diploma. Another photo depicts a young man again wearing a graduation gown in front of a university building in the act of jumping while throwing the graduation cap in the air. Yet another one presents an older couple (presumably the narrator's parents), holding each other in a tender embrace and smiling. In this case, it is interesting to note the contrast between the photo and the title of the piece, which reads 'Separation of Families'. In two of the stories the protagonist is depicted in an activist stance: either raising a fist in defiance or participating in a demonstration. Only one of the narratives does not have a personal photo as it is not signed but published anonymously.

In terms of similarities in the content of the narratives, it is important to note that many of the themes that were found in individual narratives were shared with other narratives. Very significant, for example, is the topic of family, covering family loyalty and sacrifice by parents. As we have seen, the topic of activism is also a widely shared one. In the analysis of the video narratives published in 2015, I found that all stories shared a certain number of organizing topics. Table 4.1 shows a comparison of overlapping topics.

Overlaps point to some of the recurrent themes in all stories published by the movement: in particular, the centrality of activism in the lives of those who tell their stories, the importance of family relations both in the affective sphere of Dreamers and undocumented youth, and also the presence of rupture points and moments of realization that push these youngsters to action. The topic of dreams is also significant in that stories very frequently refer to broken or realized wishes, and objectives that have been reached or elude narrators.

Table 4.1 Topics found in both sets of narratives

Topics	2015 Tot. 15	2016–17 Tot. 13
Demographic information	15	8
Crucial moment	11	6
Reasons for activism	7	7
Family history	9	5
Dreams	13	7

In order to study whether there had been significant change in the way identities were presented in the two sets of data, I ran the texts through the software AntConc to obtain word frequencies. Word frequencies are tricky because most of the frequent words are not content words; however, a comparison between some of the most frequent words up to rank 80 in the two corpora, shown in Table 4.2, reveals some interesting trends.

Table 4.2 Comparison of high frequency words in the two corpora

2016–17 Corpus			2015 Corpus		
Word	Rank	Frequency	Word	Rank	Frequency
I	1	302	I	1	727
not	13	58	me	15	203
me	14	51	just	24	117
undocumented	26	28	mom	37	80
community	35	20	not	38	75
fear	42	17	able	39	74
family	48	16	didn't	57	51
DACA	54	14	work	59	51
fight	55	14	parents	60	49
parents	57	14	action	77	35
mother	65	13	dad	78	35
children	67	12	dream	79	35
united	80	11	years	80	25

We find that some words have similar rankings. This is the case for example with 'I' and 'me' and with words referring to family or family members, which are different in distribution and kind, but similar in the sense that they are in both cases highly frequent terms. There are, however, significant differences in the terms that are frequent in one of the two corpora but not in both, as these terms reveal differences in foci in the two sets of narratives. For example, while 'fear' appears as rank 42 in the 2016–17 corpus, it has rank 104 in the 2015 corpus. On the other hand, while 'dream' appears with rank 79 in the 2015 corpus, it has rank 118 in the 2016–17 corpus. Another important difference concerns the words 'undocumented' and 'community', which are ranked 26 and 35 in the 2016–17 corpus but 106 and 162 in the 2015 corpus. Finally and most importantly, the word 'fight' has a low rank of 198 in the 2015 corpus, but a rank of 55 in the more recent corpus.

These differences are significant when considered in the light of the qualitative analysis as they point to a change in stance by the movement. While during the Obama years the stress was on the construction of a collective image as good immigrants and deserving citizens, the focus during the rise of Trump and his election has shifted towards the highlighting of a more combative stance, indexed in some of the terms circulated and widely repeated in messages and stories by members of the movement: #HereToStay, #NoBanNoWallNoRaids, Unafraid.

Together with the image of the good student and self-sacrificing youth appearing, for example, in the #undocugrad stories, we witness the emergence of more combative profiles. While activism and participation in the political arena were certainly present as themes in the 2015 stories, the more recent corpus shows narrators more focused on this aspect as shown by the frequency of the word 'community'. The frequency of the word 'undocumented' also points to a greater acceptance of one's status in conjunction with a fighting stance. We saw in the analysis that some stories end with vows to continue fighting, as in the following examples:

> And perhaps, it's just a dream, but I will fight for myself because I have the power, WE have the power.
> (United We Dream, 2016b).

> I fight because I am a fighter and I will fight for myself because I have POWER because WE have POWER.
> (United We Dream, 2016c).

Moreover, narrators start incorporating the theme of unity with other disenfranchised groups, such as undocumented migrants who are not part of the Dreamers group or muslims targeted by the Trump government, and talk about their own frustrations and failures besides those of their parents. For example, we find personal stories in which narrators present themselves as trying in many ways to find work or to get an education without succeeding, together with narratives that stress the attainment of goals. Narrative 2 presents an instance of this when the narrator talks about the frustration of the whole community about the Trump presidency in the following terms:

> My mother's pain during the month of November was not unique to her, our entire community was feeling the same way and when January came along our biggest fears became reality. We saw our communities being torn apart by ICE agents and the administration's push for mass deportation and detention. This is what our community is really facing.

Narrators in 2016–17 do not put as much stress on dreams as the authors of the narratives told in the previous years did and rather talk about actions that they want to take to effect change in society. This does not mean that the defensive stance that was so prevalent in the past has been abandoned, but that there has been a refocusing of the public image of the Dreamers. These changes have been evident in the type of content published in the same period on the UWD Facebook page. Besides uploading the types of narratives as described at the beginning of this chapter, the Facebook page constantly features live video of Dreamers protests throughout the United States, for example the demonstrations demanding a 'Clean Dream Act' (that is, a Dream Act without compromise) in different cities or irruptions by Dreamers in the US Congress, protests against deportations and so forth. The Facebook page also features news stories under the title in Spanish 'La Migra son Manipuladores' (Migration agents are manipulators), in which illegal actions and behavior by migration agents in action are detailed. Also, news stories about other abuses not only against Dreamers but also against people who help them have been part of the Facebook feed of the last six months. Many calls to action either through participation in marches and demonstrations or through financial support are also a prominent part of the postings that have been appearing throughout this period. Postings prod people to 'take action' or 'walk out' into the streets, 'tell ICE to release' someone, 'add your name now to stand up to...', and so forth. In addition, posts make public demands about releasing detained individuals or stopping anti-immigrant actions.

Discussion and Conclusions

In this chapter I have argued that storytelling as a discourse practice has a central role in the Dreamers movement's effort to construct and circulate a positive collective identity. We have seen that Dreamers engage in different kinds of storytelling, using oral and written modes and embedding narratives in online and offline contexts. We have also seen that this strategy is shared by supporters of the Dreamers through the diffusion of biographies in the press and the circulation of biographical narratives in the political arena. This strategy has emerged as a direct response to widely shared tropes about migrants as parasites and criminals that are a centerpiece of mainstream anti-immigrant Discourses. Because of the strength and the widespread character of those characterizations, telling individual stories appears to be seen as a way of humanizing migrants through highlighting their personal trajectories, their emotional connections with members of their families, their motives for leaving their countries of origins, and the suffering and sacrifices through which they have gone in order to stay in the country and attain their objectives.

Autobiographical and biographical narratives are representations of the experience of individuals, and yet they contribute to the construction of a collective identity because they are related to each other through a variety of means. One way in which they connect to each other is through their posting and telling at close intervals in time and space, as well as through the highlighting across stories of values amply shared in US society. Through their narratives Dreamers circulate similar and repeated images of themselves as hard-working, ready to sacrifice, loyal to their families and willing to attain personal success, all values that are highly regarded in US society as demonstrated by the emphasis on the same characteristics in articles of supporters in mainstream media. For example, an editorial in the *Washington Post* described Dreamers as desirable citizens because of their qualities: 'risk-taking gumption, entrepreneurial drive, a commitment to hard work and fair play and a fierce belief in a better life for their offspring' (Washington Post, 2016).

We have also seen that narratives cohere with each other through the intertextual connections that they create, with the reproduction of slogans that are circulated by the movement at specific times in order to unify themselves around political objectives. Thus, the reprisal in different narratives of the slogan '#HereToStay' links the fight of individual Dreamers with collective objectives while emphasizing their personal attitudes as fighters. At the same time, narratives establish intertextual dialogues with absent but persistent voices that declare them criminal and undesirable by explicitly or implicitly arguing against such characterizations. It is then through repetitions of themes and structural elements, contiguity in time and space, the use of the logo and other symbols of the organization and of similar imagery through photos and video elements that individual narratives contribute to creating a generalized and collective portrait of who the Dreamers are and what kinds of values they represent.

We have also seen that the traits of this collective identity have a certain stability in time, but that they reflect change in relation to shifting political realities and strategic objectives of the movement as well. And, indeed, while narratives produced in the Obama era stressed the non-threatening, good citizen aspect of these young migrants, the rise of Trump and the advent of his government have pushed the movement towards a different stance in which activism and the will to fight have taken a more substantial role. The analysis also demonstrates the highly contextualized nature of autobiographic stories that, far from embodying the aspirations and trajectories of individuals as biographical approaches to storytelling would characterize them, represent targeted and well-crafted responses to prevailing stereotypes. Thus, it is through practice-oriented conceptions of storytelling that we can really make sense of the multiple ways in which identities are created and negotiated in concrete social contexts.

Acknowledgements

I want to thank my research assistant Peri Beckerman for her insightful work on the data.

References

Appadurai, A. (1996) *Modernity*. Minneapolis: University of Minnesota Press.
Baker, P., Gabrielatos, C., Khosravinik, M., Krzyżanowski, M., McEnery, T. and Wodak, R. (2008) A useful methodological synergy? Combining critical discourse analysis and corpus linguistics to examine discourses of refugees and asylum seekers in the UK press. *Discourse & Society* 19 (3), 273–306.
Bakhtin, M. (1981) *The Dialogic Imagination: Four Esays*. Austin: University of Texas Press.
Beverly, J. (2004) *Testimonio: On the Politics of Truth*. Minneapolis: University of Minnesota Press.
Bohlmeijer, E., Roemer, M. Cuijpers, P. and Smith, F. (2007) The effects of reminiscence on psychological well-being in older adults: A meta-analysis. *Aging and Mental Health* 11 (3), 291–300.
Bruner, J. (1994) Life as narrative. *Social Research* 54 (1), 11–32.
Busch, M. and Krzyżanowski, M. (2012) Media and migration: Exploring the field. In M. Messer, R. Schroeder and R. Wodak (eds) *Migrations: Interdisciplinary Perspectives* (pp. 277–295). Vienna: Springer.
Charteris-Black, J. (2006) Britain as a container: Immigration metaphors in the 2005 election campaign. *Discourse & Society* 17 (5), 563–581.
Clement, S. and Nakumara, D. (2017) Survey finds strong support for 'Dreamers'. *Washington Post*. See https://www.washingtonpost.com/politics/survey-finds-strong-support-for-dreamers/2017/09/24/df3c885c-a16f-11e7-b14 f41773cd5a14_story.html?utm_term=.5824df73f867 (accessed 25 September 2017).
De Fina, A. (2003) *Identity in Narrative: A Study of Immigrant Discourse*. Amsterdam: John Benjamins.
De Fina, A. (2015) Narrative and identities. In A. De Fina and A. Georgakopoulou (eds) *Handbook of Narrative Analysis* (pp. 351–368). Malden, MA: Wiley.
De Fina, A. (2018a) Narrative analysis. In R. Wodak and B. Forchtner (eds) *Handbook of Language and Politics* (pp. 233–246). London and New York: Routedge.
De Fina, A. (2018b) What is your dream? Fashioning the migrant self. *Language & Communication* 59, 42–52.
De Fina, A. and Georgakopoulou, A. (2012) *Analyzing Narrative: Discourse and Sociolinguistic Perspectives*. Cambridge: Cambridge University Press.
De Fina, A., Schiffrin, D. and Bamberg, M. (eds) (2006) *Discourse and Identity*. Cambridge: Cambridge University Press.
Fetzer, A. (2010) Small stories in political discourse. In C. Hoffman (ed.) *Narrative Revisited: Telling a Story in the Age of New Media* (pp. 163–184). John Benjamins: Amsterdam.

Fivush, R. and Sales, J.M. (2006) Coping, attachment, and mother-child narratives of stressful events. *Merrill-Palmer Quarterly* 52 (1), 125–150.

Foucault, M. (1970) The order of discourse. In R. Young (1981) *Untying the Text: A Post-Structuralist Reader* (pp. 48–78). Boston: Routledge and Keagan Paul.

García Agustín, O. and Aguirre Díaz, F.J. (2014) Spatial practices and narratives. The GenkiDama for education by Chilean students. *Journal of Language and Politics* 13 (4), 732–754.

Gee, J.P. (1996) *Social Linguistics and Literacies: Ideology in Discourses*. London: Falmer Press.

Goetsch, P. (1994) Presidential rhetoric: An introduction. In P. Goetsch and G. Hurm (eds) *Important Speeches by American Presidents after 1945* (pp. 7–31). Heidelberg: Winter.

Gómez, C. et al. (2017) The President's intent: Preliminary findings of a critical discourse analysis of Trump's speeches and tweets from the date of his candidacy to mid-September 2017. 17 September 2017. See https://www.thepresidentsintent.com/full-report/ (accessed November 2017).

Gotsbachner, E. (2011) Xenophobic normality: The discriminatory impact of habitualized discourse dynamics. *Discourse & Society* 12 (6), 729–759.

Gray, M. (2009) Negotiating identities/queering desires: Coming out online and the remediation of the coming-out story. *Journal of Computer-Mediated Communication* 14 (4), 1162–1189.

Gregg, G. (2011) Identity in life narratives. *Narrative Inquiry* 21 (2), 318–328.

Gugelberger, G. and Kearny, M. (1991) Voices for the voiceless: Testimonial literature in Latin America. *Latin American Perspectives* 18 (3), 3–14.

Hamilton, K. (2017) Trump told dreamers to 'rest easy,' but here's proof that they shouldn't. *Vice News*, 3 May 2017. See https://news.vice.com/story/trump-told-dreamers-to-rest-easy-but-heres-proof-they-shouldn't (accessed 5 May 2017).

Jones, R. (2015) Generic intertextuality in online social activism: The case of the It Gets Better project. *Language in Society* 44, 317–339.

KhosraviNik, M. (2009) The representation of refugees, asylum seekers and immigrants in British newspapers during the Balkan conflict (1999) and the British general election (2005). *Discourse & Society* 20 (4), 477–498.

Kristeva, J. (1986) Word, dialog and novel. In T. Moi (ed.) *The Kristeva Reader* (pp. 34–61). New York: Columbia University Press.

Labov, W. (1972) The transformation of experience in narrative syntax. In W. Labov (ed.) *Language in the Inner City: Studies in the Black English Vernacular* (pp. 354–396). Philadelphia: University of Pennsylvania Press.

Labov, W. and Waletzky, J. (1967) Narrative analysis. Oral versions of personal experience. In J. Helm (ed.) *Essays on the Verbal and Visual Arts* (pp. 12–37). Seattle: University of Washington Press.

Leudar, I. and Nekvapil, J. (2004) Media dialogical networks and political argumentation. *Journal of Language and Politics* 3, 247–266.

Lopez, G. and Krogstad, G.M. (2017) Key facts about unauthorized immigrants enrolled in DACA. Pew Research Center, 25 September 2017. See http://www.pewresearch.org/fact-tank/2017/09/25/key-facts-about-unauthorized-immigrants-enrolled-in-daca/ (accessed 30 October 2017).

Martín Rojo, L. (2013) El poder de los discursos en sociedades en transformación. XXX Universidad d'estiu d'Andorra, 2–6 Septembre 2013. Unpublished paper. See https://uam.academia.edu/LuisaMart%C3%ADnRojo/Papers (accessed 10 November 2017).

Marwick, A.D. (2010) I tweet honestly, I tweet passionately: Twitter users, context collapse and the imagined audience. *New Media Society* 13, 114–133.

McAdams, D.P. (1988) *Power, Intimacy and the Life Story: Personological Inquiries into Identity*. New York: Guilford.
McIntyre, A. (1984) *After Virtue* (2nd edn). Notre Dame, IN: University of Notre Dame Press.
Merino, M.A., Becerra, S.Z. and De Fina, A. (2016) Narrative discourse in the construction of Mapuche ethnic identity in context of displacement. *Discourse and Society* 7, 60–80.
Nakamura, D. and O'Keefe, E. (2017) 'This is the moment': Dreamers face make-or-break push on immigration fight with Trump. *Washington Post*, 4 December 2017: A6.
Nicholls, J. (2013) *The Dreamers*. Stanford: Stanford University Press.
Ochs, E. and Capps, L. (2001) *Living Narrative*. Cambridge, MA: Harvard University Press.
Perrino, S. (2015) Performing extracomunitari: Mocking migrants in Veneto barzellette. *Language in Society* 44, 141–160.
Rhodan, M. (2017) Undocumented youths are sharing their stories online in protest. *Time*, 30 August 2017. See http://time.com/4922121/dreamers-daca-undocumented-online/ (accessed 12 September 2017).
Riessman, C.K. (1991) Beyond reductionism: Narrative genres in divorce accounts. *Journal of Narrative and Life History* 1, 41–68.
Santa Ana, O. (1999). Like an animal I was treated. Anti-immigrant metaphor in US public discourse. *Discourse & Society* 10 (2), 191–224.
Schubert, C. (2010) Narrative sequences in political discourse. Forms and functions in speech and hypertext frameworks. In C. Hoffman (ed.) *Narrative Revisited: Telling a Story in the Age of New Media* (pp. 143–162). Amsterdam: John Benjamins.
Shenav, S. (2005) Concise narratives: A structural analysis of political discourse. *Discourse Studies* 7 (3), 315–335.
Smorti, A. (2011) Autobiographical memory and autobiographical narrative: What is the relationship? *Narrative Inquiry* 21, 303–310.
Souto-Manning, M. (2014) Critical narrative analysis: The interplay of critical discourse and narrative analyses. *International Journal of Qualitative Studies in Education* 27 (2), 159–180.
Tierney, W.G. (2000) Undaunted courage: Life history and the postmodern challenge. In N. Denzin and Y. Lincoln (eds) *Handbook of Qualitative Research* (2nd edn) (pp. 537–554). London: Sage.
United We Dream (2016a) The undocumented story of Dania Torres. Medium.com, 23 May 2016. See https://medium.com/@UNITEDWEDREAM/the-undocumented-story-of-dania-torres-c298db2b0814 (accessed 30 May 2016).
United We Dream (2016b) The undocumented story of Carlos Olmo. Medium.com, 23 May 2016. See https://medium.com/@UNITEDWEDREAM/the-undocumented-story-of-juan-carlos-olmos-a2d7b8777746 (accessed 5 June 2017).
United We Dream (2016c) Deyanira – DACA and us. Medium.com, 29 May 2016. See https://medium.com/@UNITEDWEDREAM/deyanira-daca-us-98a6167784ec (accessed 1 June 2016).
United We Dream Facebook page. https://www.facebook.com/UnitedWeDream/.
Washington Post (2016) Editorial, 16 September 2018, p. A 18. Washington DC.
Wodak, R. (2015) *The Politics of Fear: What Right-Wing Populist Discourses Mean*. Thousand Oaks, CA: Sage.
Wroe, L.E. (2017) It really is about telling people who asylum seekers really are, because we are human like anybody else. *Discourse & Society*, published online 22 November 2017. See http://journals.sagepub.com.proxy.library.georgetown.edu/doi/full/10.1177/0957926517734664 (accessed 25 November 2017).

5 Moving for a Better Life: Negotiating Fitting in and Belonging in Modern Diasporas

Jo Angouri, Marina Paraskevaidi and Federico Zannoni

Introduction

Moving for a better life is common in human history and intensifies in times of (economic or natural) crises. In the current socioeconomic context, fear-based narratives associate migration with pressures on the welfare system, loss of employment, crime, and an erosion of values that summarily threaten the imagined homogeneity and perceived social cohesion of the host society. The host society becomes a contested area, split between those who are 'in' and those who are attempting to gain access. Migrants, often represented as one homogenous group including any and all, from refugees to economic migrants, are positioned as different to 'us' and debates on whether or not 'they fit in' occupy a central position in the media and everyday discourses. In this process the migrant is generalised, negatively stigmatised and often commodified as a resource, brain power, knowledge worker, manual labour and/or a burden and threat.

Accessing and successfully settling in a different context depends on being granted membership in the community and being accepted as *one of us* in at least some domains of human activity. This process is not straightforward and it involves negotiating established hierarchies and positions of power. Dominant ideologies about the *other* are projected onto the newcomer, who is expected to fit in with the norms and ways of doing of the majority group and to display belonging. This does not suggest that the majority or host is one homogenous, invariably rigid and hostile group. Research, for instance in workplace sociolinguistics (Angouri *et al.*, 2017), has shown how the majority group negotiates *with* the newcomer in the process of settling in. Equally, substantial research has shown the barriers that are imposed on those coming to new socio-cultural and linguistic contexts. Work on low-skilled migration in particular has provided evidence of such patterns of exclusion time and again (Piller, 2016; Roberts & Campbell, 2007).

In this context, this chapter focuses on the narratives of young people who moved individually or as part of their family in seeking a *better life*. In line with the scope of this volume to uncover the multi-layered interdependencies between language and migration and challenge the discourse of discrimination, we engage with the participants' lived experiences and seek to unpack the complexities of belonging as constructed in the narratives of individuals who have experienced a transition to a different geographical space, a 'land of hope' and 'promise for prosperity'. We look into the use of binaries such as *here/there*, *us/them*, *now/then* and the positions that are mobilised in the discourse of our participants. We pay special attention to the positions our participants claim for yet another binary, that of *self/other*, and in particular to how they navigate the liminal space, the *in-between*. This is a constant interplay of rejecting and aligning with the emergent categories, where sometimes *self* becomes *other* in relation to the different groups and communities that the individual claims (or aspires to claim) membership in.

We close the chapter by discussing how fitting in and belonging take place in the *in-between* position in our participants' narratives and draw on the concept of *liquid migration* to describe the complexities of categorisation processes our participants mobilise in their discourse. This is in line with studies arguing for a dynamic understanding of mobilities and immobilities and shows the limitations of dichotomies in traditional academic perspectives. We close the chapter with directions for further research. We have structured the text into five sections: we start by looking into modern diasporas to situate our participants, turn to the notions of belonging and fitting in as framed in this chapter, and then discuss our data and methodology, before moving on to the analysis of the data and our findings; finally, we present our concluding remarks.

Identity Construction in Modern Diasporas

Traditional diaspora studies were primarily concerned with the study of displacement, forced migration and movement from a fixed homeland or motherland to a new locus at a particular time. In line with the positivist and post-positivist thinking which dominated social sciences until the end of the 20th century, movement was conceptualised relatively linearly, including a definite departure and end point, and the homeland was associated with the 'mythic place of desire in the diasporic imagination' (Brah, 1996: 192). This was well reflected in definitions and the set characteristics of diasporas according to which diasporas involved a portion of the population living outside the borders of the homeland. In this, the homeland coincided with national borders and the relevant nation state (e.g. Connor, 1986). More recent work (e.g. Caldas-Coulthard & Iedema, 2008; Lainer-Vos, 2010; Tsagarousianou, 2004), influenced by constructionism, critical realism and postmodernism, questions the linearity of earlier conceptualisation of diasporic communities and the fixed boundaries of communities.

As argued by Tsagarousianou, 'diasporas should be seen not as given communities, a logical, albeit deterritorialised, extension of an ethnic or national group, but as imagined communities, continuously reconstructed and reinvented' (2004: 52). Diasporic communities operate at the interface of complex 'human and cultural segments' (Connor, 1986, cited by Safran, 1991: 83) that are intertwined and dynamically changing. Drawing on these complexities, Brubaker (2005) discussed the excessive proliferation of the meanings of diaspora and of the related concepts of *homeland* and *ethnic/religious community* and considered their traditional definitions too vague and rigid, inappropriate for the increasingly diverse and fluid world society. The thorny issue of 'return', which dominated earlier work, is still considered part of the diaspora experience, but *homeland* has become a *homing desire*, a representation, essentially placeless, rather than a physical geographical place (Brah, 1996).

As Van Hear (1998: 195) puts it, 'diasporas can be made and unmade', they are in a continuous state of formation and reformation, and the context of globalisation accelerates all of these processes, strengthening and deepening the connections between the ethno-national and trans-national dimensions. The increasing movement of people, objects and information in the global sphere is associated with several social, cultural and economic trends, such as the advent of the global economy and the development of new technologies, mass transportation and media (Genovese, 2003). These trends influence the personal and social (national and supra-national) identities of *immigrants* and *natives*, both being ideological labels, in the frail borders between hybridity and uniformity (Bauman, 1997; Castells, 1996; Giddens, 1990). In modern societies, diaspora members are 'in a better position to act as bridge between the particular and the universal' than past generations of migrants (Cohen, 2008: 148), combining cosmopolitanism and ethnic collectivism to face the gap between local and global tendencies. This makes the *migrant* simultaneously a powerful agent as well as a vulnerable and often misunderstood *outsider*. The contradictions and conflicts in these positions mirror phenomena and changes that involve the global liquid modernity (Bauman, 2000) and affect the identity construction processes of individuals and groups.

Migrant identity/ies occupy a prominent position in diasporic literature (e.g. Angouri, 2012; Ayelet *et al.*, 2017; Cheng, 2012; Jensen, 2011; Jones & Krzyżanowski, 2008). This is in line with the focus on the concept of identity in a range of disciplines and areas of study in social sciences such as psychology, sociology, anthropology, gender studies and sociolinguistics. Influential work across fields has shaped our current thinking, such as Erikson's (1968) ego-identity and sense of *self*, Butler's (e.g. 1999) work on gender and performativity, S. Hall (e.g. Hall & Du Gay, 1996) and Giddens (1991) on identity and politics, and Bell (1984) on audience design. In the past decade, identity studies have become a field in their own right in social sciences (see e.g. Côté, 2006). In sociolinguistics, the relationship between language and identity has been explored since the 1960s (see e.g. Labov, 1972). Moving from a rather static view focusing on the characteristics shared by groups to recognising it as a complex process informed by individuals' experiences, sociopolitical circumstances and specific contextual elements (Billig, 1995; Gellner, 1983; Giddens, 1991), research on identity has shifted and grown following the development of thinking in the field in particular and in social sciences more generally.

A poststructuralist perspective on identity (e.g. Bhabha, 1990; Butler, 1999; Foucault, 1983, 1984) emphasises the link between identity construction and the spatial and sociopolitical organisation of the modern nation state, exploring the constitution of *self* within a historical framework (Wodak, 2014). A constructionist reading of identity (Angouri, 2012, 2015) has allowed for a variety of approaches in capturing the complexities of individual experience, and although not all approaches agree on how 'reality' should be conceptualised, they typically converge on the anti-essentialist pole. Following a prevailing trend in social sciences, much of the current research in applied linguistics and sociolinguistics takes a constructionist approach, which is the stance we adopt in this chapter.

At the same time, a number of theorists have also problematised the inflated use of the concept of identity. Identity, as any abstract notion and *macro*-term (culture is another good example, see Angouri, 2018), can afford a wide range of meanings and the list of possible definitions is endless. Hence, theorists have questioned the explanatory power of the concept and have suggested that other terms, specifically *meso*-terms, may be more useful for explanatory frameworks. While this is a valuable criticism, and we have also raised this concern in other work (e.g. Angouri, 2015), there are two relevant points here: (a) what constitutes a *macro-*, *meso-* or *micro-* notion often rests on matters of definition rather than inherent differences between the terms themselves; (b) the concept of identity has first-order currency for the lay user and is associated with powerful membership claims to communities with which the individual self-identifies or to which s/he is granted membership. The various *identities* claimed and/or resisted are powerful resources for constructing *self/other*, and the study of migrant identity is thus simultaneously a study of membership in diasporic communities.

Although identity negotiation/construction is socially situated in the *here and now*, it does not occur in a sociospatial momentality as a topical new construct in vacuum, but is a multi-layered process of positioning *self* and *other* to which interlocutors bring their past and history, non-present agents (see also De Fina, this volume) on 'exophoric circumstances', and a series of symbolic indices beyond language (such as clothing, the characteristics of the space/location where interaction takes place etc.): 'a convoluted network with a multiplicity of highly diverse dates, places and people' (Latour, 1996: 231). In accessing this network, interactants draw on discourses available to them at the level of both the specific interaction and the broader sociopolitical context. Our focus is on how these pre-existing structures come to the fore and are made relevant in any given context. More specifically, power dynamics are inextricably linked to interactional negotiation and determine the relationship and dependencies between the speakers; indeed, not all speakers will be 'entitled' to accept or reject identities projected onto or claimed by them. Identity negotiation and construction occur at the level of both the individual and the group. The latter has been the focus of group membership categorisation, which we discuss next.

The process of categorisation involves positioning *self* or *other* in relation to in- and/or out-groups (this has been the tenet of different identity theories and most notably Social Identity Theory). Membership Categorisation Analysis or MCA (Antaki & Widdicombe, 1998; Sacks, 1972) explores how interactants, at the topical level of interaction, negotiate membership claims (acceptance or rejection) to categories which they co-construct and which are emergent in discourse (rather than pre-defined by the researcher/interviewer). This approach focuses on the analysis of a variety of discourse practices employed in lay interactions throughout the process of membership categorisation. As categories emerge (from school teacher, immigrant, national group to parent etc.), MCA proves a useful tool to explore the negotiation mechanisms in the immediate context of interaction. According to Sacks (1992), common nouns work as 'membership categorisation device(s)' (MCD) and obtain symbolic properties in 'building' relationship dynamics between the negotiated categories. This mechanism relates to the notion of indexicality, which links linguistic phenomena to their contextual inferences. Later, in light of the data, we look at how mundane notions and actions become indices of symbolic meaning and identity claims/ disidentification.

While the boundaries of the in-group and out-group solidify, *self* and *other* start shaping as distinct (imagined) conceptual entities with variable weight and significance. When there is power imbalance between the two groups, this can lead to *othering*: when the powerful *us* constructs an impassable line between *us* and *them*, and the *other* is reduced to an essentialised, stereotypical set of demeaning characteristics (Jensen, 2011). The process of *othering* entails an element of symbolic degradation, where the *other* is seen as subordinate, of less value, inferior, negatively different etc. Analysing the process of *othering* looks into 'the consequences of racism, sexism, class (or a combination hereof)' (Jensen, 2011: 65), power abuse and discrimination, which essentialise and dehumanise groups or individuals.

Us and *them*, however, are not two ends of a linear spectrum. They are positions available to the speaker that are dynamically related, juxtaposed or contrasted. As we show in the data, our speakers move between us/them, now/then, here/there categories in constructing *self* and claiming a dynamic stage which is best seen as transient and liminal. Liminality concerns an *in-between* stage in the process of transitioning 'into' a new community or context. The term is associated with the work of Van Gennep (1909) and Turner (1967), who addressed the spatiotemporal threshold between two worlds. The three phases or stages are identified in the process as: separation, margin (or limen) and aggregation (Turner, 1969/2008: 94). Turner, building on Van Gennep, argues that 'during the intervening "liminal" period, the characteristics of the ritual subject (the "passenger") are ambiguous; he [sic] passes through a cultural realm that has few or none of the attributes of the past of coming state' (Turner, 1969/2008: 94). Although our thinking has progressed considerably and the dynamics of transitions have been discussed time and again, liminality can be usefully associated with the concept of *in-between* identities. Research taking this approach (e.g. Beech, 2011; Torres & Wicks-Asbun, 2014; Ybema *et al.*, 2011) looks into the complexity of transitioning into a new context, which requires a recontextualisation of *self* in the process of acquiring new ways of doing and being. These *in-between* spaces are characterised by identity struggles, as contradictions, conflict between the old and the new, adjustment and resistance co-exist. As is well argued by Ybema *et al.* (2011: 23–24): 'In transitional liminars' identity talk, their present "self" [...] remains undefined, ambiguous, unclear, in-between, "not anymore", "not yet" or, at best, in-the-making'. We argue that this is an ongoing process which never reaches a definite 'end'. Liminality and dynamic *in-between*-ness are instrumental concepts linked to theoretical frames particularly useful for the analysis of the narratives of individuals who self-identify as simultaneously *insiders* and *outsiders*, maintaining symbolic relationships with imaginaries of particular nations and/or countries.

Claiming *in-between* spaces and positions as well as indexing membership (or not) to communities accessible to the individual are directly related to claiming and indexing belonging in the new context. Krzyżanowski and Wodak (2008) focus on migrant identity and show the perceived *threshold* position (*in-between*-ness) that individuals construct in the processes of claiming membership and 'doing' belonging. By drawing on modes of belonging (Jones & Krzyżanowski, 2008) they unpack the dynamics and contradictions of attachments the individuals mobilise in the process of renegotiating/re-establishing membership to the new community/collectivity and progressively renegotiating new normalities. We discuss this further in the next section.

Belonging and the Process of Fitting in

Research (e.g. Delanty *et al.*, 2008) has repeatedly showed belonging to be a multi-layered and multi-faceted process, related to personal/ family experience, emotional attachment to a place or a group, and the (claimed/granted) participations in professional and social activities. In the context of a diverse and globally interconnected world, fitting in and belonging are becoming fluid and dynamic as linguistic, geographical and national boundaries carry multiple meanings across time and space.

Some researchers distinguish between two levels of belonging: a personal and a political (Antonsich, 2010; Yuval-Davies, 2011). The former captures the intimate *at home* feeling of belonging to a place ('placebelongingness'); the latter refers to the discursive enactment of belonging, the negotiation of 'socio-spatial inclusion/exclusion (politics of belonging)' (Antonsich, 2010: 644). In this sense, belonging manifests at an individual level – a relationship of attachment to a place/person/context – *as well as* in multiple collective relationships (group/s) (Yuval-Davies, 2011), which have different norms, expectations of behaviour and by extension ways of granting (or not granting) membership. The sociospatial element, along with emotional attachments as well as ethical and political values are the three components which Yuval-Davies (2011) attributes to belonging; understanding the dynamic interdependencies between these elements aims at capturing the ways in which belonging is subject to the multiple structures of power and hegemony.

Discourses of national identity and ethnic fantasies are prime resources in the construction of belonging (or non-belonging) for both the individual and the group. This has been particularly visible and relevant in the past decade, in Europe and across continents, in dominant discourses on the (so-called) migration crises as well as in populist rhetoric, where hate-discourses capitalise on the fear of the *other* to explain the economic crisis and build a victim-paradigm for the 'ethnically pure' citizens, the locals, the non-migrants (for an extensive analysis of the rise of far-right populism in Europe, see Angouri & Wodak, 2014; Byng, 2010; Wodak, 2015; Wodak *et al.*, 2013). The notion of *nationality* has been prominently used in relation to migration discourses particularly in the public sphere. In the past two decades, and in the current political context, *citizenship* is of increasing prominence. The two terms share common ground; however, citizenship is correlated to the legal (or lack of) relationship between the individuals and the state and a sense of responsibility to demonstrate *belonging* in the society ('citizen') (Ayelet *et al.*, 2017). The dif/fusion of nationality, citizenship and language and the association with who has the right to (not) belong has particular consequences for migrants and for those coming new to a socio-cultural context.

In previous work (Kirilova & Angouri, 2018), we associated belonging with historicity and a state of mind/body that changes over time on the basis of cumulating and deconstructing lived experience. We distinguished between *belonging* and *fitting in*. We argued that the latter is a *meso*-concept and hence allows examining how speakers *do* fitting in, in the situated here and now of interactional encounters. Fitting in looks forward to the future, to the undiscovered, whereas belonging presupposes a pre-existing context/group/category to which the newcomer is expected to assimilate (Antonsich, 2010), and also carries strong connotations of emotional attachment and state of being. This, however, is an analytical artefact, as the two are intertwined and 'index' each other.

The concept of *fitting in* involves a process of adjusting to a new environment, a new context or situation, a new group or category. Fitting in thus entails belonging and vice versa. The concept of fitting in is analytically useful for exploring the processual aspect of transitioning and settling in a new context. Successfully indexing fitting in is also a strategy for the individual to achieve their goal in an encounter: e.g. by successfully indexing membership to the majority group, I increase my chances for securing a job and passing the 'gate' of a job interview and so on.

Both *fitting in* and *belonging* are, largely but not exclusively, discursively constructed; fitting in is primarily projected onto the newcomer, who is expected to perform in the new environment. This may entail the newcomer staying at the periphery of the new community in the process of observing and analysing dominant norms and ways of doing. Workplace research has shown (Angouri et al., 2017; Gunnarsson, 2009) cases where newcomers are empowered to move from the outer layers of a community to the centre – the latter understood as the locus of decision-making power. At the same time, however, the same research and particularly work on low-skilled migration has also shown how the workforce can be locked in a periphery, which then leads to exploitation and discrimination in the allocation of resources (see Piller & Lising, 2014). These contextual dynamics are operationalised in interaction and hence any analysis of fitting in is also an analysis of power hierarchies and structures in the target context (Kirilova & Angouri, 2017). Periphery is understood here as both material and abstract, related with claiming a position as an insider/outsider to the dominant group. We return to this point in the light of the data.

In Bourdieu's terms, *fitting in* is the process through which a *habitus* reacts and adapts to a (new) *field* (Bourdieu, 1984; Wodak, 2011). The relationship between *habitus* and *field*, as introduced by Bourdieu, is a useful concept in discerning fitting in. Sinclair (2017: 2), drawing on McNay (1999), describes the *habitus* as a 'deeply internalised system of dispositions and schemas through which we interpret and respond to the world', without being consciously aware of doing so, acquiring what Bourdieu refers to as a/the 'feel for the game' (Bourdieu, 1984). According to Bourdieu, there is a 'two-way relationship between habitus and field, where the field, as a structured space, tends to structure the habitus, while the habitus tends to structure the perception of the field' (Bourdieu, 1988: 784). Key characteristics of habitus are common behavioural dispositions and cognitive schemata, which emerge in the actions of agents in different contextual settings (*fields*). Fitting in, then, can be conceptualised as this process of recognising and acting according to situational norms which apply to any interactional encounter but also pre-exist the speakers. Both field and habitus are constantly repositioned and transformed (the latter to fit in with the former), while agents and contextual factors continually shape and re-shape them in discourse.

Data and Methodology

This chapter draws on a corpus of interviews. We zoom in on the discourse of 12 participants – five self-identified as migrating from Greece, seven self-identified as migrating to Italy – by drawing on 17 excerpts, chosen as the most illustrative of the whole corpus of the 40 interviews in total. We use pseudonyms throughout to protect the participants' anonymity.

Greece and Italy have been severely affected by the ongoing financial crisis and on this backdrop we are particularly interested in the narratives of people who im/emigrated from/to the two countries. This variety in our corpus provides a dialectical recontextualisation of the lived experience of crisis: although Italy is undergoing a financial crisis, and was so especially at the time of the interviews, the participants that moved there portrayed it as the land of opportunity. 'Migrants' are often portrayed in media as a homogenous group and this is highly problematic as it dilutes the various different needs and conditions of individuals. For our chapter, we draw on narratives of 'economic' migrants collected through ethnographic interviews in a language chosen by the participants and fully transcribed and analysed following the principles of critical discourse analysis and interactional sociolinguistics (IS). IS, associated with the legacy of John Gumperz and the analysis of spoken interaction, shares with conversation analysis (CA) an emphasis on the detailed analysis of interaction, typically using CA conventions for representing talk in writing. IS, unlike CA, however, is interested in the relationship between the situated here and now and the wider sociocultural context. In our study, the analysis went beyond content to how positions were claimed and special attention was paid to the power hierarchies associated with the positions claimed/resisted in the data set. Hence we favour the term critical IS (Angouri, 2018). Long interviews (mean 50 min) were elicited in order to obtain in-depth conversational interactions that can be valuable 'resource[s] through which we construct who we are' (Jaspal & Cinnirella, 2012: 524; Schiffrin, 2006: 111).

The analysis involved a detailed transcript which contained marked pauses, intonation features and overlapping sections as well as detailed notes of the interviewers' own reflections on their role in co-constructing the narratives. The coding followed a bottom-up approach, coding each transcript separately, then connecting cross-topic indexes and eliciting the main categories and themes. Finally, connections between the macro-categories and between the respective sub-categories were identified. The quotes we include in this chapter are selected to illustrate the ways in which positions were enacted in the data set.

We consider interviews to be co-constructions between a participant and an interviewer and hence pay attention to the role of the researcher in the process of eliciting and framing the participants' lived experience. We were particularly interested in allowing 'first-order' (or lay participant) perspectives to emerge instead of focusing solely on 'second-order' (the researcher) interpretation of the phenomena. This distinction is particularly useful, although not a simple switch between two positions. Berger and Luckmann (1966/1991: 2) argued long ago that 'the sociological understanding of "reality" and "knowledge" falls somewhere in the middle between that of the man [sic] in the street and that of the philosopher'. This quote applies directly to sociolinguistic discourse research and accurately illustrates the interplay between everyday common sense and the abstraction in the processes of research. Throughout the process of our research, we have reflected on our methodological practices and the role of the researcher in the interview process, where the situated interaction is also a space/time where identities are negotiated, co-constructed and enacted. We do not expand on this for reasons of space here, but the 'interviewer/observer' bias (Angrosino, 2007) and the ways in which positionality is actually done in the context of an interview event are particularly relevant to the way research is represented and narrated (on the politics of research interpretation, see Angouri, 2018).

Findings and Discussion

The analysis of the data shows that the participants mobilise and use binary positions as resources in constructing *self/other*. This process brings together national imaginaries as well as groups and behaviours that are attributed symbolic meaning in the narratives of our participants. Figure 5.1 represents the key actors and reference points our participants mobilise in their discourse. This figure is, evidently, an analytical artefact emerging from our data but nevertheless shows the complexity of the process and the ways in which in-between positions provide legitimate spaces for recontextualising *self* in the transition process.

Studies on migrant identities and particularly those forced into what Bailey *et al.* (2002: 238) call 'permanent temporariness', such as the case of undocumented migrants (e.g. Mountz *et al.*, 2002; Torres

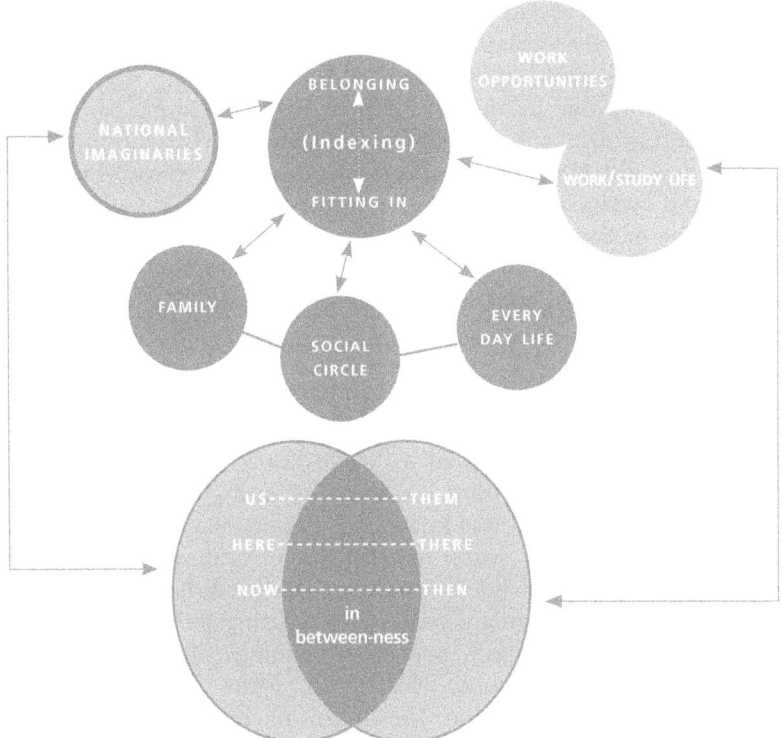

Figure 5.1 Representation of processes of claiming belonging and positioning self

& Wicks-Asbun, 2014; Lori, 2017), show the consistency of these in-between positions, which often come with the experience of being 'betwixt and between' (Newman, 1999: 91) two or more states and identities.

The diagram reflects the liminal positions negotiated across our corpus. The participants attribute, claim, reject and negotiate insider/outsider categories in their narratives of everyday experiences and challenges, remaining buoyant in the in-between fluid space which is abstract, placeless and time resistant (see also De Fina's analysis, this volume, on self-presentation in narrative). We unpack this below.

Belonging 'here' or not – the insider/outsider conundrum

The participants move between insider/outsider positions equated with 'foreignness' and 'local-ness'/'nativeness' in their discourse, drawing on points of reference in relation to their professional and social lives as well as their relationship with family in the 'here' and 'there'. 'Here' comes associated with 'opportunity' and work. This is expected, given the reason why our participants moved in the first place, linked to seeking employment, education, lifestyle or access to better options in all respects. It is also typical of diasporic narratives, even those examined in first-wave diaspora studies, where 'opportunity' and 'land of hope' are well-known motivations for leaving the 'homeland'. This orientation, which has been confirmed time and again in literature on skilled migration (Meyer, 2001), is well represented in our data. The quotes below illustrate the point.

Home is where opportunity is

In the context of the globalised professional world, moving – particularly for the skilled worker – is an opportunity, a choice and a need to remain skilled. This drives knowledge professionals from geographical spaces where work is scarce to other parts of the world on the basis of perceived offer and demand. Satisfying this need, however, is subject to the pressures of entering a profession, securing satisfying work conditions and settling in a new context (Angouri *et al.*, 2017; Baynham, 2013). Particularly in Europe, which is the locus of our studies, free movement has encouraged this. The current reterritorialisation and tendency towards separation, as evidenced by the recent rise of populist/far-right parties or the upcoming Brexit, affect population flows. This is reflected in recent mobility statistics within Europe: for instance, the number of EU citizens migrating to the UK for work post-Brexit vote has reached the lowest rate since 2012 (ONS, 2018).

Nevertheless, 'work' has always been and still is a particularly strong motivation for mobility. In the globalised world, and depending on the rights of movement available to the individual, it also influences if not determines the destination/s. Significantly, from 2010 until the end of 2015, emigration from Greece ranged between 280,000 and 350,000 people, whose main motives overwhelmingly linked to economic issues (72%) (Labrianidis & Pratsinakis, 2014). The quotes below illustrate the perceptions of market influence on individual choices.

(QUOTE 1)

```
1    Nikolas: I decided to leave I decided to leave more
2    because I started feeling I was losing the profession
```

```
3   Researcher: Ok ok I see
4   Nikolas: That if I stayed unemployed a bit longer and
5   or if I went to do something else that what I've studied
6   I would lose it
7   [...]
8   Nikolas: And it's not/ it's a technological job, for
9   instance you can't be for a long time outside of it then
10  you won't be able to re-enter
11  Researcher: Yes I understand, right
12  Nikolas: So this was also a reason why I decided to
13  leave
```

The repetition (line 1) allows Nikolas to frame the decision to move in relation to maintaining his professional skills and by extension employability. In the neoliberal economy, the need for continuous self-development and re-training adds to existing pressures to stay in the job market (Gee, 1996). With 're-enter' (line 10) Nikolas creates a movement metaphor and distances *self* from the unemployment threat (i.e. an *in-between* jobs position). Not being in the 'un/employed' is a category which the participants mobilise to both position themselves and legitimise their choices.

Decisions to move and the process of preparing for moving to the new 'home' are often taken on the basis of information available online, as illustrated by Quote 2. 'Here' (line 1) is used implicitly in comparison to an abstract/absent 'there' or a way of doing things that is different from what Fotis was used to and points to a new habit in the process of fitting in. Although media and political rhetoric often project a lack of drive to 'fit in' onto the 'migrant', our corpus systematically shows the opposite, irrespective of the age, profile or specific circumstances of the participants.

(QUOTE 2)

```
1   Fotis: So everything /here they have internet online
2   website and stuff everything so it was very easy to
3   actually check the/ the living cost in England without
4   even having ever been here
```

Moving away from a conceptualisation of diasporas as movement from place A to place B, modern mobilities involve a number of different loci. In our sample, they always involve (perceptions of) *better* opportunities for professional development and expression. The quote below by Pardeep illustrates this point.

(QUOTE 3)

```
1   Pardeep: On this side I am very happy that I came here,
2   because here I have many possibilities, I can go out
3   easily, I come to school in the morning all by myself,
4   now my parents allow me to continue even at the university
```

Across the data set, our participants associate their current locus with individual freedom, empowerment and future perspectives. Pardeep (3) talks about how moving has empowered her position: the use of 'allow' and 'even' (line 4) possibly index a shift in family moral values, a route to future potential and opportunity.

The individual situation is, in most cases, assessed as 'better' in the current locus than what it was before, particularly in the data set of younger participants in Italy. From the participants' viewpoint, the *other* is often but not always associated with attributes that are presented in a positive light, such as being open, liberal or progressive. A divide between affiliation to the 'new' versus the 'old' community is emerging and also projected onto the participants' significant identity actors, such as parents and relatives.[1]

Open-mindedness and choice – or 'too much freedom'?

The complexity of the multiple hegemonies the speakers experience and their fragile habitus, where multiple pressures and competing discourses co-exist, are represented by the two quotes below (4, 5). The participants' habitus is fluctuating in the liminal position between the imagined opposite poles of *here* and *there* as well as poles of reference in daily life, e.g. *school* and *home*. Crystalyn (4) mobilises the category 'family' by reference to 'parents', but she does not identify them as her own parents. By speaking about parents in general, she distances *self* from the act of attributing criticism of 'old' mentality to the 'former us' and signifies a process of aligning with the progressive *other*. This is a consistent move in the data, particularly for the younger participants. These opposing/conflicting pairs (here/there, now/before, school/home etc.) function as *relativising devices* in the self-positioning process. In Quote 5, home and school become the spatial binaries (*fields*) where *self* is called on to align with or reject conflicting identities, in response to pressure from significant agents (family/peers).

(QUOTE 4)

1 Crystalyn: Parents are very open here, while in my country
2 their mentality has remained a bit old.

(QUOTE 5)

1 Borana: It was a very critical period of my life because in
2 any case it was the adolescent phase. In the classroom at
3 school I felt very well, my life was the school, and when
4 I came back home, on the other hand, it was a disaster for
5 me, I always felt sad because my parents always criticised
6 me for what I was doing at school.

'Home' is a central space constructed both as a site of oppression and/or a safe space for positioning *self in-between* the contradicting poles of reference in the participants' lives. These conflicting positions form part of the tapestry of identities projected onto the *other* and claimed for the *self*. Note, for instance, how freedom is also constructed as 'too much' by another participant, who swings between subject positions in her narrative.

(QUOTE 6)

1 Erlinda: There is too much freedom here, for example
2 people go to disco when they are sixteen or seventeen
3 years old, sell drugs, while in Albania people that are
4 sixteen or seventeen years old are more limited, they
5 stay at home.

The projected positive characteristics of the *other* do not mean that our participants are not reporting experiences of exclusion or discriminatory behaviours nor does it mean unconflicted acceptance of the *other*. However, in the context of the commodified economy and the appalling working conditions that migrants often experience (Cohen, 2008), our participants position *self* as empowered to make choices and to align with the aspirations of peers from the majority group. This positive stance is further enhanced by reference to a range of situations where the participants develop choices and decide how to conduct their lives. Not all of this is commodified on the basis of economic capital available to the individual or the family. The perceived quality of everyday life plays an equally important role, linked to the size of the city/place, the engagement with the local community, the ease of commuting to/from work, the quality of services etc. The quote below illustrates the perceived significance of the mundane of daily life.

(QUOTE 7)
```
1 Petros: Yes yes I feel good, in the sense that a small
2 society makes me feel like, feel comfortable (…) some-
3 thing I had lost in Greece (…) which is unbelievable I
4 mean the feeling of being comfortable abroad and being
5 a foreigner actually and not feeling comfortable in your
6 own neighbourhood
```

In Quote 7, the phrase 'in the sense' downplays 'I feel good' (line 1) as Petros builds the reasoning behind his choice of moving. There is both an alignment (indexed by 'the feeling of being comfortable' – line 2) and a disidentification (introduced by 'unbelievable' – line 3) with belonging to the community 'abroad'. The same is true of the 'foreigner' position (lines 4–5) which disrupts the belongingness to the 'there' group (introduced by the pronoun 'your own').

Our participants index a settled-self, drawing mainly on the professional domain and the opportunities of the host society. This, however, does not come without struggles of transitioning into new ways of doing and/or feeling trapped in the 'outsider' category.

The accounts consistently report access to the target areas of activity for our sample, be it education and/or work. Although they typically paint the *other* as open and liberal (see the traits projected onto the *other* at the end of the chapter), they have also been othered and positioned at the periphery, which they have both accepted and resisted.

Derogatory or intentionally offensive comments about the 'homeland', perceived as such by our participants, have been reported as a common strategy of *othering* the newcomer. These come in different guises, from statements about the economy to comments about gender roles, religion and an endless list of attributes that are given negative meaning in context.

The quote below shows how Eleni claims membership in the non-mentioned/insinuated group of 'Greeks' and reacts to the 'crude and rude' Dutch (line 2). The financial crisis becomes a personal struggle for Eleni in negotiating the power balance with her co-workers. By projecting a trait onto 'all' Dutch (line 1) and essentialising their behaviour, Eleni is intensifying the struggle and impact of the incident she describes. The sympathetic interviewer encourages, and by extension elicits, the development of the story in which Eleni takes the position of being under attack but also able to 'fight back' (lines 10–13).

(QUOTE 8)

```
1   Eleni: (...) at work with Dutch in particular who are very
2   crude and rude eh yes I have received negative comments
3   Researcher: And how did you react?
4   Eleni: I replied
5   Researcher: What did you reply?
6   Eleni: Eh for example they had said something that we take
7   loans from Germany and the rest of Europe something like
8   that with a [missing] tone not like to state the obvious
9   Researcher: Yes yes
10  Eleni: Eh and I replied yes so we can then buy their
11  broken submarines / this didn't bother them ever eh / or
12  that yes you gain from the interest and have made profit
13  from the whole situation
```

An opposite position is also common in the data (e.g. Quote 9). Repetition affirms the stance here, which is then supported by 'not even' and 'not a word' (line 1). The claims of sympathy and empathy are subordinated as the imagined clear lines between the 'them' (British) out-group and the 'us' (Greeks) in-group fade in the face of the common underlying problem: the financial crisis; the lines are then restored with 'to our eyes' in the last phrase. Fotis aligns with the Greek interviewer in maintaining a common sense of *self*, defined by their shared ethnic background.

(QUOTE 9)

```
1   Fotis: But no no nothing, I mean not even / now not a word
2   for any offensive comments but not even judgemental (...)
3   you will hear sympathy and empathy for example because
4   they've been through (crisis) and they are perhaps going
5   out of their own financial crisis, irrespective if it is
6   not evident to our eyes
```

These contradictions are consistent with the process of identity construction and indicate the multiple pressures the speakers juggle in their professional, social and family lives.

Framing the in-between space

The participants bridge the various significant loci in their narratives. Despite being settled in their current loci, both the 'here' and the 'there' co-exist in their imaginaries. Tölölyan (2007) notes that 'diasporas are resolutely multilocal and polycentric, in that what happens to kin communities in other areas of dispersion as well as in the homeland insistently matters to them' (2007: 661).

The participants share a range of strategies to maintain affiliations with 'homeland' in the mundane world of everyday life. Unsurprisingly, new and old media play a critical role in the process.

(QUOTE 10)

```
1  Erlinda: The Albanian television helps me, it helps me feel
2  very close. [...] It's something that always accompanies
3  me, inside of me.
```

Belonging to the idealised imaginary, 'Albanian-ness' (10) is enacted here in spatial terms: 'close', 'inside' and 'accompanies' all index constructed abstract places where the 'in-group' resides, where the participant's identity is manifested. National fantasies are consistently enacted in the data, associated with *being* and a state of *belonging* to a category external to the present *self*. The 'home', as used in Quote 11 below, is again the locus of habits that merge the *old* and the *new*, the *here* and the *there*.

(QUOTE 11)

```
1  Nikolas: At home I listen to a Greek radio station but
2  foreign (music) (laughter) (...) usually eh sometimes it
3  will play some Greek too (...) I want the comment between
4  songs to be in Greek (laughter) [...] to create myself the
5  feeling that, somehow, I am not in England for a moment,
6  something like that
```

Transitioning 'between' spaces is consistent across the whole data set. Transitions are also consistent when our participants position *self* in the conventionally labelled 'homeland', the locus (region/nation/country/countries) with which they maintain a symbolic relationship. In these discourses, the dialectical relationship between field and habitus emerges: the participant shapes the *here* and *there*, and the *here* and *there* shapes the participant. The *rite of passage* between the identities negotiated in the *here* and *there* loci is not linear, but a *liminal* transition in the in-between space, always re-calibrated and re-shaped by multiple agents (Cheng, 2012; Kirilova, 2013). The use of *here* and *there*, repeated and juxtaposed, adds to the contrasting effect of the narratives. This is illustrated in the quote below.

(QUOTE 12)

```
1  Greta: I'm used to staying always here, to live as we
2  live here, when I go there and stay there too long, after
3  a while I miss Italy, I miss the habit of here.
```

Although our participants consistently claim agency in choices about professional *self*, there is also a sense of accepting the power of social networks. Research on diasporas (already from first-wave studies) has shown the importance of networks for the mobility of skilled migrants (Epstein & Hezler, 2016; Raj, 2012). These networks, however, are also painted in a negative light when they operate as a trap for moving 'out', as portrayed in Quote 13.

(QUOTE 13)

```
1  Athina: Even though I wasn't really intending to meet
2  Greeks I didn't really want to and it wasn't one of my
3  needs or priorities (...) on the contrary, I really wanted
4  to meet people from elsewhere but indeed at the end the
5  Greek network ended up trapping me in a way and I made
6  friends with lots of Greeks in the end, when I left my
7  main friends groups were Greeks
```

Athina's story is structured as an explanation/negation of the (eventual) alignment to the categories 'Greeks' and 'friends'. Introduced by 'even though' and then built throughout a choice of strongly negative pointers – 'really', 'I didn't really want to', 'it wasn't one of my needs or priorities' – Athina resists claims to membership. She portrays an unwilling, almost other-induced membership to the group, prefaced by 'on the contrary' (line 3), in saying 'ended up trapping me in a way' (line 5). The use of the 'trap' metaphor creates a visual impression of the group's physical existence and its boundaries. Her positioning denies any intentional affiliations; by naming it 'Greek network' she further intensifies the net or trap effect. This represents a struggle, common in our corpus, where participants construct an imposed top-down affiliation with 'us', which consequently becomes 'them'. The negative characteristic projected onto the group creates both the necessary distance to claim a liminal position and a *dipping-in-and-out membership*.

Negotiating and recontextualising the outsider position is recurrent in the data and associated with being at/from the periphery. On several occasions, participants distance *self* from a constructed *other* which, however, also includes the in-group (e.g. 'I am not the typical Greek' or 'Greeks do this') and they stand at the borders of the category for dis/identifying with the group. The 'permanent temporariness' of the liminal positions is strongly evident in the data. The speakers perform identity acts aligned with their perception of the interviewers' profiles and expectations, as well as with the imagined characteristics of the group to which they (do not) belong. Performative acts are in assonance with a 'rigid regulatory frame' about what minority/majority looks like. Claiming fitting in is dependent on meeting dominant imaginaries of identity performance. 'Identity is a normative ideal rather than a descriptive feature of experience' (Butler, 1990: 23) and the speakers 'do' their position as in/outsider by reference to a range of practices and behaviours that are mobilised in the discourse.

Neither here nor there – staying at the periphery

The concept of the periphery has a long history in sociolinguistic research (e.g. Pietikäinen *et al.*, forthcoming; Pietikäinen & Holmes, 2013; Wang *et al.*, 2014) and has also attracted attention in relation to the process of integration into a community. The influential 'communities of practice' framework (CoP) (Lave & Wenger, 1991) has provided a useful vocabulary for discussing the movement from the 'periphery' to the 'centre' of a new context. While that particular framework is not adopted here, we acknowledge its impact to sociopragmatic research. It is useful to note that our participants associate the *in-between* position with staying at the periphery and observing the *other*, while also claiming a central position when they position *self* in a 'glocal' international context. Quote 14 is an example of this.

(QUOTE 14)

```
1   Fotis:  (...) I observe them [the British] from outside. Even
2           if I go out and party and all I am with Greeks, so even
3           if there is a foreigner [in the group] exactly because
4           the foreigner is a minority in the group they will only
5           comment, or when you are the minority in the group, I mean,
6           once I was out with my ex-manager, who has been many years
7           in Britain and is half British, and yes he behaves like
8           a British, so if I go out with him and there are other
9           British with us, I consider myself a minority in the ways
10          of thinking, they seem to me completely different
```

Choice of words such as 'outside' clearly define the 'us' and 'them' pattern; when more British are present, the Greek either becomes the minority or the foreigner and vice versa. Fitting in with the new group of Greeks is constructed as a taken-for-granted process, whereas interaction with the *other* (British or foreigners) seems to be a laborious, long-winded process, an unmapped territory yet to be conquered, a quasi-impossible task. Membership in each group is subjected in this case to a common ethnic profile which is aligned with national identity. National identity is used as the common denominator that defines the (in/out) groups. However, the notion is left ambiguously open to a commonsensical reading. Notions such as nation, ethnicity and culture function as what Laclau and Mouffe (1985) named a 'floating signifier', a 'decidable totality' devoid of meaning (Rear, 2013). Co-constructed floating signifiers are conceptualised and deduced to 'common-sense' agreed upon notions in the 'public sphere' (Habermas, 1991). In that sense, 'nation', although it remains devoid of content, becomes a context-specific notion which exists, is operationalised and substantialised exclusively in contextual relativity to 'what nation is/is not', to 'the enemies' or 'the others' etc.; it 'symbolises an absent fullness' (Torfing, 1999: 195).

Claims of sameness/difference are in line with the positions taken or resisted in the corpus. Our participants legitimise their position by foregrounding categories to which they claim belonging compared to the majority group. Belonging to more than one linguistic, cultural, religious, ethnic (and so forth) group provides justification for *doing* 'being different'.

(QUOTE 15)

```
1  Zineb: They have an easier life, because it is the life
2  that they have lived since they were born in the same
3  city, with the same people. They have more stable roots,
4  while I feel a bit here, a little there. I feel like them
5  because I always remain Moroccan, also Muslim, but at the
6  same time different because I see things in a somewhat
7  different way from them.
```

In Quote 15, similarly to Athina (13), Zineb positions herself in the in-between status between 'them' and 'I' (lines 3–4), and 'here' and 'there', swinging between 'like them' and 'different'.

Further to the discussion of sameness/difference, being in global cities and global workplaces seems to provide spaces where 'difference' is the norm, and this allows for easier movement from the abstract periphery to the powerful centre. The quotes below show how being the 'majority local' is contrasted to a 'majority international', with the latter being constructed as 'easier' to access. This is consistent in the data set and associated with both the professional and the social lives of the participants.

(QUOTE 16)
```
1   Petros: No one I am the only one eh the only one until
2   /not only in my group but also at management level they
3   are foreigners eh and this makes me feel that we all
4   have the same / we are here with the same goal I mean
5   they are equival/ they are people like me from France
6   from Lithuania from Hungary Spanish / of course because
7   they are the majority (...) eh we just have much in common
8   and that helps me in anything that I might find weird at
9   work / weird in the sense a difficulty or in regards to
10  some habits here / other eh or / it has to do again with
11  the 'adjustment' (gestures quotes with hands)
12  (...) all this has to do with the whole / with socialising
13  which for me / because we spoke before about adjustment
14  and this helps me because they are people like me so we
15  are looking for the same things / to go out and find / to
16  do some things to
```

Petros employs the rule of the 'majority' (line 7), like Fotis above (14), to make sense of the group formation process and to distinguish 'us' and 'them'. The 'adjustment' is used here to describe the process of fitting in and to demonstrate resilience, which for Petros involves the overcoming of difficulties and different ways of doing. When referring to the ways of doing, Petros uses 'here' (line 10) to frame the space where the process of adjustment takes place. 'Here' is often 'placeless', used as an abstract denominator to distinguish a non-present/past 'there'. 'There' is framed as different and familiar, easier to navigate. In these multidimensional contexts, people develop adjusting mechanisms in order to cope with what Bauman (2000) calls the 'liquid modernity' and Sloterdjik (2004) refers to as the 'foamy present', the 'rapidly reconstituting nature of interpersonal, social and organisational spheres and associated conducts' (Caldas-Coulthard & Iedema, 2008: 1). Individuals construct the polycentricity of their own perceived reality; the negotiation of membership attribution and categorisation is thus an ongoing process embedded within everyday discourse and interaction. Petros later refers back to the 'adjustment' (line 11) when talking about socialising, which in order to be successful as a process very much depends on group attributes: 'people like me', implying foreigners, who move from an abstract periphery to the centre of a (more or less) 'glocal' group. The 'international' migrant is a consistent discourse in our corpus.

Concluding Remarks

The analysis of the data has shown how the participants claim intermediate positions and display strategies for resisting *othering*, while at the same time displaying *fitting in* with the broader, imagined context and negotiating *belonging* to imaginary communities of the 'homeland', the 'local network' or their 'peers'. A range of attributes are claimed for *self/other* in our corpus. We understand those as resources for doing identities and converging or diverging from collectivities available to the individual. They are organised around binaries which are mutually exclusive and mutually constitutive.

Studies on the politics of migration (Delanty *et al.*, 2011) have addressed the expectation the newcomer is faced with regarding becoming *one of us*: learn, adjust, adopt, assimilate, behave and perform according to a set of rules, 'values', a language or religion etc. This process moves from a position of exoticisation/othering to de-othering *and* re-culturalisation; the newcomer is expected to learn 'our' ways of doing and perform accordingly. Non-conforming comes with the penalty of exclusion from resources and, by extension, power to claim an insider position. This does not mean that the 'newcomer/s' are powerless agents; the process involves a negotiation between groups. This is a process of power negotiation which takes different guises in different contexts. In their narratives, the participants mobilise a number of strategies to index fitting in with the new environment: from observation and understanding of norms, collecting information prior to moving, scoping out and adjusting behaviour according to the context, to seeking empowerment by teaming up with the *periphery* aiming to approach/access the *centre*. This process of recontextualising *self* does not take place while moving from stage A to B in a linear way, nor do the positions form concrete solidified entireties. On the contrary, the process involves *multiple fragmentary positions in a complex matrix of interdependencies, which are constantly negotiated, claimed and rejected.*

Table 5.1 Attributes associated with *us/them*

Attributes associated with *us*	Attributes associated with *them*
Moral – traditional – inward-looking	Liberal – open-minded – immoral
At/from periphery – minority	At/from centre – majority
Supportive – oppressive	Polite – rude

Unlike *fitting in*, which looks towards the future, *belonging* presupposes a pre-existing time/space/group and because of that it is built on powerful imaginaries, to which the participants seek to affiliate, identify and connect with, such as national narratives or idealised fantasies about the 'homeland'. However, we do not see belonging as a permanent state; like fitting in, it involves a constant negotiation between individual and group: both are re-positioned, re-defined and situatedly constructed. In the sense-making process, binaries such as here/there, us/them or now/then constitute powerful resources that work as *relativising devices* in the sense of 'things work one way there, hence here it's different', for positioning *self/other* as well as for constructing and claiming an in-between space. Table 5.1 provides an overview of some of the common attributes to *self* and *other*, as evidenced by the data. We used the concept of liminality to capture the fluidity of the *in-between-ness*: hovering in the in-between space involves identity struggles, contradictions, resistance and resilience, creatively recontextualising the old in the new. Moving beyond static dichotomies to understand identity and migration, we align with a more dynamic *liquid* view of the underlying processes, with multiple in-between temporalities.

To conclude, migration is not a homogeneous linear process, and neither are 'migrants' a homogeneous group. Individuals have different needs, come from diverse starting points and conditions, and essentialising their position is highly problematic in unpacking and understanding the complexities of the issues involved and the impact to the individuals' lived experiences. The concept of *liquid modernity* describes well the constant mobility, change and interdependencies in relationships, identities and contemporary societies in general (Bauman, 1997, 2000). Expanding and building on this notion, *liquid migration*[2] describes the in-between-ness, the ever-changing positions in the process of migration (and by extension in fitting in and belonging) as well as the power of established structures and hegemonies. In the context of liquid modernity and in particular under the latest socioeconomic circumstances, on a global scale but especially in Europe, where we see the rise of far-right parties and nationalist tendencies, tensions have been brought to the fore of public discourses and political rhetoric. Normalised discourses of *othering* and master narratives dehumanising migrants are rife in mainstream media and political rhetoric (Wodak, 2015). Applied linguistic and sociolinguistic enquiry has a lot to contribute to resisting by analysing and evidencing these discourses and the underlying power dynamics within them. This may support an alternative narrative which is overdue and urgently needed.

Notes

(1) An interesting discussion is provided by Capstick (this volume) on resistance to 'freshie' identities.
(2) Liquid migration was first introduced by Engbersen *et al.* (2010) based on Bauman's concept and refers to individualised migration patterns benefiting from open borders and open labour markets, as well as 'made possible by the individualisation of family relations in Central and Eastern Europe, so that migration patterns become less network-driven, with young migrants having fewer family responsibilities in the country of origin' (Engbersen *et al.*, 2010: 3). We go beyond this definition and back to Bauman's broader conceptualisation of 'liquid' to capture the multifaceted complexities of migration in postmodernity.

References

Angouri, J. (2012) 'I'm a Greek Kiwi': Constructing Greekness in discourse. *Journal of Language, Identity, and Education* 11 (2), 96–108.
Angouri, J. (2015) Studying identity. In Z. Hua (ed.) *Research Methods in Intercultural Communication: A Practical Guide* (pp. 37–52). Chichester: Wiley.
Angouri, J. (2018) *Culture, Discourse and the Workplace*. Abingdon: Routledge.
Angouri, J. and Wodak, R. (2014) 'They became big in the shadow of the crisis': The Greek success story and the rise of the far right. *Discourse & Society* 25 (4), 540–65.
Angouri, J., Marra, M. and Holmes, J. (eds) (2017) *Negotiating Boundaries at Work: Talking and Transitions*. Edinburgh: Edinburgh University Press.
Angrosino, M. (2007) *Doing Ethnographic and Observational Research*. London/Thousand Oaks/New Delhi/Singapore: Sage.
Antaki, C. and Widdicombe, S. (eds) (1998) *Identities in Talk*. Thousand Oaks, CA: Sage.
Antonsich, M. (2010) Searching for belonging – an analytical framework. *Geography Compass* 4 (6), 644–659.
Ayelet, S., Baübock, R., Bloemraad, I. and Vink, M. (eds) (2017) *The Oxford Handbook of Citizenship*. Oxford: Oxford University Press.
Bailey, A.J., Wright, R., Mountz, A. and Miyares, I.M. (2002) (Re)producing Salvadoran transnational geographies. *Annals of the Association of American Geographers* 92(1): 125–144.
Bauman, Z. (1997) *Postmodernity and its Discontents*. New York: New York University Press.
Bauman, Z. (2000) *Liquid Modernity*. Cambridge: Polity.
Baynham, M. (2013) Postscript. In A. Duchêne, M. Moyer and C. Robert (eds) *Language, Migration and Social Inequalities: A Critical Sociolinguistic Perspective on Institutions and Work* (pp. 272–276). Bristol: Multilingual Matters.
Beech, N. (2011) Liminality and the practices of identity reconstruction. *Human Relations* 64 (2), 285–302.
Bell, A. (1984) Language style as audience design. *Language in Society* 13 (2), 145–204.
Berger, P.L. and Luckmann, T. (1966/1991) *The Social Construction of Reality: A Treatise in the Sociology of Knowledge*. Harmondsworth: Penguin Books.
Bhabha, H.K. (1990) Introduction: Narrating the nation. In H.K. Bhabha (ed.) *Nation and Narration* (pp. 1–7). London: Routledge.
Billig, M. (1995) *Banal Nationalism*. London: Sage.
Bourdieu, P. (1984) *Distinction: A Social Critique of the Judgement of Taste*. London: Routledge.

Bourdieu, P. (1988) Vive la crise! *Theory and Society* 17 (5), 773–787.
Brah, A. (1996) *Cartographies of Diaspora: Contesting Identities*. London: Routledge.
Brubaker, R. (2005) The 'diaspora' diaspora. *Ethnic and Racial Studies* 28 (1), 1–19.
Butler, J. (1990) *Gender Trouble*. London: Routledge.
Butler, J. (1999) Bodily inscriptions, performative subversions. In J. Price and M. Shildrick (eds) *Feminist Theory and the Body: A Reader* (pp. 416–422). New York: Routledge.
Byng, M.D. (2010) Symbolically Muslim: Media, hijab, and the West. *Critical Sociology* 36 (1), 109–129.
Caldas-Coulthard, C.R. and Iedema, R. (2008) Introduction. In C.R. Caldas-Coulthard and R. Iedema (eds) *Identity Trouble: Critical Discourse and Contested Identities* (pp. 1–14). London: Palgrave Macmillan.
Castells, M. (1996) *The Information Age: Economy, Society and Culture*. Vol. 1: *The Rise of the Network Society*. Oxford: Blackwell.
Cheng, N. (2012) The becoming of immigrants from outsiders to in betweens: The national identity of immigrant women in Taiwan. PhD thesis, London: SOAS, University of London. See http://eprints.soas.ac.uk/14246 (accessed 7 October 2019).
Cohen, R. (2008) *Global Diasporas: An Introduction*. Abingdon: Routledge.
Connor, W. (1986) The impact of homelands upon diasporas. In G. Sheffer (ed.) *Modern Diasporas in International Politics* (pp. 16–45). London: Groom Helm.
Côté, J. (2006) Identity studies: How close are we to developing a social science of identity? An appraisal of the field. *Identity* 6 (1), 3–25.
Delanty, G., Jones, P. and Wodak, R. (2011) Introduction: Migration, discrimination and belonging in Europe. In G. Delanty, R. Wodak and P. Jones (eds) *Identity, Belonging and Migration* (pp. 1–20). Liverpool: University of Liverpool Press.
Engbersen, G., Snel, E. and de Boom, J. (2010) A van full of Poles: Liquid migration in eastern and central European countries. In R. Black, G. Engbersen, M. Okólski and C. PanÑîru (eds) *A Continent Moving West? EU Enlargement and Labour Migration from Central and Eastern Europe* (pp. 115–140). Amsterdam: Amsterdam University Press.
Epstein, G.S. and Heizler (Cohen), O. (2016) The Formation of Networks in the Diaspora. *IZA DP* 9762, 2–29. See http://ftp.iza.org/dp9762.pdf (accessed 7 October 2019).
Erikson, E.H. (1968) *Identity: Youth and Crisis*. New York: WW Norton & Company.
Foucault, M. (1983) On the genealogy of ethics: An overview of work in progress. In H. Dreyfus and P. Rabinow (eds) *Michel Foucault: Beyond Structuralism and Hermeneutics* (pp. 229–264). Chicago: University of Chicago Press.
Foucault, M. (1984) The subject and power. In B. Wallis (ed.) *Art after Postmodernism* (pp. 417–432). Boston: David R. Godine.
Gee, J.P. (1996) *Social Linguistics and Literacies: Ideology in Discourses*. Oxford: Taylor & Francis.
Gellner, E. (1983) *Nations and Nationalism*. Oxford: Basil Blackwell.
Genovese, A. (2003) *Per una pedagogia interculturale*. Bologna: Bononia University Press.
Giddens, A. (1990) *The Consequences of Modernity*. Cambridge: Polity Press.
Giddens, A. (1991) *Modernity and Self-Identity*. Cambridge: Polity.
Gunnarsson, B.L. (2009) *Professional Discourse*. Vol. 10. London: Bloomsbury Publishing.
Habermas, J. (1991) *The Structural Transformation of the Public Sphere: An Inquiry into a Category of Bourgeois Society*. Cambridge, MA: MIT Press.
Hall, S. and Du Gay, P. (eds) (1996) *Questions of Cultural Identity*. London: Sage.
Jaspal, R. and Cinnirella, M. (2012) The construction of ethnic identity: Insights from identity process theory. *Ethnicities* 12 (5), 503–530.

Jensen, S.Q. (2011) Othering, identity formation and agency. *Qualitative Studies* 2 (2), 63–78.
Jones, P.R. and Krzyżanowski, M. (2008) Identity, belonging and migration: Beyond describing 'others'. In G. Delanty, R. Wodak and P.R. Jones (eds) *Identity, Belonging, Migration* (pp. 38–53). Liverpool: Liverpool University Press.
Kirilova, M. (2013) All dressed up and nowhere to go: Linguistic, cultural and ideological aspects of job interviews with second language speakers of Danish. Dissertation, Linguistics, University of Copenhagen, Faculty of Humanities.
Kirilova, M. and Angouri, J. (2017) Workplace communication practices and policies. In S. Canagarajah (ed.) *The Routledge Handbook of Migration and Language* (pp. 540–557). London: Routledge.
Kirilova, M. and Angouri, J. (2018) You are now one of us – negotiating 'fitting in' in the workplace. In A. Creese and A. Blackledge (eds) *The Routledge Handbook of Language and Superdiversity* (pp. 345–360). London & New York: Routledge.
Krzyżanowski, M. and Wodak, R. (2008) Multiple identities, migration and belonging: 'Voices of migrants'. In C.R. Caldas-Coulthard and R. Iedema (eds) *Identity Trouble: Critical Discourse and Contested Identities* (pp. 95–119). London: Palgrave Macmillan.
Labov, W. (1972) *Sociolinguistic Patterns*. Philadelphia: University of Pennsylvania Press.
Labrianidis, L. and Pratsinakis, M. (2014) *Outward Migration from Greece during the Crisis, 2014*. See http://www.lse.ac.uk/europeanInstitute/research/hellenicObservatory/CMS%20pdf/Research/NBG_2014_-Research_Call/Final-Report-Outward-migration-from-Greece-during-the-crisis-revised-on-1-6-2016.pdf (accessed 26 April 2018).
Laclau, E. and Mouffe, C. (1985) *Hegemony and Socialist Strategy: Towards a Radical Democratic Politics*. London: Verso.
Lainer-Vos, D. (2010) Diaspora-homeland relations as a framework to examine nation-building processes. *Sociology Compass* 4 (10), 894–908.
Latour, B. (1996) On inter-objectivity. *Mind, Culture and Activity* 3 (4), 228–245.
Lave, J. and Wenger, E. (1991) *Situated Learning: Legitimate Peripheral Participation*. Cambridge: Cambridge University Press.
Lori, N.A. (2017) Statelessness, 'in-between' statuses, and precarious citizenship. In S. Ayelet, R. Baübock, I. Bloemraad and M. Vink (eds) *The Oxford Handbook of Citizenship* (pp. 744–762). Oxford: Oxford University Press.
McNay, L. (1999) Gender, habitus and the field: Pierre Bourdieu and the limits of reflexivity. *Theory, Culture and Society* 16 (1), 175–193.
Meyer, J.B. (2001) Network approach versus brain drain: Lessons from the diaspora. *International Migration* 39 (5), 91–110.
Mountz, A., Wright, R., Miyares, I. and Bailey, A.J. (2002) Lives in limbo: Temporary protected status and immigrant identities. *Global Networks* 2 (4), 335–356.
Newman, K.S. (1999) *Falling from Grace*. Berkeley, CA: University of California Press.
ONS (2018) *Migration Statistics Quarterly Report: February 2018*, statistical bulletin. See www.ons.gov.uk/peoplepopulationandcommunity/populationandmigration/internationalmigration/bulletins/migrationstatisticsquarterlyreport/february2018#fewer-eu-migrants-coming-to-the-uk-for-work (accessed 24 April 2018)
Pietikäinen, S. and Kelly-Holmes H. (eds) (2013) *Multilingualism and the Periphery*. Oxford: Oxford University Press.
Pietikäinen, S., Kelly-Holmes, H., Coupland, N. and Jaffe, A. (forthcoming) *Sociolinguistics from the Periphery: Small Languages in New Circumstances*. Cambridge: Cambridge University Press. Introduction available online, see https://www.researchgate.net/

publication/279959854_Introduction_Mainstreaming_the_Periphery_in_ Sociolinguistics (accessed 22 April 2018).
Piller, I. and Lising, L. (2014) Language, employment, and settlement: Temporary meat workers in Australia. *Multilingua* 33 (1–2), 35–59.
Piller, I. (2016) *Linguistic Diversity and Social Justice: An Introduction to Applied Sociolinguistics.* Oxford: Oxford University Press.
Raj, A. (2012) The Indian diaspora in North America: The role of networks and associations. *Diaspora Studies* 5 (2), 107–123.
Rear, D. (2013) *Laclau and Mouffe's Discourse Theory and Fairclough's Critical Discourse Analysis: An Introduction and Comparison.* See www.academia.edu/2912341/Laclau_ and_Mouffe_s_Discourse_Theory_and_Faircloughs_Critical_Discourse_Analysis_ An_Introduction_and_Comparison (accessed 26 April 2018).
Roberts, C. and Campbell, S. (2007) Fitting stories into boxes: rhetorical and textual constraints on candidates' performances in British job interviews. *Journal of Applied Linguistics and Professional Practice* 2 (1), 45–73.
Sacks, H. (1972) On the analyzability of stories by children. In J.J. Gumpertz and D. Hymes (eds) *Directions in Sociolinguistics: The Ethnography of Communication* (pp. 325–345). New York: Holt, Rinehart & Winston.
Sacks, H. (1992) *Lectures on Conversation*, Vol. 1, ed. G. Jefferson. Oxford: Basil Blackwell.
Safran, W. (1991) Diasporas in modern societies: Myths of homeland and return. *Diaspora: A Journal of Transnational Studies* 1 (1), 83–99.
Schiffrin, D. (2006) From linguistic reference to social identity. In A. De Fina, D. Schiffrin, M. Bamberg (eds) *Discourse and Identity* (pp. 103–132). Cambridge: Cambridge University Press.
Sinclair, A. (2017) 'It's a real negotiation within yourself': Women's stories of challenging heteronormativity within the habitus. *Women's Studies International Forum* 64, 1–9.
Sloterdjik, P. (2004) *Sphären III – Schäume, Plurale Sphärologie.* Frankfurt am Main: Suhrkamp.
Tölölyan, K. (2007) The contemporary discourse of diaspora studies. *Comparative Studies of South Asia, Africa and the Middle East* 27 (3), 647–655.
Torfing, J. (1999) *New Theories of Discourse: Laclau, Mouffe and Žižek.* Oxford: Blackwell.
Torres, R.M. and Wicks-Asbun, M. (2014) Undocumented students' narratives of liminal citizenship: High aspirations, exclusion, and 'in-between' identities. *The Professional Geographer* 66 (2), 195–204.
Tsagarousianou, R. (2004) Rethinking the concept of diaspora: Mobility, connectivity and communication in a globalised world. *Westminster Papers in Communication and Culture* 1 (1), 52–65.
Turner, V.W. (1967) Betwixt-and-between: The liminal period in rites de passage. In *The Forest of Symbols: Aspects of Ndembu Ritual* (pp. 4–20). Ithaca, NY & London: Cornell University Press.
Turner, V.W. (1969/2008) *The Ritual Process: Structure and Anti-Structure.* Piscataway, NJ: Transaction Publishers.
Van Gennep, A. (1909) *Les rites de passage.* Paris: Nourry.
Van Hear, N. (1998) *New Diasporas: The Mass Exodus, Dispersal and Regrouping of Migrant Communities.* London: UCL Press.
Wang, X., Spotti, M., Juffermans, K., Cornips, L., Kroon, S. and Blommaert, J. (2014) Globalization in the margins: Toward a re-evaluation of language and mobility. *Applied Linguistics Review* 5 (1), 23–44.

Wodak, R. (2011) *The Discourse of Politics in Action: Politics as Usual*. London: Palgrave Macmillan.
Wodak, R. (2014) Discourse and politics. In J. Flowerdew (ed.) *Discourse in Context* (Contemporary Applied Linguistics, Vol. 3) (pp. 321–346). London: Bloomsbury.
Wodak, R. (2015) *The Politics of Fear: What Right-Wing Populist Discourses Mean*. London: Sage.
Wodak, R., Khosravinik, M. and Mral, B. (eds) (2013) *Right-Wing Populism in Europe: Politics and Discourse*. London: Bloomsbury Academic.
Ybema, S., Beech, N. and Ellis, N. (2011) Transitional and perpetual liminality: An identity practice perspective. *Anthropology Southern Africa* 34 (1–2), 21–29.
Yuval-Davis, N. (2011) *The Politics of Belonging: Intersectional Contestations*. London: Sage.

6 Building 'Fortress Europe': Legitimizing Exclusion from Basic Human Rights

Markus Rheindorf and Ruth Wodak

Introduction

This chapter presents a discourse-historical analysis of mediatized border and asylum politics in Austria during the key months of the so-called refugee crisis of 2015/16, viewed in the context of attitudes towards refugees and migrants in postwar Austria, more specifically since 1989 and the fall of the Iron Curtain (Krzyżanowski & Wodak, 2009; Matouschek et al., 1995; Wodak & Pelinka, 2002; Wodak, 2015). During those months, the Austrian government's stance shifted from a policy of open borders to building a border fence and setting an annual limit on asylum applications, both recontextualized as positive contributions to building 'Fortress Europe'. While some distinct events, such as the march of thousands of refugees from Hungary to Austria, the gruesome death of 71 refugees at the hands of people smugglers, and the incidents in Cologne during New Year's Eve 2015/16, have been considered turning points for the extended debates over how to handle migration, the above-mentioned reversal was gradual and publicly negotiated as mediatized politics (Rheindorf & Wodak, 2017; Triandafyllidou, 2017).

More specifically, we investigate the legitimization of restrictive asylum policies, including restricting access to basic human rights and closing borders, indicating the normalization of far-right discursive positions. In this, we are guided by the following research question:

(1) Which strategies are used to argue for and legitimate new, more restrictive asylum policies in the so-called refugee crisis of 2015–16?

Taking into account recent methodological advances in combining qualitative and quantitative approaches to meet the challenges of analysing substantial corpora, we also ask:

(2) How can existing methodological approaches be elaborated to a systematic and comprehensive multi-level analysis that integrates qualitative and quantitative methods?

Our work draws on a number of fields, i.e. media representation of refugees (Baker *et al.*, 2008; KhosraviNik, 2009, 2010; Rheindorf & Wodak, 2017); research on discrimination and exclusion (in Austria and elsewhere; Reisigl & Wodak, 2000, 2001; Wodak & van Dijk, 2000); on legitimation and argumentation (van Leeuwen & Wodak, 1999; van Leeuwen, 2007; Wodak, 2018); and on border and body politics (Lehner & Rheindorf, 2018; Triandafyllidou *et al.*, 2017; Wodak, 2015). Among approaches to critical discourse studies, the discourse-historical approach or DHA is distinguished inter alia by its attention to different levels of context and its adherence to the principle of methodological triangulation (Reisigl & Wodak, 2016). The former includes (a) historical and social context, (b) immediate situational context, (c) intertextual and interdiscursive relationships, and (d) text-internal co-text. Focusing on the short-term development, this chapter first addresses the historical and social context. It then turns to the immediate situational and co-textual context relevant to the analysis. We then review pertinent literature on legitimation, argumentation and topoi in order to establish the conceptual framework for our empirical study. In the next section, we develop our research design, which integrates quantitative methods of corpus linguistics with qualitative methods, specifically legitimation and argumentation analysis. We then present the results of our quantitative and qualitative analyses and draw conclusions in the final section.

Historical Context

After World War II, Austria gradually became a country of immigration (Mourão Permoser & Rosenberger, 2012). In the 1960s, the so-called guest workers were invited to provide labour for Austria's fast-growing economy. Beyond this, Austria admitted over 400,000 refugees in the course of the crises in the former communist countries Hungary, Czechoslovakia and Poland in 1956, 1968 and 1981, respectively. After 1989, however, migration became an increasingly divisive aspect of Austrian politics, with the right-wing populist Austrian Freedom Party

(FPÖ) in particular campaigning for strict immigration and naturalization laws, closing borders and limiting asylum applications (Matouschek et al., 1995; Reisigl & Wodak, 2000; Wodak & Matouschek, 1993). Overall, stricter requirements for obtaining residency as well as naturalization were implemented in the early 1990s (Kraler, 2011; Perchinig, 2010). In contrast to the policy focus on learning German, the FPÖ reinforced negative prejudices and cultivated the image of the 'lazy immigrant' and 'bogus refugee' whose main interests in Austria were said to be social welfare and unemployment benefits (Sedlak, 2000).

Between 2000 and 2006, the government coalitions between the FPÖ and the Austrian People's Party (ÖVP) introduced the 'Integration Agreement' in 2002 (de Cillia & Dorostkar, 2013). Applicable to all third-country nationals, this document intimates a contract between the respective immigrant and the Austrian state, detailing the immigrant's obligations and commitment to integrate. Said obligations consist largely of language requirements (Mourão Permoser & Rosenberger, 2012; Wodak, 2012, 2017). The FPÖ's campaigns, meanwhile, became more nativist and recontextualized migration as a burden on the welfare state and as an issue of security, not just in terms of crime (as before) but of terrorism in the wake of 9/11 (Krzyżanowski & Wodak, 2009). When the legal provisions for asylum and residency were revised in 2005, the declared aim was to prevent the abuse of asylum, to expedite the processing of asylum seekers, and to simplify the deportation of those who refused cooperation, were convicted of a criminal offence, or should have been processed by another country according to the Dublin regulations. The subsequent coalition governments between the ÖVP and the Austrian Social-Democratic Party (SPÖ) continued to implement stricter measures (e.g. restricting the movement of refugees). Integration rather than migration became the focus of official policy manifested in the form of institutionalization, first as a State Secretariat (since 2011) and then a Ministry for Integration (since 2014). Since 2013, refugees have become an increasingly salient topic of political debate (e.g. in the form of deplorable conditions in the refugee camp Traiskirchen), as evidenced by the official minutes of parliamentary debates (Rheindorf, 2017).

In the more immediate context of the so-called refugee crisis in 2015 and 2016, mediatized debates intensified on the two salient issues of building a border fence to control the movement of refugees and limiting the human right to asylum by setting a maximum limit on asylum applications per year. Discursively, the crisis thus presented a field of struggle over radical policy changes, both issues raising serious ideological and legal concerns. Responding to ever-increasing pressure from the far-right, the governing mainstream parties also began to endorse these policies as signals to voters. Both policy changes were adopted in early 2016, and the preceding months were characterized by increasingly intense efforts to legitimate them (and delegitimate current policies) in mediatized discourse. Ultimately, extensive efforts at legitimation thus led to several legal changes in laws and regulations, increasing control over borders (i.e. Border Control Law or 'Grenzkontrollgesetz') and asylum applicants (i.e. Asylum Law or 'Asylgesetz').

Immediate Context

The immediate context of the discourse we analyse comprises numerous national and transnational events in a period characterized by a strong overall increase of refugees arriving in or moving through Austria. Each of these events was identified as potentially influencing the discourse on refugees, asylum seekers and migrants: The deteriorating housing situation for refugees in Austria in early 2015, followed by an inspection by Amnesty International, led to a moral outrage and call for political responsibility. The federal government's ensuing difficulty in (re)distributing refugees across Austria's provinces due to the latter's reluctance to provide housing culminated in heated debates over a federal 'crackdown' in spring. The closing of Hungary's eastern and southern borders in summer by means of fences was initially rejected by the government but adopted as a model by the ÖVP. The tragic death of 71 refugees locked in an air-tight van, discovered on an Austrian highway in August, and the widely mediatized death of Alan Kurdi near Bodrum on 2 September led not only to sympathy for refugees but also to the blanket vilification of people smugglers as murderers as well as strengthened calls for strict border controls to save the lives of refugees (see Figure 6.1 below for a detailed timeline).

On a different level, there were regional influences linked to election campaigns in the Austrian regions of Styria, Burgenland, Upper Austria and Vienna. In these campaigns, increasing pressure from the FPÖ – driven by opinion polls indicating its rising popularity – led all mainstream parties with the exception of the Vienna chapter of the SPÖ to align more and more with the FPÖ's positions on asylum and migration. Meanwhile, civil society became very active in providing support for arriving refugees and organized several demonstrations of solidarity, the largest of which was a free concert under the motto of 'Voices for Refugees', performed on Vienna's prestigious Heldenplatz on 3 October and attended by 150,000. When none of the re-location, distribution or border control policies discussed on the EU level were implemented by

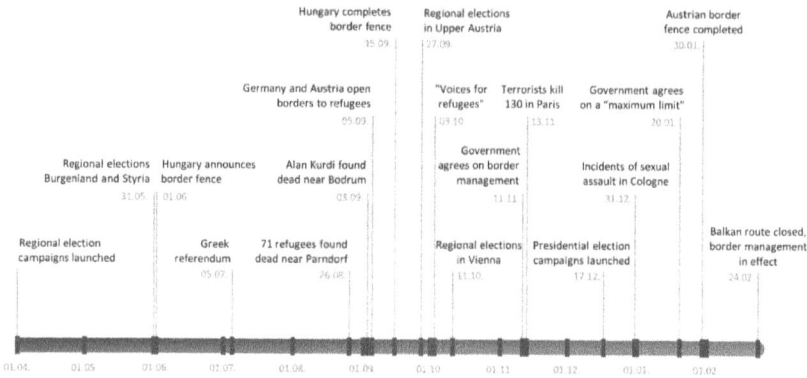

Figure 6.1 Timeline of events in 2015–16

late 2015, Austria's foreign minister and now chancellor Sebastian Kurz (ÖVP) proposed to close the Balkan route.

Other major events linked to the discourse were the terrorist attacks in Paris in November 2015 and the incidents of sexual harassment on New Year's Eve in Cologne, which foregrounded issues of security and gender, i.e. 'protecting our women from illegal migrants'. In Austria, the increasing polarization manifested most clearly in the campaigns for the Austrian presidential election of 2016, with candidates publicly taking position on the issues of border fences as well as maximum limits. The discourses thus intersect and cut across regional and national elections, national and EU politics, as well as national and international crime and terrorism.

Discourse, Legitimation and Argumentation

Like other approaches in critical discourse studies, the DHA regards discourse as a form of social practice (Reisigl & Wodak, 2016). More specifically, it assumes a dialectical relationship between discourses and the situations, institutions and social structures in which they are embedded: on the one hand, the historical, social and situational contexts shape and affect discourses; on the other hand, discourses constitute social reality. Social actors use and act within discourse to constitute and negotiate knowledge, identities, social relations and, in the special context of politics, political measures and policies. Especially in the face of social change and upheavals such as the so-called refugee crisis of 2015/16, social actors in the field of politics often call and argue for radically changing/adapting existing policies. In Western democracies, politicians must seek the approval of the population for such policy changes and such appeals largely depend on the mass media to convince the electorate, hence mediatized politics. The discursive practices used to reach this aim thus have a strong strategic aspect and have been studied as strategies of *legitimation*.

Martín Rojo and van Dijk (1997: 528) define legitimation as practices by which a powerful group or institution such as political leadership or government seeks 'normative approval for its policies or actions [and] does so through strategies that aim to show that such actions are consistent with the moral order of society'. As a sociopolitical act, legitimation is characteristically accomplished through discourse using persuasive and sometimes manipulative means. Regarding the linguistic realization of legitimatory acts, Martín Rojo and van Dijk distinguish between pragmatic, semantic, stylistic, interactional and social dimensions. Importantly, the propositions employed in legitimation are commonly organized by complex argumentative schemata, including premises that concern the nature of the proposed action and the phenomena it relates to (usually presented or established in descriptive or narrative modes) as well as conclusions that concern said action's social, moral or political acceptability (Martín Rojo & van Dijk, 1997: 531–532). Careful microanalysis of such argumentative schemata must acknowledge and seek to identify not only explicit argumentation but also presupposed knowledge.

Ietcu-Fairclough (2008: 133–135) foregrounds the argumentative dimension of legitimation in defining it as 'a social, political and argumentative practice, a form of strategic maneuvering which aims to reconcile successfully various conflicting demands and pressures acting on political actors'. Significantly, the concept of strategic manoeuvring links argumentation to domains (or fields) of society, requiring analysis to include context. In Ietcu-Fairclough's terms, the political field creates 'field-specific dialectical constraints on' as well as 'rhetorical opportunities for strategic maneuvering' within legitimation. Zarefsky (2008) lists relevant contextual (historical) constraints in the US political field and elaborates some relevant argumentation strategies, some of which have been extensively discussed elsewhere, such as Lakoff's (2004) concept of 'framing' or Hansson's (2015) work on strategies of blame avoidance. Zarefsky's (2008: 118) emphasis on the latent knowledge of broad and narrow sociopolitical and historical contexts in the analysis of argumentation schemes in specific political debates is very much in keeping with the discourse-historical approach.

Given its sociopolitical nature, it follows that legitimation routinely draws on recurring argumentation schemata in order to persuade the public of the acceptability or necessity of a specific action or policy. Van Leeuwen (2007) and van Leeuwen and Wodak (1999) distinguish between four broad types: authorization, moralization, rationalization and mythopoesis. Legitimation by authorization depends on reference to personal, impersonal, expert or role model authority, but may also appeal to custom in the form of tradition or conformity. Legitimation qua moralization is based on abstract moral values (religious, human rights, justice, culture and so forth), straightforwardly evaluative claims, or analogy to assumedly established moral cases. Legitimation through rationalization references either the utility of the social practice or some part of it (i.e. instrumental rationalization by way of goals, means or outcomes) or assumed 'facts of life' (i.e. theoretical rationalization by way of definition, explanation or prediction). Rationalization may be established as 'common sense' or by experts in the domains of knowledge used for legitimation, e.g. economics, biology or technology. In legitimation through mythopoesis, the proponents of the policy in question will rely on telling stories that may serve as exemplars or cautionary tales (see Table 6.1).

In a more specific elaboration of the relationship between legitimation (argumentation) and normative values ('common sense' as used in political legitimation), van Eemeren (2010) uses the Aristotelian term 'endoxon' to define the presupposed common-sense knowledge of a specific epistemic community. Through the notion of endoxa as commonly held beliefs, van Eemeren (2010: 111) corroborates Habermas's (1992) thesis that legal systems ultimately depend on moral systems, even if morality infiltrates law through whatever room it leaves for interpretation (e.g. van Leeuwen & Wodak, 1999: 111).

In the formal analysis of argumentation, which relies on a functional model of argumentation, the three basic elements investigated are *argument, conclusion rule* and *claim* (Reisigl, 2014: 75). Conclusion rules (also referred to as topoi) are seen as central to the premise inasmuch as they justify the transition from argument to conclusion (Wodak, 2015: 51–54 for an extensive discussion). The notion of topos has been conceptualized in different ways, elaborating and modifying Aristotle's seminal approach (Reisigl, 2014). Wengeler (2015), for instance, distinguishes between context-specific topoi that are applicable only within a specific content-related area (such as discourses about migration) and general topoi that are context-independent.

A key strategy of discourse analysis is to make tacit or implicit topoi explicit in the form of conditional or causal paraphrases (Reisigl & Wodak, 2001: 69–80). Focusing on such conclusion rules, Kienpointer (1996: 194) identifies several formal topoi, such as topos of analogy,

Table 6.1 Types of legitimation

Authorization		
Authority		*Personal Authority*: Based on institutional status of individuals/groups
		Impersonal Authority: Originating from laws, policies, regulations etc.
		Expert Authority: Academic, scientific or other type of credible expertise
		Role Model Authority: Popularity and acceptability of positions held by role models or opinion leaders
Custom		*Authority of Tradition*: Acceptability of what is claimed to have always been done
		Authority of Conformity: Acceptability of what everyone or most people do
Moralization		
		Abstraction: Abstract depiction of practices that links them to moral values
		Evaluation: Legitimation of positions and practices via evaluative adjectives
		Analogy: Legitimation relying on comparisons and contrasts
Rationalization		
Instrumental Rationalization		*Goal Orientation*: Focused on goals, intentions, purposes
		Means Orientation: Focused on aims embedded in actions as means to an end
		Outcome Orientation: Focused on outcomes of actions as if already known
Theoretical Rationalization		*Definition*: Characterizing activities in terms of already moralized practices
		Explanation: Characterizing people as actors because the way they do things is appropriate to the nature of these actors
		Prediction: Foreseeing outcomes based on some form of expertise
Mythopoesis		
		Moral Tales: Narrating rewarding decisions and practices of social actors
		Cautionary Tales: Linking nonconformist practices to undesirable consequences

authority, consequence, contradiction or definition. While topoi are often 'shortcuts' and not explicated in discourse, they are not necessarily fallacious. In the context of legitimation, the analysis of topoi may reveal flawed logic, manipulative and erroneous conclusions inasmuch as what they ignore or sidestep can be fallacious. Previous work in critical discourse analysis has identified a large number of content-related topoi in legitimizing immigration control. Due to space restrictions, we cannot comment on the many different taxonomies and have to refer readers to Reisigl and Wodak (2001) and Reisigl (2002, 2007, 2012).

Most recently, Lehner and Rheindorf (2018) – analysing political discourse in Austria but using a much smaller data set – identified the following topoi in relation to refugees and asylum seekers (see Table 6.2 below).

Table 6.2 Topoi in Austrian media during the 'refugee crisis' (Lehner & Rheindorf, 2018)

Topos	Warrant
Topos of abuse/definition	Most of the people arriving at the moment are not in danger or being persecuted; therefore, they are not refugees but (economic) migrants
Topos of burden	Providing for so many refugees places an inordinate burden on Austria and Austrians; therefore, Austria should only accept a limited number
Topos of culture/burden	The people arriving at the moment are mostly uneducated and/or illiterate; therefore, they are an inordinate and unacceptable burden on the welfare state
Topos of culture/burden	The people arriving at the moment do not share 'our' values and are therefore difficult/impossible to integrate; therefore Austria should only accept a limited number
Topos of culture/male nature and burden	The people arriving at the moment are mostly young men who have never learned to or cannot exercise restraint; therefore, they are a danger to Austrian women
Topos of economic resource limitation	Austria does not have the resources (money, housing) to provide for so many refugees; therefore, Austria should only accept a limited number
Topos of historical dissimilarity/conditionality	The Geneva Convention was designed for a different (historical) situation and does not apply to the current situation; therefore Austria is not bound by it
Topos of law and order	According to international treaties (Dublin II, Geneva Convention), refugees must apply in the first safe state they reach; therefore, most of the people arriving at the moment are not eligible to apply for asylum in Austria
Topos of national borders	Austria has a natural right to control its borders and know the identity of everyone who is in the country; therefore, borders must be closed entirely and strictly policed
Topos of national responsibility	If the EU does not control its external borders, Austria must take national measures
Topos of reality	The universal human right to asylum is a theoretical ideal, not a reality like limited resources; therefore, granting this right is optional for Austria
Topos of solidarity (within the group/charity begins at home)	Because they are Austrian (like us), homeless or poor Austrians deserve our help more than refugees; therefore, Austria should help them instead
Topos of (potential) threat/danger	Some of the people arriving at the moment are/may be/may in the future become radicalized and commit acts of terrorism; therefore, Austria should close its borders and police them strictly

From a methodological point of view, qualitative analyses have traditionally been used to identify topoi, but with the increasing use of corpus linguistic methods in critical discourse analysis (CDA), attempts have been made to use quantitative methods to detect topoi in large data sets. Arguably the most comprehensive efforts to do so were taken in

RASIM, a research project investigating the representation of refugees, asylum seekers, immigrants and migrants in the British press (e.g. Baker et al., 2008). In several ways, our approach here builds on the methodological experiments of RASIM while seeking to improve upon it. In particular, we see as problematic the operationalization of 'topos' on a predominantly lexical level and the related lack of qualitative verification of topoi found through quantitative methods, neglecting the text and co-text as linguistic units of analysis. While we use corpus linguistic methods to generate results (mainly regarding nomination and collocation), these results are also used for downsampling the data, i.e. 'picking the right cherries', for the qualitative analysis which serves to corroborate and complement the quantitative results. Specifically, we ask:

- Which nominations and predications are used in the course of legitimizing new, more restrictive asylum policies?
- Which topoi are used to legitimate new, more restrictive asylum policies?

For both levels of analysis, we also ask:

- How do these patterns change across the time-frame of our study?
- How do these changes reflect sociopolitical changes on the global, European and national context?

Research Design: Data and Methods

Legitimation strategies use both explicit and implicit argumentation, especially the latter relying on nomination and predication. While argumentation must ultimately be identified through close qualitative analysis and can therefore be analysed only in a limited number of texts (necessitating the use of downsampling strategies), nomination and predication patterns can be effectively gleaned through corpus linguistic methods which can be applied to the entire corpus. Initially, we conducted statistical analysis of the recurring nominations of refugees as well as a set of methods focused on collocational patterns (Baker & McEnery, 2005: 223). In this context, the notion of *discourse prosody* is particularly useful insofar as it conceptualizes the relationship between key terms and the recurring, habitual patterns of their usage in context (Gabrielatos & Baker, 2008: 10). Indeed, it captures how collocational patterns can help create and invoke topoi, i.e. lead the reader from premise to conclusion without explicit argumentation, in that readers are more likely to attend to the connotational rather than the denotational level of specific frequent collocations. The qualitative analysis can thus be guided by integrating qualitative and quantitative methods: collocations categorized into semantic fields can be used to represent the (changing) topical macro-structure of discourse around key terms, and the dominant argumentative patterns can be taken to relate to this structure (Baker et al., 2008).

Following the principles of triangulation (Bryman, 2006: 105–106; Creswell, 2014), we thus combined quantitative and qualitative methods (1) to *off-set* respective weaknesses in providing *complementary* results and (2) to use the results obtained by quantitative methods for *down-sampling* the substantial corpus for qualitative analysis. All results are given in the following sections.

(1) Corpus compilation: We compiled a *corpus of Austrian newspaper and magazine articles* using search terms covering the often conflated social actors 'refugee', 'migrant', 'asylum seeker' and 'immigrant' (Baker et al., 2008) using the German lemmas: *flüchtling*, *migrant*, *asylwerber*, *asylant*, *asylsuchende*, *schutzsuchend*, *geflüchtete*.[1] We included 11 news media with wide distribution and representing the full spectrum of journalistic quality and political views. For the period of January 2015 to February 2016, this yielded a total of 5739 texts, running to 8,008,536 tokens. These texts were also tagged for date and publication.

(2) Frequency and dispersion: We conducted *quantitative analyses on the nomination patterns* associated with the relevant social actors, situated on the lexical level of legitimation strategies. The corpus linguistic approach used the methodology developed in Baker et al. (2008) and Baker et al. (2013), adapting it for our more focused research interest in legitimation and taking into account the specifics of German (e.g. compounding, nominalization). This included *total and monthly frequency* of search term lemma and compounds relevant to the representation of refugees, asylum seekers, immigrants and migrants.

(3) Semantic fields: To gain an overview of the discourse prosodies associated with *refugees* and related terms, we conducted a *semantic field analysis* (or 'key categories', see Baker, 2006: 143) for the collocates of each search term, adapting the qualitative categories used in Gabrielatos and Baker (2008). Comparison of the relative frequency of these fields highlights the different discourse prosody of each term.

(4) Intercollocation: Drawing on Baker and McEnery (2005) and Gabrielatos and Baker (2008), we investigated the *intercollocations* (i.e. overlap of collocates) between search terms in order to test the possible conflation of terms regarding their usage.

(5) Key collocates per month: Further elaborating the collocates-in-fields approach, we computed the *month-to-month change of key collocates* for each field (keyness relative to the preceding month, using restrictive cut-off points of keyness >100 and frequency in that month of >2). This approach modifies the consistent-collocates or c-collocates approach developed by Baker *et al.* (2008), yielding a nuanced map of the ebb and flow of collocational patterns. The procedure can be used to reveal how specific events are immediately reflected in the attributive patterns associated with refugees as distinct from more consistent, long-term patterns.

(6) Downsampling: The quantitative results thus obtained were then used for *downsampling the corpus for qualitative analysis* (Baker, 2006: 90; Baker, 2012: 248). At this first stage, we selected 70 texts with typical usage of search terms, i.e. typical collocational patterns, five for each month, for identification of argumentative patterns.

(7) Qualitative analysis of legitimation strategies: The close analysis of these texts identified topoi used in legitimizing either changing or adhering to current asylum policies, including related welfare and border policies. This is necessary because the analysis of collocations alone cannot reliably reveal the use of topoi. Given a shared definition of topoi as 'conclusion rules that connect the argument with the conclusion', a lexis-focused approach identifying topoi as 'related to a specific word or cluster' (Baker *et al.*, 2008) is error-prone and likely to overlook larger or implicit and indirect argumentative schemes; and extending it to concordance lines is insufficient to address these concerns inasmuch as it still neglects the text as the key unit of argumentation analysis.[2]

(8) Saturation: The final analytical step was to *expand the qualitative sample for each month by five texts*, adding texts featuring typical changes (significant increase or decrease) in collocations of the search terms. These were in turn analysed and any new topoi identified added to the list. This step was repeated at least twice for each month or until the saturation point was reached. These steps were taken to avoid the downsampling issue of privileging dominant (i.e. very frequent) patterns over infrequent ones, thus potentially overlooking minority discourses or counter-discourses (Freake *et al.*, 2011: 39–43; Baker, 2006: 125, for a detailed methodological discussion).

Results

Quantitative results

The number of articles on refugees, asylum seekers and migrants published each day of the 14-month period under investigation fluctuates

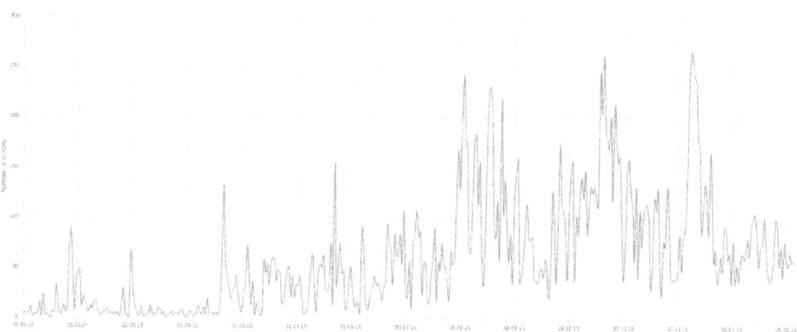

Figure 6.2 Number of articles on refugees, migrants and asylum seekers

wildly. In addition to notable peaks in reporting, each of which corresponds roughly to an event of national or international significance during the 'refugee crisis', there is an overall increase of media attention. Figure 6.2 shows the highly context-sensitive intensity of news reporting on refugees through this time period (see also Figure 6.1).

The individual frequencies of the search term lemmas reveal a strong focus on refugees (*flüchtling**), followed by the less frequent cognates asylum applicant (*asylwerber**), asylum seeker (*asylsuchende**) and nouns denoting those seeking protection (*schutzsuchende**), those who have fled (*geflüchtete**) and successful applicants (*asylberechtigte**). Derogatory terms such as bogus asylum seeker (*scheinasylant**, *asylant**) are comparatively rare. However, compounding of *flüchtling** points to more indirect delegitimation as in economic refugee (*wirtschaftsflüchtling**).[3] Terms related to migrants (*migrant**, *wirtschaftsmigrant**), in contrast, are much less frequent. Table 6.3 lists all search term lemma and related compounds by individual frequency; compounds with any of the search terms as head are listed in separate rows; compounds combining a search term with other heads are given in the final column of the respective row.

Viewed on a monthly basis, the frequency of individual search term lemma broadly corresponds to the number of articles published. In absolute numbers, there is thus a clear peak of *flüchtling** in September, which slowly abates in the course of the following months. However, Table 6.4 also indicates a relative increase of *migrant** and *wirtschaftsflüchtling** towards the end of 2015 and an even stronger relative increase of *migrant** in the early months of 2016. This suggests a *discursive shift* in the way the same group of people is represented: After the brief surge

Table 6.3 Total frequency of search term lemma and notable compounds

Lemma	Frequency	Related lemma referencing the social actor
flüchtling*	19,164	Flüchtlingsgruppe (34), Flüchtlingswelle (161), Flüchtlingsstrom/ströme (646), Flüchtlingszustrom (84), Flüchtlingsbewegung (102), Flüchtlingskatastrophe (50), Flüchtlingskrise (1423), Flüchtlingsfrage (264), Flüchtlingsproblem (134), Flüchtlingssituation (107), Flüchtlingstragödie (100), Flüchtlingsdrama (325), Flüchtlingszahlen (164)[4]
asylwerber*	4068	
migrant*	1430	Migrantenkind (8), Migrantenfamilie (1), Migrantengruppe (7), Migrantenströme (6), Migrantenwelle (5), Migrantenleid (6), Migrantenzustrom (13), Migrationsfluss (4), Migrationsfrage (14), Migrationskrise (20), Migrationsprobleme (15), Migrationsströme (111), Migrationstragödie (4), Migrationswelle (14)[5]
asylsuchende*	541	
asylbewerber*	512	
wirtschaftsflüchtling*	494	
schutzsuchende*	459	
asylberechtigte*	266	
asylant*	140	Aslylantenflut (3), Asylantenfamilie (2), Asylantenschwemme (2), Asylantenheim (28)[6]
schutzbedürftige*	112	
geflüchtete*	78	
bootsflüchtlinge*	74	
wirtschaftsmigrant*	56	
scheinasylant*	34	
asylantragsteller*	20	
bürgerkriegsflüchtling*	19	
asylanwärter*	2	
asylbetrüger*	2	

of solidarity in summer, clearly emphasizing the label 'Flüchtling', the discourse thus starts to shift to 'Migrant' as the political debate begins to focus on closing the border and numerically limiting the right to asylum; this intensifies further after the incidents of sexual harassment in Cologne.

Because this might, after all, simply signify a *topical* shift away from refugees in a narrow sense to migrants of any sort, we undertook an extensive collocational analysis to determine whether and to what degree *flüchtling** and *migrant** are used interchangeably.

Table 6.4 Monthly frequency of search term lemma

	1/15	2/15	3/15	4/15	5/15	6/15	7/15	8/15	9/15	10/15	11/15	12/15	1/16	2/16
flüchtling*	250	174	144	125	252	228	471	814	4591	3759	3164	2253	1712	1227
asylwerber*	53	37	31	26	53	48	101	173	975	798	672	478	363	260
migrant*	19	13	11	9	19	17	35	61	182	190	196	218	248	212
asylsuchende*	7	5	4	4	7	6	14	23	130	106	90	64	48	34
wirtschaftsflüchtling*	2	8	6	4	12	14	21	31	57	74	68	62	73	61
schutzsuchende*	2	0	3	2	8	12	19	22	24	110	91	76	54	32
asylant*	2	1	1	1	2	2	4	6	14	28	23	21	18	19
geflüchtete*	1	0	1	0	1	1	2	3	19	15	11	10	8	5

Merging refugees and migrants: Conflation of social actors

We obtained a broad overview in terms of semantic fields realized by the search term lemmas' collocates. Adapting the categories developed by Gabrielatos and Baker (2008), we distinguish between: abuse of system, burden, entry (mode, place, route), legality of claim, number, personal traits, plight, positive effect, residence, threat (crime, terrorism) and welcome. Categorization was done manually and concordance lines were used to disambiguate usage.

The results, given in Table 6.5, reveal striking contrasts, e.g. between the frequency with which refugees and migrants (but even more so economic refugees) are represented as abusing the asylum and welfare systems. Given the fluidity with which the two terms are used in referring to the same group of people, this suggests a specific role of nomination in a (de)legitimizing strategy. Interestingly, the pattern is very different regarding the semantic field of *burden*: although economic refugees are most frequently associated with burdens for Austria as a host country, this is very similar to the way refugees and asylum seekers are represented – but in contrast to migrants.

Both refugees and migrants are more often represented in terms of their *entry* or *origin* than economic refugees. The *legal status* of asylum seekers and refugees in general is less frequently discussed than that of migrants (but even more so economic refugees). Refugees, asylum seekers

Table 6.5 Number and percentage of collocates (five left/five right) by semantic fields

	flüchtling*	asylwerber*	migrant*	asylsuchende*	wirtschafts-flüchtling*
Abuse of system	186; 0.1%	25; 0.06%	77; 0.54%	–	156; 3.16%
Burden	9834; 5.13%	1508; 3.96%	249; 1.74%	279; 5.16%	320; 6.48%
Entry	8689; 4.53%	447; 1.09%	680; 4.76%	126; 2.33%	39; 0.79%
Legality of claim	1899; 1%	510; 1.25%	464; 3.24%	21; 0.39%	196; 3.97%
Number	9462; 4.94%	1936; 4.74%	823; 5.76%	297; 5.49%	24; 0.49
Origin	813; 0.42%	159; 0.39%	47; 0.33%	22; 0.41%	5; 0.1%
Personal trait	1133; 0.59%	474; 1.16%	186; 1.30%	79; 1.46%	181; 3.66%
Plight	2467; 1.29%	56; 0.14%	60; 0.42%	8; 0.15%	4; 0.08%
Positive effect	53; 0.03%	31; 0.08%	14; 0.1%	14; 0.26%	–
Residence	546; 0.29%	794; 1.94%	10; 0.07%	32; 0.59%	28; 0.57%
Threat	2502; 1.31%	487; 1.19%	157; 1.1%	55; 1.02%	13; 0.26%
Welcome	597; 0.31%	134; 0.33%	40; 0.28%	29; 0.54%	57; 1.15%

and migrants are all commonly aggregated or collectivized in terms of *numbers*; indeed, numbering is the single most common and consistent way all search terms are used in our data. A substantially larger segment of collocates for economic refugees relates to their *personal traits* and their *welcome* than with any other search term lemma. And, finally, refugees and asylum seekers as well as migrants are significantly more likely to be represented in the context of *threats* than economic refugees. Given these broad contrasts and similarities, it seems pertinent to ask if, e.g. the burdens and threats associated with specific terms are qualitatively similar or distinct. While not all collocational patterns of the search term lemmas can be compared here, the three most common, i.e. *flüchtling**, *asylwerber** and *migrant**, warrant some discussion.

For *abuse of system*, the comparison shows refugees and asylum seekers to be (infrequently) attributed with wrong or false claims, forgery, pretence and lies, while migrants are (overall much more frequently) associated with abuse, fraud, cheating and parasite-like behaviour. Much of this is reflected in the different collocates for *burden*: refugees are very strongly represented as a burden, but mostly in terms of expenses (money, costs, budgeting) due to housing, medical treatment, provisions and education. Specifically, the overcrowding of quarters and distributing refugees across Austria are seen as burdensome. Refugees' inability to provide for themselves is also seen as an unacceptable burden. In contrast, the burden caused by migrants is focused on their unemployment and resulting poverty, their wilful dependence on welfare or support, the number of children, as well as their alleged unwillingness to integrate (Rheindorf, 2017).

In terms of their *entry*, refugees and asylum seekers are strongly associated with the routes they take, the means of transportation used, the crossing of specific borders, and places of arrival. Specifically, narratives about crossing the Austrian border at Spielfeld and Nickelsdorf as well as of arrival at Vienna train stations dominate. Significantly, migrants are associated with similar routes and forms of entry.

The *legality* of refugees' and asylum seekers' stay is associated with applying, deportation, recognition/rejection of asylum, being picked up and registered by police, rights and laws (specifically the Dublin treaties). Significantly, this overlaps largely with the way in which migrants are represented: Here, too, asylum, asylum applications, deportation, the Dublin treaties and processing feature prominently. In addition, illegal and illegality itself are frequent collocates, as are papers and passports.

The *numbering/quantification* of refugees is not simply higher but also more emphatic, dramatic and evaluative (e.g. record numbers), often resorting to aggregation (groups, droves, masses) as well as natural catastrophes (stream, flood). While migrants are also frequently counted, none of the latter collocates were found for them.

The reference to similar *origins* – Afghanistan, Africa, Iraq, Syria – further indicates an overlap between the individuals referenced as refugees, asylum seekers and migrants. However, the former are also associated with Somalia, while the latter group is linked to Morocco and the Maghreb.

In terms of attribution, *personal traits* are particularly revealing. Refugees and asylum seekers are associated with age categories (young, old, underage), with religious identity (Islamic, Muslim) as well as with moralizing traits: honest, grateful, decent, friendly or ungrateful, cowardly and reckless. This overlaps with migrants' representation as being young, male and Muslim, but contrasts sharply with the traits of being educated or (more frequently) uneducated, unqualified, lazy and having illusions.

In summary, *plight and hardship* is a dominant collocational pattern for refugees, with a wide variety of collocates. This includes fleeing and escaping, reasons for fleeing (civil war, war, inhumane conditions, persecution), adverse conditions (cold, hunger, exhaustion, being stuck, obstacles, being ill, falling victim, agony, trauma, injury, fear, desperation, hopelessness), life-threatening or fatal events (catastrophe, being abandoned, distress at sea, suffocating, drowning, dying) or needing help. In contrast, both asylum seekers and migrants are largely associated with generic terms such as flight, help or plight.

The lexical realization of *threats* associated with refugees is much more varied than with asylum seekers and migrants. The former are linked to threatening movements or natural forces (storm, stream, push, pressure), lack of control and order (chaos, uncontrolled, unregistered, unchecked, infiltration), transgressive and violent behaviour (assault, aggressive, break through, escalation, violent, beat, threaten, sexual harassment, rape, wrangling), military or armed conflict (tear gas, invasion, fighters, hostile, army, soldiers), criminality, law enforcement and security (damages, delinquent, stealing, police, arrest, fingerprints, suspect, monitor, control, safety risk, punishment), religious extremism and terrorism (Jihadist, extremist, Islamist, terrorist, radicalize). Asylum seekers are associated with many of the same threats (conflict, criminality, stream and incident). In contrast, migrants are often linked to being sniffed out, picked up or arrested by police, being a threat to security (so-called Islamic State) and criminal behaviour or chaos (unchecked, uncontrolled).

As a second step to verify possible conflation of terms, we also investigated the search terms' intercollocations. In developing that approach, Gabrielatos and Baker (2008) concluded that an overlap of 40% was significant for distinct terms while some cognates (e.g. migrant and immigrant) show an overlap of 60% and higher. To test this hypothesis, we compared collocates not only for search terms (i.e. *flüchtling**, *migrant**, *asylwerber**), but also for selected cognates, where the overlap was expected to be particularly high (e.g. *asylbewerber** for *asylwerber**, *geflüchtete** for *flüchtling**). The results are given in Table 6.6, with overlap rates below 33% in white shading, between 34% and 65% in light grey, and above 66% in dark grey shading.

Results confirm that cognates, e.g. *asylwerber** and *asylbewerber**, show an overlap of collocates in the range of 60% and higher. A 'misuse of terminology' (Greenslade, 2005) in the sense of conflating the groups of refugees, asylum seekers and migrants is indicated by the relatively high ratio of overlap between collocates of *migrant** and *flüchtling** as well as *asylwerber** and *asylsuchende**.

Longitudinal development of discourse prosodies

To obtain a longitudinal map of how the discourse prosody of the key search term *flüchtling** changed in the course of the 14 months which saw a reversal of Austria's refugee and border policies (Rheindorf & Wodak, 2017), we calculated the key collocations of each monthly sub-corpus relative to that of the preceding month, starting with February 2015 relative to January 2015. While some changes are no doubt more gradual, this technique reveals stark changes in how *refugees* were presented in the press. Because the resulting tables are massive, we categorized the results in the same semantic fields as before and only show the results for *burden* and *threat* here.

So far, our largely quantitative analyses have confirmed: Austrian news media's reporting on refugees, asylum seekers and migrants was highly sensitive to events related to the refugee crisis – not just in quantity but in terms of nomination and attribution as well. We have found indications of a discursive shift from refugees to migrants towards the end of 2015, continued in early 2016. By way of semantic field analysis, we have characterized the attributive patterns associated with refugees, asylum seekers and migrants, and, focusing on intercollocations, have shown a significant overlap between the usage of the search terms and their cognates. Finally, the key collocations per month add a semantic layer to the news' observed sensitivity to events of the refugee crises,

Building 'Fortress Europe': Legitimizing Exclusion from Basic Human Rights   135

Table 6.6 Intercollocations between search terms and cognates

	migrant*	flüchtling*	wirtschaftsflüchtling*	asylwerber*	asylbewerber*	asylant*	asyl-suchende*	schutz-suchende*	geflüchtete*
migrant*	–	45%	28%	32%	29%	26%	34%	30%	32%
flüchtling*	35%	–	34%	65%	62%	42%	62%	60%	72%
wirtschaftsflüchtling*	22%	43%	–	38%	35%	51%	22%	24%	21%
asylwerber*	27%	69%	45%	–	75%	52%	78%	62%	41%
asylbewerber*	24%	64%	41%	79%	–	49%	72%	59%	38%
asylant*	43%	45%	38%	46%	49%	–	51%	24%	28%
asylsuchende*	31%	47%	32%	67%	66%	42%	–	71%	42%
schutzsuchende*	25%	51%	18%	71%	68%	22%	74%	–	42%
geflüchtete*	42%	63%	21%	58%	59%	31%	37%	35%	–

showing short-term shifts in collocational patterns: the death of 71 refugees being smuggled into Austria, for instance, effectively shifted the way the media reported on refugees, asylum seekers and migrants, emphasizing their plight for a brief period; the November terrorist attacks in Paris, however, shifted the discourse towards threats (see Table 6.7). In contrast, some semantic fields, such as burden, seem to be comparatively stable even though they are also likely candidates for topoi used in legitimizing immigration control.

Qualitative Results: Legitimizing Immigration Control

After using the downsampling procedure outlined above, we analysed a total of 210 texts (15 per month) for topoi used in (de)legitimizing current or proposed asylum and border policies. In the following, for each topos found, we provide a brief definition and exemplary analysis in context, discuss its interdependence (clusters of topoi) and longitudinal development. In doing so, we begin with the most constant topoi, i.e. those present in most months, and end with more complex clusters of topoi.

- Numbers: *If the numbers prove a specific claim, a specific action should be taken.*
  (1) The coalition is acting 'irresponsibly', not least regarding the refugee crisis. Which, in Strache's view, is not a crisis but a 'mass migration'. (Kurier, 2015a, December)
  While absolute numbers and statistics are frequently invoked, aggregation as in the above example and metaphors of natural catastrophe are also used to legitimize qua authority the closing of borders. The topos of numbers occurs throughout the period investigated and invokes enormous dangers which threaten the country. Strache's authority and common knowledge are contrasted with the government which is delegitimized as being irresponsible.
- Burden: *If a person, an institution or a country is burdened by specific problems, one should act in order to diminish those burdens.*
  (2) A German study on the costs of asylum is causing controversy in Austria. 50 billion. [...] Adjusted to Austria, that would be 5 billion in two years. In fact, the government is calculating – even with a maximum limit – 210,000 refugees, about the same number as in ten times larger Germany. (Österreich, 2016, February)
  In our data, the topos of burden (and responsibility) is often combined with topoi of number and reality. In particular, the

Table 6.7 Key collocates for *flüchtling for each month in the corpus, relative to the preceding month (keyness of >100, frequency of >2).

	1/15	2/15	3/15	4/15	5/15	6/15	7/15	8/15	9/15	10/15	11/15	12/15	1/16	2/16
burden	—	lodging places	money provision	capacity places quarters	tent barracks capacity container housing overcrowded space	distribution jobs unemployed welfare	housing burden costs	courses crisis	integration crisis overwhelmed	capacity cost money pay burden	capacity expenses financial increased costs overwhelmed	cost economic cope burden unemployed welfare budget pay	unacceptable money capacity medical care expensive problems	providing housing distribution crisis expenses
threat	—	police pressure security terrorism threaten	pressure	arrest chaos criminal criminality damage extremists fears fighters harass Islamists police pressure punishment push rape security soldiers storming stealing storm suspected tear gas terrorism terrorists threaten violent	arrest beat up chaos criminal criminality damage delinquent escalate fighters hostile Jihadists police pressure security storm suspected violent	control damage fears Islamists police pressure terrorist threaten wrangling	arrest beat up chaos escalate invasion Jihadists police pressure rape soldiers storm suspected tear gas terrorism violent	army break through criminal soldiers suspected tear gas unchecked	arrest break through chaos control criminality escalate fears police pressure push security sexual soldiers storming tear gas threaten wrangling unchecked	aggressive army beat up damage Islamists pressure soldiers stealing storm violence	arrest assault beat up control criminal criminality delinquent escalate extremists fears fighters fingerprints hostile invasion Islamists Jihadists police pressure punishment radicalize security soldiers stealing storm suspected terrorists terrorism threaten violent unchecked unregistered	assault chaos concerns criminal criminality fingerprints fighters Islamists pressure radicalize security risk stealing storm	arrest aggressive army assault fears fears harass monitor molesters police punishment rape security stop suspected terrorist threaten unchecked violent worries unregistered	concerns control criminal extremists fighters fingerprints infiltration Islamists Jihadists problems stealing terror terrorism

argument that Austria is bearing an inordinately high burden is based on often hypothetical or projected comparisons to Germany, invoking a sense of unfairness and/or positive self-presentation as generous. The topos of burden can be found as early as April 2015 but gains great prominence in the following months. Here, we encounter moralization (the contrast of fairness and unfairness) substantiated by the topos of burden.

- Humanitarianism: *If people are suffering, it is our duty as fellow human beings to provide humanitarian aid.*
  (3) The tragedy of up to 50 dead refugees in Burgenland leaves many politicians in shock. [...] The human rights expert of the Green Party, Alev Korun, said that it was Europe's responsibility to open legal routes for refugees and end the death of war refugees. (Österreich, 2015, August)

  The topos of humanitarianism is related to moralization legitimation and strongly present in the news reporting through most of 2015 but could not be found after November 2015, i.e. the time of the terrorist attacks in Paris. The values, and hence, moralization change as the primary value after the terrorist attacks concerns the protection of the country and its people, and not of the refugees.

- Reality (limited resources): *Because reality is as it is, a specific action should be taken.*
  (4) For Haslauer, the 'factual limit' to accepting asylum applicants is 'where we simply are no longer able to. Therefore this consideration, that asylum is a basic human right, is theoretical thought game, which has its limits in the factual', so Haslauer. (Kurier, 2016, January)

  Towards the end of 2015, the 'facticity' of 'limits' and the topos of reality are often invoked in legitimizing border controls and limiting asylum applications, simply as expert authority and theoretical rationalization. Obviously, the Geneva Convention is challenged; governments should thus deal with realities and facts and not attempt to fulfil utopian demands. There is a notable play on words with 'Grenze' meaning both border and limit. Typically, no evidence is offered to corroborate said facticity; instead, the topos of burden is frequently invoked alongside the topos of reality.

- Abuse: *If a right, help or support is abused, that right should be modified, restricted or withheld.*
  (5) Someone who leaves their country for economic reasons and immigrates illegally to another can well be called an economic refugee. But critics object that the term is often used in a derogatory

way and should therefore be rejected. 'Economic refugee' is said to imply that someone has no reason for asylum and therefore no right to remain. However, in reality this very accurately describes who is seen as an economic refugee: that is, someone who applies for asylum but does not meet any of the required criteria. (Profil, 2015, August)

The topos of abuse appears predominantly in relation to so-called economic refugees or migrants. The earliest instances we found were in July 2015 and often related to topoi of burden and definition. The argument concerns who could be rightly defined as a true refugee, and who not. Then, quasi-objective reasons and criteria are listed for this definition, thus creating an appeal to expertise and theoretical rationalization legitimation.

- Nature/Culture: *Since it is the nature of members of a specific group/ culture to be/act/behave in a specific way, specific problems arise in certain situations.*

  (6) In the Federal Republic of Germany [...] more than two thirds of the 1.1 million asylum applicants are single men – with all the problems resulting from that. But one must be clear that the immigration also changes the cultural environment. How far the people will accept this change is more than doubtful. (Presse, 2016, January)

The topoi of nature and culture often blend into one another in our data, as some biological trait of refugees or migrants seems to be culturalized or vice versa, but also linked to threats and burdens. For instance, the culture (or religion) of asylum seekers might be described as dangerously misogynist, but might also be linked to the testosterone levels of young men who are presupposed to be dangerous and potential rapists. Such topoi appear as early as July but intensify in late 2015 and early 2016, especially after the events of 31 December in Cologne. This includes a fallacy of hasty generalization, in the sense that all young foreign men are assumed to be necessarily and per se dangerous and thus a threat to 'our' women. The declarative mode suggests that the article presents clear evidence, thus expert authorization legitimation is invoked even if the source of the evidence remains vague.

- Threat: *If there are specific dangers or threats, one should do something to counter them.*

  (7) 'Whichever measures gives the chance to reduce the number of refugees', was Mikl-Leitner's description of her guiding principles. The minister referred to 2015 as the 'toughest year' for the police.

The refugee issue had contributed to that as well as the increased threat of terrorism. (DerStandard, 2016, January)

The topos of threat appears throughout the period investigated, but with an important qualification: in the early months of 2015, it refers only to threats to refugees, for instance from smugglers. More and more, the discourse then shifts to threats caused by refugees, combining these with topoi of burden, numbers, reality and security; in this way, obvious facts legitimize (instrumental rationalization) restrictive measures. Ultimately, these point to the responsibility of government and police to actually implement such legitimate measures.

- Pressure: *If something creates pressure on someone or something, steps should be taken to reduce or relieve that pressure.*
  (8) The influx of refugees has strongly increased just recently. Asylum applicants are being accommodated in three tent cities in Upper Austria and Salzburg as well as the new deportation centre in Styrian Vordernberg. (Presse, 2015, May)

Often linked to topoi of burden and numbers, the topos of pressure appears throughout the period investigated, expressing the sense of a mounting pressure often in metaphorical terms (e.g. influx, stream or tide). These topoi are related to instrumental rationalization: obviously, tents (even if hotly debated) are necessary to deal with the huge numbers of refugees.

- Law and Order: *If current law dictates/forbids a specific action, that action must be taken/foregone.*
  (9) It is inadmissible to lure refugees 'with promises of salvation and offers of welcome'. It would be better to help them in their own regions in camps. The government 'is constantly breaking the law'. There are 'giant problems concerning welfare', lodging and the labour market. (Heute, 2015, December)

Towards the end of 2015, the topos of law and order becomes increasingly common in our data, often linked to topoi of number, threat and burden, and legitimized both morally and rationally. Usually, the lack of law and order is blamed on the government or the EU, who are accused of criminal negligence. As several of the examples above have already shown, the topoi we found frequently occur in clusters, more and more so towards the height of the so-called refugee crisis.

  (10) In light of the massive wave of refugees currently rolling over Europe, Austria's government is working on changing the law to bring decisively stricter rules for asylum applicants. [...] Minister

of Interior Johanna Mikl-Leitner comments: 'We want to provide protection to those who need it. What is happening right now, however, is often no longer a search for protection, but the search for the economically most attractive country. I have no sympathy for that. That is why it is important to re-focus our laws on the core of asylum.' (Kurier, 2015b, October)

In the above segment, the topoi of burden and numbers are offset with the limited topoi of responsibility and humanitarianism; expert authority legitimation is appealed to as well as moral legitimation. As arguments that justify limiting responsibility and humanitarian obligations, the minister uses the topoi of abuse and reality. Moreover, topoi of definition and reality are present which substantiate the discursive shift: from a moral obligation towards refugees to the expert authority which is acting in a responsible way.

Discussion

On the most descriptive level, our analyses confirm the findings of related work on media reporting on refugees in Austria and elsewhere: it is a prime site of political legitimation and delegitimation of the status of refugees. More specifically, we have shown that reporting during the so-called refugee crisis reproduced topoi and legitimation strategies well known from previous work (e.g. Martín Rojo & van Dijk, 1997; van Leeuwen & Wodak, 1999; Reisigl & Wodak, 2000; Baker *et al.*, 2008; KhosraviNik, 2010), even if giving them specific articulations and interdiscursive links in the context (e.g. comparisons to Hungary and Germany). In the longitudinal development made so pertinent by the new laws implemented at the end of the period under investigation, we were able to identify several shifts in terms of the topoi and legitimation strategies employed: while refugees were always seen as a burden, this was in conjunction with the humanitarian obligation and the refugee's plight; even early in 2015, however, a perceived crisis in the housing provided for refugees that brought to the fore long-standing tensions between the federal government and Austria's states shifted the focus to *burden, threat, law and order*, but above all to rising *pressure* on Austrian institutions. Mass crossings in the summer of 2015 were represented as requiring a *humanitarian* response but also regulation; only then was there notable reporting about *abuse* and bogus (economic) refugees. At the end of the year, this is accompanied by a shift towards the topos of the *real*, arguing economic and resource limitations. Throughout the period, topoi of *nature* and *culture* gained in prominence, closely related to *threats* of crime and terrorism, peaking in 2016 after the incidents in Cologne. The topos of a *humanitarian* obligation, in contrast, recedes more and more toward the end of 2015 and virtually disappears in 2016. Throughout all this, there is a constant increase in topoi of *pressure* and *burden*, probably the most persistent characteristic of the discourse studied.

We see distinct advantages in the combination of corpus linguistic and qualitative discourse analysis in our research design. In terms of triangulation, quantitative methods gave us (1) a broad overview of how refugees, asylum seekers and migrants were represented and (2) a nuanced longitudinal perspective on how this representation changed due to sociopolitical developments. This, in turn, allowed us to downsample the data set for detailed analysis on the text level, grasping linguistic and rhetorical structures beyond collocations and concordance lines. Unlike previous work that relied more heavily on quantitative analyses, we were thus able to capture the complexity of clusters of topoi in the data.

At the time of writing, more than two years after the period analysed in this chapter, we encounter a changed legal situation in the form of concrete laws that are supposed to protect Austria from future 'migration movements': for example, they refer specifically to the potential burden of asylum applicants on Austrian institutions which might be compromised in their functioning as well as the threat posed to public order (AsylG, 2005: §36 (2), 8.1.2018) as the criteria for limiting the number of asylum applications. While this is not always the case, our study shows that the topoi employed in legitimation can quickly become part of legal regulations and thus policy.

Notes

(1) In that order, these terms correspond roughly to English 'refugee', 'migrant', 'asylum applicant', 'asylum holder', 'asylum seeker', 'those seeking protection' and 'those who fled'. Most of these terms are established in the relevant legal contexts, except for *asylant*, which is a derogatory term that vaguely refers to recognized refugees and/ or asylum seekers. The greater lexical variety in German is partly achieved by nominalization and compounding, although there is de jure no greater variety of legal distinctions. The exact legal definition of each term does not enter into this discussion – indeed, the lack of a clear distinction in media discourse is the focus of our interest.
(2) In this regard, care must also be taken to avoid conflating 'discourse' with 'topos': Baker (2006: 86) claims that semantic preference or discourse prosody reveals 'a range of discourses: refugees as victims, as the recipients of official attempts to help, as a natural disaster and as a criminal nuisance'. While such patterns of nomination and attribution are significant, they do not, in our understanding, translate directly to topoi or discourses.

(3) Indeed, dissociation by compounding may play an important role in delegitimizing: Such implicit argumentation strategies have been discussed by van Rees (2005: 64): '1. from an existing conceptual unit, expressed by a single term, one or more aspects are split off; 2. through this operation a contradiction or paradox is resolved because now a proposition can be considered true in one interpretation of the original term and false in the other; 3. the reduced and the split off concept are assigned a different value'.

(4) These terms correspond, in order, to English 'refugee group', 'refugee wave', 'refugee stream/s', 'refugee influx', 'refugee movement', 'refugee catastrophe', 'refugee crisis', 'refugee question', 'refugee problem', 'refugee situation', 'refugee tragedy', 'refugee drama' and 'refugee numbers'.

(5) These terms correspond, in order, to English 'migrant child', 'migrant family', 'migrant group', 'migrant streams', 'migrant wave', 'migrant suffering', 'migrant influx', 'migrant river', 'migrant question', 'migrant crisis', 'migrant problems', 'migration streams', 'migration tragedy' and 'migration wave'.

(6) These terms correspond, in order, to English 'asylum seeker flood', 'asylum seeker family', 'asylum seeker flooding' and 'asylum seeker home'.

References

AsylG (2005) Bundesgesetz über die Gewährung von Asyl (Asylgesetz 2005). See https://www.ris.bka.gv.at/GeltendeFassung.wxe?Abfrage=Bundesnormen&Gesetzesnummer=20004240 (accessed 11 October 2019).

Baker, P. (2006) *Using Corpora in Discourse Analysis*. London & New York: Continuum.

Baker, P. (2012) Acceptable Bias? Using corpus linguistics methods with critical discourse analysis. *Critical Discourse Studies* 9 (3), 247–56.

Baker, P. and McEnery, T. (2005) A corpus-based approach to discourses of refugees and asylum seekers in UN and newspaper texts. *Journal of Language and Politics* 4 (2), 197–226.

Baker, P., Gabrielatos C., KhosraviNik, M., Krzyżanowski, M., McEnery, T. and Wodak, R. (2008) A useful methodological synergy? Combining critical discourse analysis and corpus linguistics to examine discourses of refugees and asylum seekers in the UK press. *Discourse & Society* 19 (3), 273–305.

Baker, P., Gabrielatos, C. and McEnery, T. (2013) *Discourse Analysis and Media Attitudes: The Representation of Islam in the British Press*. Cambridge: Cambridge University Press.

Bryman, A. (2006) Integrating quantitative and qualitative research: How is it done? *Qualitative Research* 6 (1), 97–113.

Creswell, J.W. (2014) *Research Design: Qualitative Quantitative and Mixed Methods Approaches*. London: Sage.

de Cillia, R. and Dorostkar, N. (2013) Integration und/durch „Sprache". In J. Dahlvik, C. Reinprecht and W. Sievers (eds) *Migrations- und Integrationsforschung – wissenschaftliche Perspektiven aus Österreich* (pp. 143–161). Göttingen: V&R.

DerStandard (2016) Mikl-Leitner: Ohne Obergrenze bis zu 120.000 Asylanträge. 9 January 2016. See https://www.derstandard.at/story/2000028754024/mikl-leitner-ohne-obergrenze-muss-mit-bis-zu-120-000 (accessed 11 October 2019).

Freake, R., Guillaume, G. and Sheyholislami, J. (2011) A bilingual corpus-assisted discourse study of the construction of nationhood and belonging in Quebec. *Discourse & Society* 22 (1), 21–47.

Gabrielatos, C. and Baker, P. (2008) Fleeing, sneaking, flooding: A corpus analysis of discursive constructions of refugees and asylum seekers in the UK press, 1996–2005. *Journal of English Linguistics* 36 (1), 5–38.

Greenslade, R. (2005) *Seeking Scapegoats: The Coverage of Asylum in the UK Press.* London: Institute for Public Policy Research.

Habermas, J. (1992) *Faktizität und Geltung. Beiträge zur Diskurstheorie des Rechts und des demokratischen Rechtsstaates.* Frankfurt a.M.: Suhrkamp.

Hansson, S. (2015) Discursive strategies of blame avoidance in government: A framework for analysis. *Discourse & Society* 26 (3), 297–322.

Heute (2015) Robert Lugar für Aufnahmestopp bei Flüchtlingen. 6 December 2015. https://www.heute.at/s/-12897977 (accessed 11 October 2019).

Ietcu-Fairclough, I. (2008) Legitimation and strategic maneuvering in the political field. *Argumentation* 22, 399–417.

KhosraviNik, M. (2009) The representation of refugees, asylum seekers and immigrants in British newspapers during the Balkan conflict (1999) and the British general election (2005). *Discourse & Society* 20 (4), 477–498.

KhosraviNik, M. (2010) The representation of refugees, asylum seekers and immigrants in British newspapers: A critical discourse analysis. *Journal of Language and Politics* 9 (1), 1–28.

Kienpointer, M. (1996) *Vernünftig argumentieren. Regeln und Techniken der Diskussion.* Reinbek: Rowohlt.

Kraler, A. (2011) Immigrant and immigration policy making in Austria. In G. Zincone, R. Penninx and M. Borkert (eds) *The Making of Migration and Integration Policies in Europe: Processes, Actors and Contexts in Past and Present* (pp. 21–59). Amsterdam: Amsterdam University Press.

Krzyżanowski, M. and Wodak, R. (2009) *The Politics of Exclusion: Debating Migration in Austria.* New Brunswick, NJ: Transaction Publishers.

Kurier (2015a) Fischers Appell zu Weihnachten: Wir schaffen das. 24 December 2015. See https://kurier.at/politik/inland/heinz-fischers-appell-zu-weihnachten-wir-schaffen-das/171.368.332 (accessed 11 October 2019).

Kurier (2015b) Scharfes Asyl-Gesetz der ÖVP. 3 October 2015. See https://kurier.at/politik/inland/oevp-legt-scharfes-asyl-gesetz-vor/156.416.088 (accessed 11 October 2019).

Kurier (2016) Asyl: Landeschef Haslauer stellt Grundrecht infrage. 2 January 2016. See https://kurier.at/politik/inland/asyl-landeschef-haslauer-stellt-grundrecht-infrage/172.821.224 (accessed 11 October 2019).

Lakoff, G. (2004) *Don't Think of an Elephant! Know your Values and Frame the Debate.* White River Junction, VT: Chelsea Green.

Lehner, S. and Rheindorf, M. (2018) 'Fortress Europe': Representation and argumentation in Austrian media and EU press releases on border policies. In G. Dell'Orto and I. Wetzstein (eds) *Covering the European Refugee Crisis* (pp. 40–55). London: Routledge.

Martín Rojo, L.M. and van Dijk, T.A. (1997) There was a problem, and it was solved: Legitimating the expulsion of illegal migrants in Spanish parliamentary discourse. *Discourse & Society* 8 (4), 523–566.

Matouschek, B., Wodak, R. and Januschek, F. (1995) *Notwendige Maßnahmen gegen Fremde? Genese und Form von rassistischen Diskursen der Differenz.* Vienna: Passagen.

Mourão Permoser, J. and Rosenberger, S. (2012) Integration policy in Austria. In J. Frideres and J. Biles (eds) *International Perspectives: Integration and Inclusion* (pp. 39–58). Montreal & Kingston: McGill-Queen's University Press.

Österreich (2015) Schlimmster Massenmord der 2. Republik. 27 August 2015. See https://www.oe24.at/oesterreich/politik/Schlimmster-Massenmord-der-2-Republik/202075409/print (accessed 11 October 2019).
Österreich (2016) Flüchtlinge: Kosten bis zu 5 Milliarden? 1 February 2016. See https://www.oe24.at/oesterreich/politik/Fluechtlinge-Kosten-bis-zu-5-Milliarden/222397243/print (accessed 11 October 2019).
Perchinig, B. (2010) All you need to know to become an Austrian: Naturalisation policy and citizenship testing in Austria. In R. van Oers, E. Ersbøll and T. Kostakopoulou (eds) *A Re-Definition of Belonging? Language and Integration Tests in Europe* (pp. 25–50). Leiden & Boston: Martinus Nijhoff.
Presse (2015) „Notstand" Zeltstädte für Flüchtlinge. 14 May 2015. See https://www.diepresse.com/4731554/notstand-zeltstadte-fur-fluchtlinge (accessed 11 October 2019).
Presse (2016) Zornige junge Männer sind in Europa angekommen. 14 January 2016. See https://www.diepresse.com/4904687/zornige-junge-manner-sind-in-europa-angekommen (accessed 11 October 2019).
Profil (2015) Wirtschaftsflüchtlinge: Die (ganz besonders) Unerwünschten. 27 August 2015. See https://www.profil.at/ausland/wirtschaftsfluechtlinge-unerwuenschten-5830954 (accessed 11 October 2019).
Reisigl, M. (2002) „Dem Volk aufs Maul schauen, nach dem Mund reden und angst und bange machen". Von populistischen Anrufungen, Anbiederungen und Agitationsweisen in der Sprache österreichischer PolitikerInnen. In W. Eismann (ed.) *Rechtspopulismus. Österreichische Krankheit oder europäische Normalität?* (pp. 149–198). Vienna: Cernin.
Reisigl, M. (2007) The dynamics of right-wing populist argumentation in Austria. In F.H. Van Eeemeren, J.A. Blair, Ch.A. Willard and B. Garssen (eds) *Proceedings of the Sixth Conference of the International Society for the Study of Argumentation* (pp. 1127–1134). Amsterdam: International Center for the Study of Argumentation.
Reisigl, M. (2012) Zur kommunikativen Dimension des Rechtspopulismus. In A. Pelinka and B. Haller (eds) *Populismus als Herausforderung oder Gefahr für die Demokratie* (pp. 141–162). Vienna: Braumüller.
Reisigl, M. (2014) Argumentation analysis and the discourse-historical approach: A methodological framework. In C. Hart and P. Cap (eds) *Contemporary Critical Discourse Studies* (pp. 67–95). London: Bloomsbury.
Reisigl, M. and Wodak, R. (2000) 'Austria First': A discourse-historical analysis of the Austrian 'anti-foreigner-petition' in 1992 and 1993. In M. Reisigl and R. Wodak (eds) *The Semiotics of Racism: Approaches in Critical Discourse Analysis* (pp. 269–303). Vienna: Passagen.
Reisigl, M. and Wodak, R. (2001) *Discourse and Discrimination. Rhetorics of Racism and Antisemitism*. London: Routledge.
Reisigl, M. and Wodak, R. (2016) The discourse-historical approach. In R. Wodak and M. Meyer (eds) *Methods of Critical Discourse Studies*. (3rd revised edn) (pp. 23–61). London: Sage.
Rheindorf, M. (2017) Integration durch Strafe? Die Normalisierung paternalistischer Diskursfiguren zur „Integrationsunwilligkeit". *Zeitschrift für Diskursforschung* 2, 182–206.
Rheindorf, M. and Wodak, R. (2017) Borders, fences, and limits. Protecting Austria from refugees: Metadiscursive negotiation of meaning in the current refugee crisis. *Journal of Immigrant and Refugee Studies* 1–24.

Sedlak, M. (2000) 'You really do make an unrespectable foreigner policy': Discourse on ethnic issues in the Austrian parliament. In R. Wodak and T.A. van Dijk (eds) *Racism at the Top: Parliamentary Discourses on Ethnic Issues in Six European States* (pp. 107–168). Klagenfurt: Drava.

Triandafyllidou, A. (2017) A 'refugee crisis' unfolding: 'Real' events and their interpretation in media and political debates. *Journal of Immigrant and Refugee Studies* 16 (1–2), 198–216.

Triandafyllidou, A., Krzyżanowski, M. and Wodak, R. (eds) (2017) Special Issues of *Journal of Immigrant and Refugee Studies*.

van Eemeren, F.H. (2010) *Strategic Maneuvering in Argumentative Discourse: Extending the Pragma-Dialectical Theory of Argumentation*. Amsterdam: Benjamins.

van Leeuwen, T. (2007) Legitimation in discourse and communication. *Discourse & Communication* 1 (1), 91–112.

van Leeuwen, T. and Wodak, R. (1999) Legitimizing immigration control: A discourse-historical analysis. *Discourse Studies* 1 (1), 83–118.

van Rees, M.A. (2005) Indicators of dissociation. In F.H. van Eemeren and P. Houtlosser (eds) *Argumentation in Practice* (pp. 53–68). Amsterdam: Benjamins.

Wengeler, M. (2015) Patterns of argumentation and the heterogeneity of social knowledge. *Journal of Language and Politics* 14 (5), 689–711.

Wodak, R. (2012) Language, power and identity. *Language Teaching* 44 (3), 215–233.

Wodak, R. (2015) *Politics of Fear: What Right-Wing Populist Discourses Mean*. London: Sage.

Wodak, R. (2017) Integration and culture: From 'communicative competence' to 'competence in plurality'. In R. Bauböck and M. Tripkovic (eds) *The Integration of Migrants and Refugees: An EUI Forum on Migration, Citizenship and Demography* (pp. 116–137). Florence: European University Institute.

Wodak, R. (2018) 'Strangers in Europe': A discourse-historical approach to the legitimation of immigration control 2015/16. In S. Zhao, E. Djonov, A Björkvall and M. Boeriis (eds) *Advancing Multimodal and Critical Discourse Studies: Interdisciplinary Research Inspired by Theo Van Leeuwen's Social Semiotics* (pp. 31–50). London: Routledge.

Wodak, R. and Matouschek, B. (1993) 'We are dealing with people whose origins one can clearly tell just by looking': Critical discourse analysis and the study of neo-racism in contemporary Austria. *Discourse & Society* 4 (2), 225–248.

Wodak, R. and Pelinka, A. (eds) (2002) *'Dreck am Stecken': Politik der Ausgrenzung*. Vienna: Czernin.

Wodak, R. and van Dijk, T.A. (eds) (2000) *Racism at the Top: Parliamentary Discourses on Ethnic Issues in Six European States*. Klagenfurt: Drava.

Zarefsky, D. (2008) Strategic maneuvering in political argumentation. In F.H. van Eemeren (ed.) *Examining Argumentation in Context: Fifteen Studies on Strategic Maneuvering* (pp. 115–130). Amsterdam: Benjamins.

Appendix: Examples in German

(1) Die Koalition agiere ‚unverantwortlich', nicht zuletzt in der Flüchtlingskrise. Die nach Straches Ansicht keine ist, sondern eine ‚Massenwanderung'.

(2) Eine deutsche Studie über Asylkosten sorgt jetzt für Aufregung in Österreich. 50 Milliarden. [...] Umgerechnet auf Österreich wären das 5 Mrd. in zwei Jahren. Tatsächlich rechnet die Regierung ja auch – trotz „Obergrenze" – mit 210.000 Flüchtlingen, etwa gleich viel wie im zehn Mal so großen Deutschland.

(3) Die Tragödie um bis zu 50 tote Flüchtlinge im Burgenland lässt auch die Politik-Szene schockiert zurück. [...] Grünen-Menschenrechtssprecherin Alev Korun meinte, es liege in der Verantwortung Europas, legale Fluchtwege zu öffnen und dem Sterben von Kriegsflüchtlingen ein Ende zu setzen.

(4) Für Haslauer liegt die ‚faktische Grenze' bei der Aufnahme von Asylwerbern dort, ‚wo wir schlicht und einfach nicht mehr können. Daher ist diese Überlegung, Asyl ist ein Grundrecht, ein theoretisches Gedankenspiel, das eine Grenze im Faktischen hat', so Haslauer.

(5) Jemand, der sein Land aus wirtschaftlichen Gründen verlässt und illegal in ein anderes immigriert, kann wohl als Wirtschaftsflüchtling bezeichnet werden. Doch Kritiker wenden ein, der Begriff werde häufig abwertend verwendet und sei deshalb abzulehnen. ‚Wirtschaftsflüchtling' impliziere, dass jemand keinen Asylgrund geltend machen könne und deshalb kein Recht habe zu bleiben. Tatsächlich beschreibt dies jedoch sehr zutreffend, wer als Wirtschaftsflüchtling gilt: nämlich jemand, der Asyl beantragt, jedoch keines der dazu erforderlichen Kriterien erfüllt.

(6) In der Bundesrepublik Deutschland [...] sind über zwei Drittel der 1,1 Millionen Asylwerber alleinstehende Männer – mit allen sich daraus ergebenden Problemen. Aber man muss sich auch im Klaren sein, dass sich durch die Zuwanderung das kulturelle Umfeld wandelt. Wie weit die Menschen diesen Wandel mittragen, ist mehr als fraglich.

(7) ‚Welche Maßnahme gibt die Chancen, die Flüchtlingszahlen zu reduzieren', beschrieb Mikl-Leitner als Handlungsmaxime. 2015 bezeichnete die Ministerin als ‚härtestes Jahr' für die Polizei. Die Flüchtlings-Thematik habe dazu ebenso beigetragen wie die höhere Terrorbedrohung.

(8) Der Zustrom von Flüchtlingen ist zuletzt wieder stark gestiegen. Asylwerber werden in drei Zeltstädten in Oberösterreich und Salzburg sowie im neuen Schubhaftzentrum im steirischen Vordernberg einquartiert.

(9) Man dürfe Flüchtlinge nicht ‚mit Heilsversprechungen und Willkommensangeboten' anlocken. Besser wäre es, ihnen in ihrer Region in Auffanglagern zu helfen. Die Regierung ‚bricht permanent das Recht'. Es gebe ‚Riesenprobleme bei der Versorgung', bei der Unterbringung und auf dem Arbeitsmarkt.

(10) Angesichts der massiven Flüchtlingswelle, die derzeit über Europa rollt, arbeitet Österreichs Regierung an einer Gesetzesnovelle, die wesentlich härtere Regeln für Asylwerber bringen soll. [...] Innenministerin Johanna Mikl-Leitner sagt zur Novelle: ‚Wir wollen jenen Menschen Schutz geben, die ihn brauchen. Was derzeit stattfindet, ist aber oft keine Schutzsuche mehr, sondern die Suche nach dem wirtschaftlich attraktivsten Land. Dafür habe ich kein Verständnis. Darum ist es wichtig, dass wir unsere Gesetze wieder auf den Kern des Asylrechts eingrenzen.

7 'Youth should be sent here to absorb Zionism': Jewish Farmers and Thai Migrant Workers in Southern Israel

Iair G. Or and Elana Shohamy

Introduction

The present chapter examines the discursive interrelations between farmers, migrant workers, citizens and the state, by looking into a specific geopolitical and social context of agricultural migrant workers employed in a southern region of Israel. As a result of state policy and bilateral agreements with the government of Thailand, the majority of agricultural workers in the region (and elsewhere in Israel) are young Thai men who come to Israel without their families and are required to leave after a predetermined period. They have no viable way of becoming permanent residents, let alone citizens, and their overall quality of life often depends on the means and dispositions of their employers.

The Central Arava region, 100–150km north of Israel's southernmost city of Eilat, is an elongated desert area stretching along the road bordering with Jordan. With an area of 1400km^2 and a population of 3144 (mostly Jewish) inhabitants (in 2016), this is one of the most sparsely populated regions in Israel, and the economy there is mainly based on greenhouse agriculture. In the greenhouses, which belong to numerous farms (*meshakim*) in five *moshavim* (loosely cooperative community settlements) along the main road, Thai migrant workers are employed. What makes the region special is the fact that Thai migrant workers outnumber (or nearly outnumber) the Jews living in the region, creating a unique configuration that calls for ethnographic, sociolinguistic and discourse research (Shani, 2015). According to some reports (for example Blum, 2013), there are 4500–5000 workers in the region, consisting almost exclusively of Thai migrant workers and approximately 1000 trainees (*mishtalmim*), who come to the region from various countries to study and practice agriculture, but also occasionally do some of the work without getting the usual worker benefits. The numbers of work permits fluctuate and are regulated by the state, as farmers constantly struggle to recruit more workers.

Most of the Jews in the region are farm owners or make a living by providing services such as health, education and food supply to the farmers. Since the 1990s, many farmers have chosen to move to one main crop, peppers, which proved to be extremely lucrative thanks to vast demand in Europe. This led to an economic crisis in the mid-2010s, as the rates of the euro and ruble dropped; today, farmers are still working hard to overcome this crisis and readjust their crops. As the present study shows, the discourse of Jewish farmers typically celebrates the pioneering, entrepreneurial spirit of Zionism; the farmers see themselves as pioneers (*halutzim*) whose presence in the arid territories is important for Israel's security and economy. A large sign written on a row of silos at the entrance of one of the agricultural settlements reads: 'Agriculture protects the borders of the state' (Figure 7.1). With this argument taken

Figure 7.1 'Agriculture protects the borders of the state'. A sign at the entrance of Hatzeva.

from the domain of security due to the proximity to the Jordanian border, farmers hope to obtain more public support, which they expect to help them in their struggle to get more workers, subsidies and state support on the one hand, and less taxation and regulation on the other.

In recent years, the discourse of the farmers has become more apologetic, firstly because they were required to explain why they had relinquished the Zionist ideal of Jewish labor and started to rely on migrant workers; secondly, and more broadly, farmers have grown defensive because many Israeli citizens apparently view them as 'capitalist pigs' who exploit migrant workers and charge exaggerated prices for their produce. The farmers' difficulties may result from what Kaminer (2016) designates as 'an impossible demand: to carry on a self-sufficient settler-colonial form of agriculture in the context of a global market in which cheap, copious labor is the norm' (2016: 37). The apologetic discourse of the farmers and the critical, antagonistic spirit of some citizens create a setting in which public opinion is constantly shifting, variously (and, at times, coincidentally) serving the interests of farmers, workers, consumers and the state.

From 2007 to 2011, the US State Department *Trafficking in Persons Report* ranked Israel as a Tier 2 country; in direct response to its mediocre standing, the Israeli government founded a special government unit to coordinate measures against human trafficking and has taken various steps that led to the improvement of its ranking to the highest Tier 1 level from 2012 to 2017. The 2017 report stated that 'the government continued to demonstrate serious and sustained efforts' that justify maintaining its high ranking. Nevertheless, the report points to numerous problems, including the fact that 'some Thai men and women are subjected to forced labor in Israel's agricultural sector, where their passports were withheld, and they experience long working hours, no breaks or rest days, and difficulty changing employers due to limitations on work permits' (US Department of State, 2017). The 2013 report also hints at some serious language problems in addition to other labor issues, mentioning that 'NGOs remained concerned about a lack of Thai interpreters during inspections in the agriculture sector, which left inspectors unable to communicate with and receive complaints from the predominantly Thai migrant workers in this sector' (US Department of State, 2013).

It may be helpful to consider the status of Thai migrant workers in terms of what Brysk and Shafir (2004) qualify as 'citizenship gaps'. Israel's policy of migration follows the 1950 'Law of Return', which grants the right to citizenship only to Jewish immigrants or immigrants with a Jewish background. Palestinian Arabs who were born in (but not those who immigrate to) Israel are also citizens, but their citizenship is often claimed to entail a lesser degree of privileges and has been described by Jamal (2007) as a 'hollow citizenship' (cf. Shohamy & Kanza, 2009). Thus, since Israel's establishment very few non-Jewish immigrants have been granted citizenship. Several studies were conducted on the 'citizenship gaps' in Israel in relation to groups such as refugees and asylum seekers (coming mainly from Eritrea and Sudan), as well as migrant workers who are employed as caretakers of old, disabled people, in construction and agriculture (Elias & Kemp, 2010; Jaradat, 2017; Kemp, 2007; Kemp & Raijman, 2008; Kemp et al., 2000; Yonah & Kemp, 2008). It is interesting to compare these groups of 'foreigners', especially today, as there is a growing debate about the government's plan to deport people of African origin regarded by human rights organizations as refugees or asylum seekers, but considered by the state to be 'illegal immigrants' or 'infiltrators'. While most of the 'infiltrators' are deemed illegal and face a great deal of uncertainty regarding their future, migrant workers are considered to be legal, and their future is markedly planned and prearranged. However, the fact that migrant workers cannot normally become citizens or extend their stay actually means that their fate is similar to that of 'illegal immigrants'. The only main difference is that their deportation is known in advance and is part of the deal they need to accept in order to work in Israel.

The presence of migrant workers in Israel dates back to a government decision from 1989 aiming to reduce the country's dependence on Palestinian workers and increase the separation between Israeli Jews and Palestinians following the outbreak of the Intifada, as Palestinian workers began to be perceived as a menace. The government started to approve quotas of work permits for migrant workers, backed by bilateral agreements with countries such as Romania, China, the Philippines and Thailand, with Thailand being the main source of workers in the agricultural sector. Since the arrival and stay of migrant workers, unlike those of refugees and asylum seekers, are governed by state regulations, their problems and difficulties are not typically seen as a major issue. Migrant workers are often excluded from discourse and not seen as part of Israeli society or its immigration policy (see the contributions of Savski and De Fina in this volume).

Scope and Methodology

The present chapter is part of a larger study on working conditions and discrimination in the Central Arava region which includes the analysis of linguistic landscape (LL) (Jaworski & Thurlow, 2010; Shohamy, 2012; Shohamy & Gorter, 2009) as well as the discourse analysis of a wide range of materials such as local websites and fora, municipality periodicals and newsletters, and news items in the national press. In this chapter, we focus mainly on the discourse of the national press and the comments posted by web users, which allows us to explore the dynamic between various social players. The list of news items that form the basis of the present study will be detailed in the following section.

Using critical discourse analysis (CDA) (Fairclough, 2010; Wodak, 2011) inspired by the discourse-historical approach (DHA) (Reisigl & Wodak, 2009), this chapter strives to expose the varying interests and agendas behind the argumentation related to this field, focusing on the viewpoints of all the various forces at play. Following Reisigl and Wodak (2009), the analysis involves the discovery of *nominations* and *predications* in the discourse, which allow us to discern the main entities involved and their basic attributes according to what the participants in the discourse have to say about these entities. Then, the *argumentation* of various participants is examined, followed by an analysis of *mitigation* and *intensification* strategies employed in the discourse, which may make some of the arguments seem stronger or weaker to serve the participants' interests. Additionally, *perspectivization* allows some of the participants to signal how they relate to their arguments and to other stakeholders, and is therefore taken into account as part of the analysis. Lastly, the analysis also strives to point to some of the *topoi* (argumentation schemes) used in the discourse, either plausibly or fallaciously.

The findings show how the discourse of farmers is positioned in relation to those of migrant workers, the state, the citizens, and NGOs that criticize the farmers' behavior. Thus, the findings reveal the tense relationship between the different parties, the discursive construction of a better, superior 'us' by the farmers, and some unexpected convergences and collaborations between the government and the workers, between workers and the public, as well as between farmers and the public.

Thai Migrant Workers in the Israeli News and Media

The present study examines 10 news items and articles discussing Thai migrant workers and/or the situation in the Arava region, published between 2009 and 2015 on Israeli news websites. Most of the items are followed by user comments, mostly posted by Hebrew-speaking Israeli Jews, which serve as a valuable additional resource for the analysis of the entities, interests and arguments that can be traced in the discourse.

Broadly speaking, three different phases in the lifespan of this discourse field can be detected, and the sources were selected so that all of them are represented.

In the initial phase, to which the first three news items belong, attention was drawn to the existence of Thai agricultural workers in the Arava region (and other parts of Israel), but the working conditions of these workers were not yet brought into focus. The first item, published on the *Haaretz* newspaper website, is titled 'A visit to the farmers of the Arava, in fields that yearn for working hands, and in greenhouses that transform foreign workers into family' (Ben-Simhon, 2009). Written by a journalist born in the Arava region, the son of a farmer, the article mainly represents the Jewish farmers' perspective, claiming that they are in need of migrant workers and collaborate with them harmoniously. The second article, published on a social activists' website on 28 November 2010 (Mell, 2010), criticizes the fact that the employment of Thai workers in agriculture comes at the expense of (mostly female) Israeli Palestinian workers, who are no longer wanted on most farms. The third item, dated 2 February 2011 (Esterkin, 2011), discusses the reality behind a popular TV drama series, which was among the first to highlight life in the region. In all three items it is evident that the working conditions of Thai migrant workers are not at the center of attention and are mostly unknown to Israeli news readers.

The TV drama series *Yellow Peppers*, premiered in 2010, played a major role in drawing Israelis' attention to the Thai population in the Arava region. The series depicted the life of a Jewish couple in the region who raise an autistic boy. Reviews of the series commended the fact that it did not ignore the Thai workers. Commonly featured in the series are conversations in Thai among the workers, whereby they relate to the lives of their employers' families and friends. This feature, which was likened to the role of the chorus in Greek tragedy, encapsulated the recognition that the workers were not a faceless, dehumanized 'workforce', but knew a lot about and were interested in what was going on. It should be noted, though, that the role of Thai workers in the series was secondary, subservient to the main plot line of the Jewish farm owners. The life events of Thai workers appeared to be secondary even in the eyes of the workers themselves. The closeness between Jews and Thais as well as the level of involvement of Thais in the lives of their Jewish employers seemed exaggerated, as some commentators claimed (Esterkin, 2011).

In 2013, a new phase in the history of this discourse began, with various reports revealing the harsh working conditions, at least on some of the farms. An article in *Haaretz* from 20 June 2013, titled 'A sad visit to the agricultural workers from Thailand who grow our food' (Kashti, 2013), reminiscent of the title of Ben-Simhon's (2009) article on the farmers, took the perspective of the workers and showed their harsh living conditions, low salaries and lack of security. Three months afterwards, a news item on the *Maariv NRG* website (Goren, 2013) described some of the complaints farmers have about the government policies regarding migrant workers and the low-quality workers they seem to be getting due to these policies. An item from 28 March 2014, titled 'A mysterious syndrome claims the lives of tens of agricultural workers from Thailand' (Kashti & Efrati, 2014), threw a spotlight on the sudden unexplained bed death of 43 Thai workers in five years, aged 23 to 42, possibly linked to sudden arrhythmic death syndrome (SADS), which some link to stress, lack of sleep, poor working conditions, lack of access to medical services or exposure to pesticides. This phase culminated in substantial public criticism of the farmers, both for exploiting migrant workers and for selling their produce at a very high price.

Lastly, the third phase in the history of the discourse on Thai migrant workers was affected by the economic crisis that hit the Arava farmers in 2014. Farmers' almost exclusive focus on the cultivation of peppers, then marketed in Europe and Russia, proved to be disastrous as the ruble as well as the demand dropped. An article published in *The Marker* titled 'Sad peppers: This is how the Arava farmers' gold mine collapsed' (Starkman, 2014) viewed the public criticism of the farmers and the position of the government as two additional culprits of the crisis. In 2015, two further articles discussed the farmers' protests asking the government to bail them out (Yagana, 2015) and included a more extensive analysis of the crisis (Gabison, 2015). In January 2015, following a report by Human Rights Watch on the abuse of Thai migrant workers in Israel (Human Rights Watch, 2015), attention was again temporarily drawn to the working conditions on the farms. One of several news items that covered the report (Frankel, 2015) is included in the present analysis.

The Findings: Main Entities and Attributes

The discourse of news items, articles and their respective web user comments enables us to reconstruct intricate relationships among four main entities: farmers, Israeli citizens, the state and Thai migrant workers.

Farmers seem to combine capitalism and Zionist ideology. As capitalists, they wish to maximize their profits and minimize workers' wages and social rights; they also want to minimize state interference and regulations, but in times of crisis they do expect the state to support them and bail them out. Their self-image, however, is more closely linked to national ideology: because they chose to settle in and cultivate the desert areas of southern Israel, they see themselves as pioneers who 'make the desert bloom', fulfilling one of the imperatives of the founder of the nation, David Ben-Gurion, who chose to live in the southern desert of Israel to set an example for others to follow. Because their settlements are close to the Jordanian border, farmers also see themselves as protectors of the state. Historically, their presence there did play a part in the security of Israelis, especially before Israel and Jordan signed a peace agreement in 1994. Hence, they tend to see themselves as pioneers who chose to sacrifice the comfort of living in central Israel in order to substantially contribute to the nation. As a whole, farmers tend to show the positive, harmonious sides of collaboration with Thai migrant workers: They mainly downplay the criticisms or their attempts to reduce the costs of their labor and portray these workers as a necessity to Israel's agriculture. They expect the state to increase the numbers of work permits so that more workers can be recruited.

It appears that most Israeli citizens share the Zionist ideology reflected in the discourse of the farmers. They seem to prefer Jewish labor and Jewish agriculture, usually resenting migrant workers for supposedly (but not really) taking their jobs. As a consequence, most political parties in Israel state that they wish to reduce Israel's reliance on any 'foreign' workforce. Despite this ideological background, evidence from the comments written by Israelis in response to some of the news items shows they do not always believe that the farmers are genuine ideologues. They often see them as cynical capitalists who abuse Zionist ideology to cover up their greed for money. The fact that farmers employ Thai migrant workers to increase their profits undermines the Zionist ideological preference for Jewish workers and makes farmers appear less credible. The Israeli citizens who participate in the discourse also present themselves as consumers who want to buy cheap produce in the supermarkets. They suspect the farmers of being responsible for the high prices of produce, and this seems to reinforce the farmers' image as greedy, opportunistic capitalists. Finally, Israeli citizens who participate in the discourse show some moral concerns and social agendas when it comes to the exploitation and working conditions of migrant workers. They voice their concerns, which contribute to putting more pressure on the farmers.

The state is at the center of the nexus between farmers, citizens and migrant workers. It has brought migrant workers to Israel in the first place and also profits from their cheap labor through taxation. Israeli politicians feel they have obligations to the agricultural lobby and/or to consumers. Since the social protests of 2011, which focused on the taxation burden and cost of living of the middle class, there has been increased pressure on the government to reduce the prices of goods, which some believe could be achieved by reducing regulations and customs on imported goods and others believe should be accomplished by price regulation, either at the expense of farmers. The state also acknowledges its obligation to protect workers' rights, although most politicians claim they mainly want to minimize 'foreign labor' and let Israelis have these workers' jobs. In recent years, the state has increased regulation to ensure that migrant workers get all the benefits required by law. While this is seen as a favorable move in terms of workers' rights, which may be partly motivated by Israel's desire to improve its status in the eyes of the US State Department or human rights organizations, this move is usually seen negatively by the farmers, who consequently need to pay a lot more to their workers and make sure they are legally employed. In fact, it may well be the case that regulations and social benefits mandated by the state are meant to exert pressure on the employers in an attempt to reduce their reliance on non-Israeli workers. Despite increased regulation, workers' rights activists maintain that enforcement is too weak, whereas farmers tend to claim there is too much enforcement.

Finally, the Thai migrant workers themselves are the least represented group in the discourse, both because of a language barrier excluding them from participating in Hebrew-language discourse and because of other layers of exclusion which leave them outside most discussions of Israeli society. Migrant workers pay huge amounts of money to travel to Israel. They come for a limited time period of five years and three months, after which they must leave the country. They cannot come with their families or become permanent residents or citizens. They usually have no say in their work or living conditions. Farmers tend to stress the fact that despite all these limitations, work in Israel still pays off for the workers, since they earn a lot of money compared to what they would have earned in Thailand, and thus become 'rich' and can build their own houses in Thailand. Workers' rights activists expose cases of extremely poor working and living conditions, wishing to increase public awareness so that the state will intervene and increase enforcement.

In the following sections, the relationships between these four entities will be exemplified by examining the discourse and argumentation of news media and user comments in three different areas: the farmers' accounts about their pioneering mission, the exploitation of migrant workers, and the economic crisis that hit the region.

Farmers' arguments about their heroism and the lack of state support

Ben-Simhon (2009), written by the son of a farmer, is the most extensive media report representing the farmers' point of view. The farmers, and especially the writer's 61-year-old father, are given an opportunity to present their narrative of how they founded one of the first agricultural settlements in the Arava region. 'We were a group of agricultural school leavers and *moshav* (a community settlement; pl. *moshavim*) people who dreamed to establish a settlement in the desert ... We were 18-year-old kids, inherently optimistic, with a will to succeed and strong resilience,' says the father, styling the events as heroic, pioneering, groundbreaking and naïve.

According to Ben-Simhon's father, the founders' idealism was matched by support from the state and other national organizations. In his own words, he misses the days in which the farmers were the establishment's protégés *(bnei ha-tipuhim shel ha-mimsad)*. 'We were pioneers,' he recounts, 'setting out to establish a new settlement in the Arava, so we were helped and given credit. I remember the backwind that came from the Jewish Agency, from the *Moshavim* Movement, from ministers and members of the parliament. I remember visits by David Ben-Gurion and Golda Meir, and their good will. We felt we had who to count on' (Ben-Simhon, 2009).

According to the farmers' point of view, the growing dependency on migrant workers in recent years has not diminished the pioneering idealism of agriculture in the region. The state's attempts to regulate the work of Thai migrant workers are not interpreted as policies designed to safeguard workers' rights, but as unwanted intervention in an otherwise harmonious relationship between farmers and workers, proving that the state is no longer on the farmers' side. Ben-Simhon's (2009) father refers to an occasion on which inspectors from the Ministry of Interior came with immigration police forces to arrest two migrant workers on his farm:

> They came at 6 a.m. and told me and mom they came to see how many Thai workers we have and how many are missing. Gullibly, I felt they were nice people and since I have nothing to hide, I took them to the field ... Suddenly, the inspectors changed their skin and demanded to

take two Thai workers for investigation ... I suggested that the investigation take place in the field ... I was amazed by the reaction of the cops. I thought people with some sensitivity would be able to see beyond the orders they get, the real situation on the ground ... The attitude of the immigration police toward my Thai workers was disgraceful and rude. They didn't understand, and perhaps never will, that for me these workers are part of the family. Although I'm their employer, they live near my house and we spend our lives together. I have to protect them. (Ben-Simhon, 2009)

This farmer's narrative is instructive because it elucidates the speaker's attitude both toward the state and the Thai migrant workers. With the latter, very close intimacy is suggested that borders on ownership-taking ('my Thai workers'), while the former's intervention is seen as hostile and unwanted. The state's organs are perceived as extraneous and treacherous (they 'changed their skin'), and the undesirability of their intervention is justified by the family-like intimacy farmers have with their workers, which excludes any regulation or policing, making them appear as 'disgraceful and rude' meddling in family matters. The police forces are required 'to see beyond the orders they get', i.e. to discard or suspend considerations of lawfulness and formality because they are dealing with extremely delicate family relationships to which policing simply does not belong. The topos of privacy and private 'family' life as a space where policing is unwanted is complemented by a topos of protection, which views the farmer's actions against the police as an act in favor of the workers, keeping them in the custody of the 'family', even if they are not employed or paid as required by law.

The truth behind the interviewee's story may be that the state only holds a secondary interest in the workers' wellbeing, and that the workers themselves would rather have stayed on the farm, even if illegally employed, than been deported or moved to another workplace. For the farmers, there is constant struggle against the state for getting more work permits for migrant workers and for removing regulation and requirements. The interviewee moves on to tell how farmers from all over the region helped to physically prevent the immigration police from taking the workers. 'In this situation, when the government shows insensitivity to the catastrophe going on here, it doesn't matter if it hits you or your neighbor – you feel it in your bones' (Ben-Simhon, 2009). Like the topos of family intimacy, the topos of danger or catastrophe suggests another metaphor for the moral duty not to act strictly according to the law but show more sensitivity to an unusual situation. The catastrophic circumstances are also manifest in the speaker's concluding remarks, which use various intensification devices to show how dramatic the situation is:

> Till now people held back and kept the anger to themselves. Till now. Now something else happened, people finally realized that the government, with its insensitivity, is going to lead this region to ruin ... the situation is extreme ... We feel that the dream that we have been nurturing since our 18-year-old days, which lived for almost 50 years, is on the edge of an abyss. (Ben-Simhon, 2009)

Yona Mazor, another farmer interviewed in the article, relates more directly to workers' rights. He shows disbelief that the money farmers are required to pay by the state actually goes to the workers, and claims that this financial burden on the farmers is some sort of punishment:

> The government has recently decided that for each worker, the farmer is going to pay 500 shekels (ca. US$ 140) a month that will be allocated to pension funds, which I don't know if he [the worker] is ever going to get. This regulation will become effective in January. I employ 20 workers and all of a sudden, I need to pay 10,000 shekels every month, which is 120,000 shekels (ca. US$ 34,200) a year. And for what? What am I guilty of? What did I do wrong? It looks as if the farmers are a nuisance for this country. (Ben-Simhon, 2009)

Some of the topoi that can be detected in this excerpt have to do with abusive and wasteful behavior by the authorities and the cost paid by farmers. The heavy burden of costs, combined with the supposition that they are not justified and may not serve the purpose they are claimed to serve, creates an image of uncertainty and abuse that encourages the thought that these are indeed arbitrary punishments by the government, which lacks the sensitivity required to deal with the dire situation in the region and sees farmers as a mere 'nuisance'. The insinuation of punishment intensifies the arguments and produces clear perspectivization, placing the farmers at the lower end of the power relations with the state, where they can be the recipients of punishments. Thus, the point of view of farmers as reflected in this article (as well as other materials analyzed) shows a sharp contrast between an idyllic past, where state support was strong and unequivocal, and a grim present, in which the state seems to have abandoned the farmers and starts to burden them with requirements and regulations.

In May 2011, a new contract between Israel and Thailand was signed, regulating the migration and employment of Thai workers in

Israel. A news report from 2013 states that while the contract achieved its main goal of protecting workers by capping the fees they were required to pay to various mediators in order to come to Israel, the farmers employing the workers were unhappy with the new conditions. One of the farmers' main complaints was that the quality and training of the workers are not sufficient. As one of the farmers stated:

> More and more workers come not from rural areas as it used to be before this contract, but from cities ... The Thai Ministry of Labor is exclusively the one who decides which workers will arrive in Israel ... The quality of workers is inferior, and the workers who come are younger than before, many of them spoiled guys from urban areas. (Goren, 2013)

For the farmers, this new contract represented yet another imposition, since farmers can no longer control the identity and origin of the workers, unlike previously, when employment was based on personal relations. This new arrangement accentuates the clash between the protective 'family' worldview of the farmers and the often impersonal, faceless policies of state bureaucracy and regulations, which the farmers tend to resent.

The exploitation of workers

Attention was drawn to the living and working conditions of Thai migrant workers mainly thanks to the activism of Israeli NGOs such as Worker's Hotline (*Kav la-Oved*), which helps migrant workers solve problems with their employers and the authorities and advocates workers' rights in the local media. In a 2013 YouTube video produced by another NGO, called Social TV (SocialTV, 2013), Noa Schauer, then the coordinator of agricultural workers for Worker's Hotline, discusses some of the workers' rights infringements, which include work and life in the greenhouses under extreme heat conditions, inappropriate lodging places such as chicken coops and caravans, poor sanitation and protection from pesticides and other chemicals, lack of safety measures in transportation and construction, and extremely long work days six days a week with very low wages. 'If the State of Israel decides to bring 22,000 workers from Thailand to work in Israel, it is obligated to protect their rights,' Schauer asserts. 'Labor laws are fully applicable to foreign workers, and the state must enforce workers' rights violations and ban unsuitable housing conditions'. Her call for action mainly addresses Israeli citizens:

'Help us bring this issue to public attention and pressure the state to fulfill its obligations,' she pleads.

While the 2009 report on the quandaries of Jewish farmers was titled 'A visit to the farmers of the Arava...' (Ben-Simhon, 2009), the 2013 *Haaretz* article describing the poor conditions in which Thai migrant workers live and work is similarly titled 'A sad visit to the agricultural workers from Thailand who grow our food' (Kashti, 2013). The article is based on data from Worker's Hotline and official data from state authorities. The author describes a long list of violations that are commonplace in some of the farms where Thai workers are employed, including very poor living conditions, a 10-hour work day, lack of protective measures against pesticides, very low salaries, failure to compensate workers for their sick days, and more. This article allows us to explore some of the reactions to the exploitation and discrimination of Thai agricultural workers.

Firstly, in the article itself, the owner of one of the farms which the reporter visited discards all of these claims, stating that workers' monthly salaries reach 6,000 shekels (ca. USD 1,700), that extra working hours are adequately paid, and that there are enough protective suits and masks. As in Ben-Simhon's (2009) article, farmers tend to claim that the main problem is over-regulation and excessive protection of the workers:

> Because of all kinds of laws, I'm no longer the workers' employer but their slave [...] There are always two or three workers who cause trouble and complain constantly. I'd love to send them back [to Thailand], but I can't because of the law. And they do what they like – they sometimes go to work, sometimes travel to Tel Aviv. They became even more lordly than the Israeli workers.

Here, again, the accusations against the state are obvious, because the state is responsible for the laws and regulations. There is an attempt to avoid any generalization regarding the migrant workers signaled by the quantifier 'two or three', but at some point the quantifier is replaced by the personal pronoun 'they', which suggests a discussion of a broader population, especially when compared to 'Israeli workers' as a whole. While some parts of the argument are intensified, for example by using the emotionally charged term 'slave', other parts are mitigated, e.g. by limiting the problems with workers to just 'two or three' of them.

Secondly, the comments added by users to the web version of the article allow us to explore some of the additional voices and attitudes toward this issue. Some of the comments criticize the farmers and support the agenda of workers' rights, such as the comment by 'Amiram' titled 'It's a shame they treat humans this way':

> This human trafficking must be stopped. If employers pay them legally and grant them humane conditions, it won't kill us.

Other comments represent the point of view of farmers, such as the comment by 'Yosi' titled 'Go see how they live in the villages'. This user claims that, compared to the living conditions in their country of origin, Thai migrant workers are treated reasonably well:

> In the villages of northern Thailand they live in much worse conditions. The wage in the Thai market is usually around 9,000 baht, which are equivalent to 300 (US) dollars, and even this is after a 90% wage increase mandated by a law from last year. These workers are satisfied with these conditions, and the money they get here is much much more than what they could have earned in Thailand. So enough with these tendentious articles.

Another comment is conspicuous because it is supposedly written by a Thai worker who has some basic command of Hebrew (or used help to write the comment). The language of the comment (with various typos and grammatical aberrations) suggests that the comment is authentic, but even if it is not, it was clearly written by someone who wanted this voice to be heard. The comment by 'Takky' is titled 'No one in Thailand lives this way':

> I'm a villager from Thailand[;] there is no such life in Thailand. Before we come to Israel we think it will be good. But employers treat us as if we are not humans. The fact that we want to earn money doesn't mean we want to live like animals!!!

The topos of comparison plays an important role in the discourse about workers' rights violations. Thai migrant workers are compared to Israeli workers to claim that Thai migrant workers are more 'lordly' and get excessive protection. Then, the living and working conditions of Thais in Israel are compared to those in Thailand to show that they are well paid and even get rich while working in Israel. Lastly, the treatment of Thai migrant workers is compared to that of animals with the intention of defining a minimum standard of living conditions suitable for humans. The topos of pressure or compulsion is also central, mainly relating to the pressure by NGOs, citizens, the media and the state to protect workers' rights, which is seen by activists as necessary and by farmers as excessive and 'tendentious'.

The economic crisis

Reports about the economic crisis in the Arava region's agriculture began in 2014. The main reason for the crisis was the policy of pepper monoculture and the decline in demand for this specific produce as well as the devaluation of the euro and the Russian ruble, the main currencies in the markets to which the peppers were exported. In one of the reports (Starkman, 2014), titled 'Sad Peppers', the public criticism of the employment of migrant workers and the lack of state support are mentioned as additional reasons for the crisis. It seems plausible that the employment of migrant workers was one of the components of the crisis, although it is hard to determine its overall weight. Farmers began to stress their need for the state to bail them out, and the burden of labor regulations was one of the topics they wished to bring to public attention. As in the report on the discrimination against migrant workers, the comments added by web users are indicative of the agendas and themes at play.

One of the comments, written by 'Oren' and titled 'Salt of the earth', may serve to exemplify the framing of national ideology according to which the farmers are true idealists and heroes:

> The people of the Arava are the salt of the earth. They are an example of true Zionism. Instead of sending youth to Poland [i.e. the Nazi concentration camps] to absorb Zionism, urban youth should be sent to the Arava, in order to strengthen our belief in our capabilities as a nation, in our strength as a community and the values instilled in [this region's] people.

The opposite opinion is presented in comments such as the one titled 'Let's tell the truth', written by 'Shlomo'. The author of this comment questions the idealism of the farmers, since they do not fulfill the Zionist ideal of Jewish labor but rather rely on migrant workers:

> All of them are foreign workers and only the bosses (*ra'isim*) are Israeli. The epitome of slavery, Israel, 2014. It's true they're the salt of the earth but........

In Gabison (2015), several Arava farmers are interviewed, talking about the crisis. Some of them look back and discuss the (ideologically problematic) transition from Jewish to 'foreign' labor, which they ascribe to the changing economic reality. For most of them, this is the third year in a row they are in the red. The interviewed farmers point at various culprits, such as the lack of state support and subsidies, the disintegration of Agrexco, a company that used to coordinate and manage agricultural exports from Israel, and the 10% employer's tax they were required to pay on top of the salaries of Thai workers. Farmers also protest the fact that they are permitted to deduce no more than 237 shekels (ca. USD 70) a month from the salaries of their workers for housing, electricity, water, gas, internet, cable television and laundry, even though they estimate the actual cost of these services to be at least 1,000 shekels a month. One additional complaint by the farmers concerns what they regard as an 'industry of lawsuits' by Thai workers for wages below the minimum wage and other violations of labor laws and regulations. Most such lawsuits end in settlements that cost the farmers large amounts of money.

Among the comments on this article, two deserve mention because they express public sentiments that oppose the point of view of the farmers. The title of a comment posted by 'Doron' discards the narrative presented in the article and strives to expose the farmers as rich capitalists: 'They're multi-millionaires. They earned millions, no need to feel pity for them', the title says. Somewhat surprisingly, the body of the comment reveals that as much as the author resents the farmers, he is even more fervently antagonistic toward the litigation by Thai migrant workers and their lawyers:

> As for the lawsuits, which became a lucrative industry, the courts of law only care about the lawyers. They don't care about justice. It's time to deal with the legal system, take off the gloves and start acting [...] The legal system is solely preoccupied with how to rob the people of Israel for the benefit of lawyers, not the citizens.

The second comment, written by 'Someone', contains a bare title with no content: 'But why is everything so expensive at the supermarket???' These two comments, together with the ones appended to the previous article, allow us to discern a wide range of reactions among Israeli citizens. From the point of view of national ideologies, farmers are seen as 'salt of the earth', a prime example of idealism and fulfillment, even after they sacrificed a major part of this ideology by hiring non-Jewish workers. For the youth, to visit the Arava agricultural settlements is perceived as instructive as visiting the death camps in Poland in terms of forming Israelis' sense of history and identity. Critical views claim that the farmers are capitalists who exploit their workers and only want to make money. In terms of Zionist ideology, this means that they completely relinquished said ideology and do not deserve to be seen positively, or even to be pitied. Lastly, once the national ideology is put aside, the citizens' viewpoint becomes the viewpoint of the consumers, who wish to purchase cheap goods. Implicitly, the farmers' capitalist greed is claimed to be the reason for the high prices of goods in the supermarket, so their interests are not just in conflict with those of migrant workers, but with those of citizens-consumers. Topoi of morality, cost, and abuse thus play a central role in the discourse of the crisis.

Discussion and Conclusions

The discourse analysis of Israeli news media is instrumental in exposing the tensions among the state, farmers, consumers and workers. These tensions result from the superposition of various conflicting planes, most predominantly those of national ideology, economy and workers' (human) rights. On the national-ideological plane, old-school nationalism and renationalization processes perpetuate the positive image of the Jewish farmers, who materialize the colonial ideal of inhabiting remote parts of the country, Judaizing the territory, and making the desert bloom – a major component of Zionist ideology promoted by Israel's founder David Ben-Gurion. Unlike the Jewish settlements in the West Bank and other territories occupied during the 1967 war, which are seen by settlers as an extension of this ideal but have never reached a full consensus, the Central Arava settlements are perceived in public opinion as much less contentious, since they belong to the pre-1967 territory of Israel. The fact that Bedouin families used to live in some parts of the region does not blemish the positive image of the settlers. In the discourse of the news media and comments, this ideologically driven image of the settler-farmers is mobilized for arguments defending the farmers' interests.

National ideology is also one of the reasons why farmers are criticized by public opinion. Farmers are accused of abandoning the Zionist principle of self-sufficiency or reliance on 'Jewish labor', which was an essential ingredient in the formation of Israel's economy. This ideology is also shared by the farmers, who maintain that the reliance on non-Jewish workers is an economic necessity, as well as the state, which equally views migrant workers as a necessary evil. Despite this shared ideology, the interests of the farmers and the state are not mutual, since the farmers constantly look for ways to recruit more workers with less regulation, whereas the state claims it wishes to reduce the number of migrant workers and sets various barriers and requirements for migrant workers' labor; these barriers and requirements limit the farmers' possibilities, cost them money, and make them liable to lawsuits if they do not comply with the law.

The farmers often claim that the state has abandoned them, after having supported them generously for decades. This may be due to the fact that the agricultural sector, which used to be central and closely linked to the circles of power, is now just another sector among the many that the state is trying to cater to. For instance, the state may be under pressure by certain groups to increase the minimum wage, which the farmers find detrimental. The state is also interested in taking measures to protect workers' rights and fight forced labor, which from the farmers' point of view are additional taxes and regulations. Thus, in practice, the state plays a complex role that goes beyond the mere fulfillment of national ideology, and farmers, too, are motivated by their economic interests as employers and business owners, which vastly exceeds the usual boundaries of national ideology discourse. It is on this plane of economy that citizens no longer necessarily perform as practitioners of the national ideology but display a variety of sentiments, including disdain toward the farmers for being rich, exploitative capitalists, or adopt a consumerist attitude against farmers who charge exorbitant prices for their produce.

The remoteness of the Central Arava lands plays an interesting dual role in the discourse. Numerous rhetorical devices serve to discursively signal the remoteness of the place, such as the use of the word 'visit' (the visit of a Tel-Avivian reporter) in the titles of two articles. Workers' rights activists argue that the enforcement in remote areas such as the Arava region is particularly weak, leading to more violations and problems. The farmers, on the other hand, would probably agree that the region is to some extent an extraterritorial frontier land, but they would view this as positive, claiming that the state's grip should remain weak. Although they do wish to receive subsidies and benefits from the state, they reject most forms of intervention and seem keen to preserve their sense of self-sufficiency and autonomy. This sense of autonomy is also reflected in the farmers' notion of a 'family' that encompasses both them and their workers. These conceptualizations of autonomy and 'family' provide the rationale for the rejection of what could be seen as the state's 'meddling' in personal matters; at the same time, these notions of autonomy are constantly disrupted by state policies, the global economy and the public opinion in Israel, making it harder for the farmers to claim that they still apply.

In sum, the critical analysis of news media discourse about agricultural workers reveals the conflicting interests among different actors or agents such as the state, citizens, farmers and workers. These conflicting interests may be due to economic considerations, human rights concerns and group-based interests competing with national ideology. Renationalization and national ideology are rarely questioned and remain dominant in slogans in the public sphere, in the arguments used by farmers, and in comments by web users; however, in the age of late capitalism they do not seem powerful enough to overcome conflicts and bring about sufficient social cohesion. This state of affairs makes it difficult for farmers to mobilize state ideology, especially once their credibility is questioned and their ulterior motives are claimed to be exposed. The discrimination against Thai migrant workers is reported and, when not denied, is used to form arguments about the farmers' waning commitment to and cynical use of ideology. Despite the seemingly open discussion of labor law violations, the voices of migrant workers themselves are barely heard, either because the Hebrew-language discourse excludes the workers from taking part in it (see the contributions of Capstick and Angouri *et al.* in this volume) or because, at the end of the day, they are of little importance to the internal struggles between interest groups in Israeli society.

References

Ben-Simhon, K. (2009) A visit to the farmers of the Arava, in fields that yearn for working hands, and in greenhouses that transform foreign workers into family. *Haaretz*, 5 November. See https://www.haaretz.co.il/misc/1.1289606 (accessed 7 March 2018).

Blum, E. (2013) *December 2013 – Update*, Central Arava Regional Council webpage, 22 December. See http://old.arava.co.il/cgi-webaxy/item?573 (accessed 7 March 2018).

Brysk, A. and Shafir, G. (2004) Introduction: Globalization and the citizenship gap. In A. Brysk and G. Shafir (eds) *People out of Place: Globalization, Human Rights, and the Citizenship Gap* (pp. 3–9). New York: Routledge.

Elias, N. and Kemp, A. (2010) The new second generation: Non-Jewish Olim, Black Jews and children of migrant workers in Israel. *Israel Studies* 15 (1), 73–94.

Esterkin, Y. (2011) The Thais from 'Yellow Peppers' are gossiping on you too. *NRG Maariv*, 23 February. See https://www.makorrishon.co.il/nrg/online/54/ART2/213/301.html (accessed 7 March 2018).

Fairclough, N. (2010) *Critical Discourse Analysis: The Critical Study of Language* (2nd edn). Abingdon: Routledge.

Frankel, B. (2015) Low wages and death: Thais in agriculture in Israel. *Ynet*, 21 January. See https://www.ynet.co.il/articles/0,7340,L-4617232,00.html (accessed 7 March 2018).

Gabison, Y. (2015) 'I lost 600 thousand shekels in two years. What am I, Yitzhak Tshuva?'. *The Marker*, 3 April. See https://www.themarker.com/markerweek/1.2606633 (accessed 7 March 2018).

Goren, Y. (2013) Farmers: The workers from Thailand are spoiled. *NRG Maariv*, 12 September. See https://www.makorrishon.co.il/nrg/online/1/ART2/506/559.html (accessed 7 March 2018).

Human Rights Watch (2015) *A Raw Deal: Abuse of Thai Workers in Israel's Agricultural Sector*, 21 January. See https://www.hrw.org/report/2015/01/21/raw-deal/abuse-thai-workers-israels-agricultural-sector (accessed 7 March 2018).

Jamal, A. (2007) Nationalizing states and the constitution of 'hollow citizenship': Israel and its Palestinian citizens. *Ethnopolitics* 6 (4), 471–493.

Jaradat, M.G. (2017) *The Unchosen: The Lives of Israel's New Others*. London: Pluto Press.

Jaworski, A. and Thurlow, C. (eds) (2010) *Semiotic landscapes: Language, Image, Space*. London: Continuum.

Kaminer, M. (2016) A lonely Songkran in the Arabah. *Middle East Report* 279, 34–37.

Kashti, O. (2013) A sad visit to the agricultural workers from Thailand who grow our food. *Haaretz*, 20 June. See https://www.haaretz.co.il/news/education/.premium-1.2051826 (accessed 7 March 2018).

Kashti, O. and Efrati, I. (2014) A mysterious syndrome claims the lives of tens of agricultural workers from Thailand. *Haaretz*, 28 March. See https://www.haaretz.co.il/news/health/1.2281881 (accessed 7 March 2018).

Kemp, A. (2007) Managing migration, reprioritizing national citizenship: Undocumented migrant workers' children. *Theoretical Inquiries in Law* 8 (2), 663–691.

Kemp, A. and Raijman, R. (2008) *Migrants and Workers: The Political Economy of Labor Migration in Israel*. Jerusalem: Van Leer Institute & Hakibbutz Hameuchad (in Hebrew).

Kemp, A., Raijman, R., Resnik, J. and Schammah-Gesser, S. (2000) Contesting the limits of political participation: Latinos and black African migrant workers in Israel. *Ethnic and Racial Studies* 23 (1), 94–119.

Mell, I. (2010) We don't need any workers, thank you. *Haokets*, 28 November. See https://bit.ly/30RhFNT (accessed 7 March 2018).

Reisigl, M. and Wodak, R. (2009) The discourse-historical approach (DHA). In R. Wodak and M. Meyer (eds) *Methods of Critical Discourse Analysis* (2nd edn) (pp. 87–121). London: Sage.

Shani, L. (2015) Red peppers and acacia yellowing: Man and nature in the tension between agriculture and environment in the Arava. PhD dissertation, Tel Aviv University (in Hebrew).

Shohamy, E. (2012) Linguistic landscapes and multilingualism. In M. Martin-Jones, A. Blackledge and A. Creese (eds) *The Routledge Handbook of Multilingualism* (pp. 538–551). Abingdon & New York: Routledge.

Shohamy, E. and Gorter, D. (2009) Introduction. In E. Shohamy and D. Gorter (eds) *Linguistic Landscape: Expanding the Scenery* (pp. 1–10). New York & Abingdon: Routledge.

Shohamy, E. and Kanza, T. (2009) Language and citizenship in Israel. *Language Assessment Quarterly* 6, 83–88.

SocialTV (2013) Microphone for democracy – Noa Shauer from 'Worker's Hotline'. *YouTube*, 13 July. See https://www.youtube.com/watch?v=N6gaWQC4c0g (accessed 7 March 2018).

Starkman, R. (2014) Sad peppers: This is how the Arava farmers' gold mine collapsed. *The Marker*, 2 June. See https://www.themarker.com/news/macro/1.2338985 (accessed 7 March 2018).

US Department of State (2013) *ISRAEL: Tier 1. 2013 Trafficking in Persons Report*. See https://www.state.gov/j/tip/rls/tiprpt/countries/2013/215486.htm (accessed 7 March 2018).

US Department of State (2017) *ISRAEL: Tier 1. 2017 Trafficking in Persons Report*. See https://www.state.gov/j/tip/rls/tiprpt/countries/2017/271210.htm (accessed 7 March 2018).
Wodak, R. (2011) Critical discourse analysis. In K. Hyland and B. Paltridge (eds) *Continuum Companion to Discourse Analysis* (pp. 38–53). London and New York: Continuum.
Yagana, Y. (2015) The Arava farmers' protests: 'Almost half of us will go bankrupt this year'. *Walla!*, 28 February. See https://news.walla.co.il/item/2833718 (accessed 7 March 2018).
Yonah, Y. and Kemp, A. (2008) *Citizenship Gaps: Migration, Fertility and Identity in Israel*. Jerusalem: Van Leer Institute and Hakibbutz Hameuchad (in Hebrew).

Index

Abuse 81, 91, 118, 131–2, 138–9, 141, 154–5, 159, 165
Argumentation, argument 10, 117, 120–2, 125, 127, 129, 152, 156
Asylum-seekers 2
Authorization 122, 139

Belonging 5, 11, 86, 92–4, 96, 104, 109–10
Biography, biographical, autobiographical 2, 11–12, 64, 66–8, 71–7, 81–2
Borders 2–3, 7, 11–12, 18–19, 26, 54, 69, 76, 88, 105, 111, 116, 119, 127, 129, 132, 134, 136, 138, 148–9, 155, 158
Burden 7, 86, 118, 131–2, 134, 136, 138–42, 156, 159, 163

CDA, Critical Discourse Analysis 12, 95, 123–4, 152
Christian, Christianity 1
Citizenship, citizenship test 4–5, 9–10, 25, 43–6, 70, 93, 150–1
Communist, Communism 19–20, 23, 25, 35, 117
Competence, competency, competencies 5, 7, 9, 22, 58–9
Conservative 23, 25
Corpus linguistic, corpus linguistics 12, 117, 124–6, 142
Counter-discourse 46, 54, 71, 127
Crisis, crises 1, 11–12, 19, 21, 93, 95, 102–3, 116–18, 120, 124, 128, 134, 137, 140–1, 143, 149, 154–5, 157, 163, 165
Culturalization 2–5, 7, 9
Culture 2–6, 8–9, 18–19, 22–3, 25, 27, 30–2, 34, 89, 107, 122, 124, 139, 141

DHA, Discourse-Historical Approach 13, 42, 117, 120–1, 152

Diaspora, diasporas 86–8, 98–9, 104–5
Discrimination, discriminatory 10, 13, 41, 44, 46–7, 49, 52, 54, 56, 60–1, 66, 87, 91, 94, 117, 151, 161, 163, 167
Discursive shift 12, 128, 134, 141
Displacement 87

Economy, economic 1, 3, 5, 7–8, 10–12, 18–20, 23, 27, 29, 35–7, 41, 44, 49, 64–5, 71, 86, 88, 93, 95, 98–9, 101–2, 117, 122, 124, 128, 131–2, 137–9, 141, 148–9, 154, 157, 163–4, 165–7
Ethnic, ethnicity 17–23, 28–9, 36–7, 44, 46, 49, 52, 54, 56, 60, 88–9, 93, 103, 107
Ethnography, ethnographic 10–12, 41–2, 48, 61, 95, 148
Exclusion, exclusionary 1, 5, 7, 10–11, 13, 87, 92, 101, 109, 116–17, 156
Exploit, exploitation 5, 94, 150, 155, 157, 160–1, 165

Facebook 41, 47–8, 56, 58–9, 61, 72–5, 81
Far-right 5–6, 93, 98, 110, 116, 118
First language 20–2, 26–7, 29, 32, 57
Fitting in 86–7, 92–4, 99, 106–10
Forced migration 87
Frame, framing 4, 64, 67, 96, 99, 103, 106, 108, 121, 125, 163

Globalization 1

Habitus 94–5, 100, 104
Home 11–12, 43–4, 49–50, 54–6, 58, 92, 98–101, 104, 124, 143
Human rights 4, 12–13, 25, 32, 116, 122, 138, 151, 154, 156, 165, 167
Human trafficking, trafficking 150, 162

Identity, identity construction 3, 5–6, 8, 11–12, 28–9, 35, 45, 49, 54, 56, 58, 64, 67–8, 71, 81–2, 87, 89–93, 100, 103–4, 106–7, 110, 124, 133, 160, 165
Ideology 28, 32, 57, 154–5, 163–7
Illegal 3, 19, 76–7, 81, 120, 132, 151
Imagined community, communities 8, 11, 17–18, 22–3, 25–9, 31–7, 44, 46–7, 64, 68, 72, 76, 80, 87–8, 90, 92, 104, 106, 109
Immigrant 26, 34–6, 57, 64, 69, 77, 81, 91, 118, 126, 134
Indigenous, indigeneity 11, 26, 31, 33, 35–7
Integration 1, 5–6, 10, 46–7, 105, 118, 137, 164
Islam 6

Language acquisition 10, 22
Language ideology, language ideologies 28, 31–2
Language policy, language policies 3, 7–9, 11, 17–19, 26, 31–3, 36
Language test 9, 44
Left, left-wing 3, 25, 27–8, 34–5, 105, 107, 131, 150
Legal 3–5, 12, 19, 25, 35, 66, 70, 93, 118–19, 122, 131, 138, 142, 164, 151
Legitimation, legitimization 10, 12, 43, 116–17, 119–23, 125–7, 138–9, 141–2
Liberal, liberalism 3, 6–7, 25, 100, 102, 109
Liminal 87, 91, 97, 100, 104–6
Literacy, literacies 11–12, 49, 54, 60, 41–2, 45–8, 55–7, 59, 61

Macro-topic, topic 48, 57, 78, 96, 118
Media 1–2, 4–6, 9–13, 20, 31–3, 43, 65, 69, 72–4, 82, 86, 88, 95, 99, 104, 110, 117, 121, 124, 126, 128, 136, 141, 152, 156–7, 160, 163, 165, 167
Mediatized, mediatization, mediatized politics 11–12, 116, 118–19, 121
Migrants 1–13, 17, 20–5, 28–30, 36–7, 41–9, 53, 57, 59–61, 64–6, 68, 71–2, 74–6, 80–2, 86, 89, 93, 95–6, 101, 105, 110, 116, 119–20, 124–9, 131–4, 136, 139, 142

Migration 1–7, 9–13, 17–18, 20, 35–6, 41–2, 44, 47–50, 53–6, 60–1, 64–5, 69, 71, 81, 86–7, 93–4, 98, 109–10, 116–19, 122, 136, 142, 150, 159
Minority, minorities 6, 11, 26, 31–7, 43, 46, 60, 66–8, 71–2, 106–7, 109, 127
Mobility 11–12, 30, 98, 105, 110
Moralization 122–3, 138
Multilingual 5, 8
Muslim 1, 6, 45, 107, 133
Mythopoesis 122–3

Narrator 76–7, 80
Nationalism, nationalist 5–6, 19–20, 22–3, 25, 110, 165
Nationalization 1, 7
Native 26
Naturalization 9, 43, 118
Newspaper, newspapers 22, 50, 126, 153
Nomination 53, 125–6, 131, 134, 142
Normalization, normalize, normalized 1, 13, 43, 116

Othering 1, 91, 102, 109–10

Periphery 94, 102, 105–7, 109
Politics 2, 3–7, 9–10, 12, 19–20, 27, 50–1, 65, 89, 92, 96, 109, 116–17, 120–1
Populist, populism 1–3, 5–6, 64, 93, 98, 117
Predication 53, 125, 152
Prestige 11, 22, 27–8

Qualitative 2, 12, 79, 117, 124–7, 132, 136, 142
Quantitative 2, 49, 117, 124–7, 134, 142

Racist, racism 44, 91
Rationalization 122–3, 25, 138–40
Refugees 1–4, 7, 9–12, 27, 36, 71, 86, 116–19, 123, 125–9, 131–4, 136, 138–42, 151
Religion, religious 2–7, 10, 18–19, 47, 102, 107, 109, 122, 133, 139
Re-nationalization 1, 7
Representation 2, 9–12, 25–6, 29, 33–6, 44, 65–8, 81, 88, 117, 125–6, 133, 142
Resistance 3, 11–12, 19, 29, 31, 41–2, 45–7, 54–7, 59, 60–1, 92, 110–11

Right, right-wing 4–6, 11–13, 18, 20–1, 25–7, 31–6, 51, 53, 64, 68–9, 71
Rights 4, 11–13, 18, 25–6, 32–3, 35–6, 64, 68, 71, 98, 116, 122, 132, 138, 151, 154–7, 159–60, 162–3, 165–7

Second language 10, 19, 22–3, 28
Second language acquisition 10, 22
Securitization 3, 9
Security 3–4, 6, 69–70, 118, 120, 133, 137, 140, 149–50, 154–5
Social class, class 22–3, 29, 53, 57, 69, 71, 91, 101, 156
Social media 65, 69, 73
Socialist, Socialism 17–19, 23, 35
Sociolinguistic, sociolinguistics 1–2, 4, 9–13, 22, 27, 29, 45, 64, 67, 87, 89, 95–6, 106, 110, 148

Storytelling, narrative 65–8, 70–2, 74, 81–2
Strategy 8–9, 52–3, 68, 72, 81, 94, 102, 122, 131
Symbolic 3, 5–7, 27, 65, 90–2, 96, 104

Terrorism, terrorist, terror 3, 6, 43, 71, 118, 120, 124, 131, 133, 136–8, 140, 142
Threats 2, 6–7, 25, 43, 71, 132–3, 136, 139–40, 142
Topos, topoi 117, 122–5, 127, 136, 138–42, 152, 158–9, 162, 165

Undocumented 12, 64, 69–70, 72, 74–80, 96

Values, European values 2, 4, 6, 76, 82, 86, 93, 100, 109, 122–4, 138, 163

For Product Safety Concerns and Information please contact our EU Authorised Representative:

Easy Access System Europe

Mustamäe tee 50

10621 Tallinn

Estonia

gpsr.requests@easproject.com